About Island Press

Since 1984, the nonprofit organization Island Press has been stimulating, shaping, and communicating ideas that are essential for solving environmental problems worldwide. With more than 1,000 titles in print and some 30 new releases each year, we are the nation's leading publisher on environmental issues. We identify innovative thinkers and emerging trends in the environmental field. We work with world-renowned experts and authors to develop cross-disciplinary solutions to environmental challenges.

Island Press designs and executes educational campaigns, in conjunction with our authors, to communicate their critical messages in print, in person, and online using the latest technologies, innovative programs, and the media. Our goal is to reach targeted audiences—scientists, policy makers, environmental advocates, urban planners, the media, and concerned citizens—with information that can be used to create the framework for long-term ecological health and human well-being.

Island Press gratefully acknowledges major support from The Bobolink Foundation, Caldera Foundation, The Curtis and Edith Munson Foundation, The Forrest C. and Frances H. Lattner Foundation, The JPB Foundation, The Kresge Foundation, The Summit Charitable Foundation, Inc., and many other generous organizations and individuals.

The opinions expressed in this book are those of the author(s) and do not necessarily reflect the views of our supporters.

The Heart of the City

The Heart of the City

Creating Vibrant Downtowns for a New Century

Alexander Garvin

ISLANDPRESS

Washington | Covelo | London

Library of Congress Control Number: 2018959603

All Island Press books are printed on environmentally responsible materials.

Manufactured in the United States of America
10 9 8 7 6 5 4 3 2 1

Keywords: business district, business improvement district (BID), community development corporation (CDC), deindustrialization, entertainment center, historic preservation, immigration, mixed-use development, public realm, public transportation, real estate development, tax increment financing (TIF), tourism, urban parks, urban plazas, walkability

Contents

Preface

Fifteen years after I left my position as vice president for planning, design, and development at the Lower Manhattan Development Corporation, where I was in charge of planning the reconstruction of the World Trade Center (WTC), I decided to evaluate the results of the rebuilding.

I was stunned. Lower Manhattan, which for half a century had been a declining agglomeration of single-use office buildings, was becoming a resurgent, mixed-use, 24-hour community. Not because of the rebuilding of the WTC, however.

Millions of square feet of office space at the new WTC were either unoccupied or unbuilt, yet there were 9,000 more private sector jobs in lower Manhattan than had been there before the terrorist attack. There also were 38,000 additional residents living in 18,000 apartments and 6,000 more hotel rooms.[1]

How, I wondered, could lower Manhattan be resurgent when it had been in decline since the end of World War II, when, like other American downtowns, it had lost tens of millions of customers to competing business districts and suburbs that were burgeoning everywhere? I knew that other downtowns were resurgent. Were the reasons the same as for lower Manhattan?

In fact, the story was the same in other major American downtowns. Today, 40,000 more people work in downtown Atlanta than did 25 years ago. The number of people working in downtown Phoenix nearly doubled during those same 25 years. But not all downtowns were thriving.

There were three trajectories. Two had been going on for half a century. Downtowns such as San Jose, Houston, Indianapolis, and Jacksonville had never stopped growing. Detroit, St. Louis, Buffalo, and Bridgeport, on the other hand, were in decline or struggling. A third trajectory appeared in the last decade of the 20th century. Lower Manhattan, downtown Los Angeles, Seattle, and a large group of downtowns had become resurgent.

Whether a downtown had been continuously growing or had become resurgent, if it was thriving, it also was rapidly changing. These vibrant downtowns were being transformed from single-use business districts into high-density, mixed-use downtowns. In fact, the American people had been voting since the 1990s on the future of these downtowns with their feet. As professor Eugenie Birch pointed out more than a dozen years ago, "During the 1990s, downtown population grew by 10 percent, a marked resurgence following 20 years of overall decline. . . . Downtown homeownership rates more than doubled during the thirty-year period, reaching 22 percent by 2000."[2] Lower Manhattan, for instance, which had a resident population of 800 in 1950, by 2017 was home to 61,000 people.[3] The new residents lived in converted commercial buildings and newly erected residential structures, in rented apartments and resident-owned condominiums. Before 1999, for example, there were only 11,600 residential units in downtown Los Angeles; in 2017, there were 65,000, with an additional 21,000 apartments in construction.[4]

Residents and office workers are not the only people downtown. There are many tourists as well. In 2017, Chicago was the destination for 45.6 million visitors, Miami for 38.1 million, and Atlanta for 35.4 million.[5] They are the customers who keep downtown sidewalks busy and provide jobs for the people who work in the hotels, restaurants, and stores they patronize.

Downtowns are more than economic engines; they are repositories of knowledge and culture; they are generators of new ideas, new technology, and new ventures. Jane Jacobs explained half a century ago that cities are "the vast and intricate collections of ideas and institutions called civilization."[6] Those ideas and institutions thrive downtown. That is why Yale, the University of California at Los Angeles, the University of Pennsylvania, and countless other international universities are major occupants of high-density, mixed-use downtowns. So are the nation's most important museums, libraries, and medical centers. All of them are changing the downtowns around them.

The importance of such institutions is evident in many downtowns, particularly so in the recent resurgence of Pittsburgh. Ideas about robotics, artificial intelligence, digitally focused medicine, and other innovations generated at Carnegie Mellon University, the University of Pittsburgh and its Medical Center, gave rise to important startup companies. They, in turn, transformed Pittsburgh, which had lost 190,000 manufacturing jobs in the collapse of the steel industry, into a thriving innovation center that, from 2007 to 2017, gained 25,900 new professional and business service jobs, 22,900 new education and health services jobs, 4,900 new financial jobs, and 29,300 other new jobs in the past decade alone.[7]

As long as downtowns continue to thrive, we can be certain of a prosperous and thrilling future for the 21st-century American city. They are the heart of the city that drives its future. For example, 44 percent of Philadelphia's jobs are located downtown and generate 32 percent of its property taxes, from only 6 percent of the city's land. The situation is similar in downtown Pittsburgh, where 41 percent of the city's jobs are located on only 5 percent of its territory. Thus, the future of our cities is inescapably moored to the health of their downtowns.

If we are to have healthy downtowns, we need to understand what downtown is all about and how and why some American downtowns are in trouble while others are thriving. We need to identify the strategies that are successfully enhancing already-thriving districts, such as downtown Dallas; improving previously declining areas, such as the Boston Seaport; and transforming unoccupied territory, such as the Hudson Yards in Manhattan, into vibrant downtowns for a new century. This book provides the answers to those questions, identifies the elements of a great downtown, explains why some strategies have been working while other approaches have failed, and proposes additional activities that can guarantee vibrant downtowns for a new century.

.   .   .

Writing in 1932, F. Scott Fitzgerald conveyed the essence of our changing downtowns, explaining that lower Manhattan, which had experienced the worst Wall Street financial disaster in history, "had all the iridescence of the beginning of the world," confessing that he "had erroneously thought that there were no second acts in American lives" but that "there was certainly to be a second act" for New York City.[8] In fact, there have been many more than two acts for lower Manhattan and downtowns across America. That is why downtowns are constantly changing, as are the policies and programs for their improvement.

Lower Manhattan did not create its second or third act. Like all downtowns, it is inanimate. Downtowns are unable to change anything. People change downtowns, and those people are the audience to whom this book is directed. Chapters 1 and 2 describe what is happening *now* in downtown America and why we go there, and they discuss changes in the amount and location of territory that downtowns occupy and the buildings that occupy that territory.

Cities do not change themselves. Chapter 3 explains why and how downtowns are changing. Chapters 4 and 5 describe the people, businesses, institutions, and public agencies that are responsible for what happens downtown and how they go about making changes. However, people who want to improve a downtown must do more than identify opportunities. They need to know which actions have *not* been successful and what we should be doing to improve downtowns (the contents of Chapters 5 and 6). Chapter 7 presents five exemplary recent efforts to expand 21st-century downtowns.

The final chapter proposes additional, often controversial actions that can be taken to keep the heart of the city healthy so that our emerging 21st-century downtowns can continue to thrive for centuries to come. I hope that the nation will adopt them so that many downtowns can have even better second, third, and fourth acts.

Acknowledgments

The publication of every one of my books has been the result of the persistent support of my friend, student, and literary agent, Arthur Klebanoff. He has given me the backbone to persevere in the face of adversity, and I am forever grateful to him for doing so.

The increasing amount of personal observations in my recent writing is due to my friend Rick Rubens. He has continued to insist that it is not enough for me to present the facts. With each book he has pushed me further toward expressing my opinions. This one even contains recommendations for national action.

As with my previous book *What Makes a Great City*, Heather Boyer has provided more ongoing challenges, questions, and suggestions than is common in the publishing industry. She, Sharis Simonian, Katharine Sucher, and the entire production team at Island Press have helped to create a work that I hope will astonish and fascinate its readers.

This book is as good as it is because of my research assistant, Andrew Sandweiss, who scoured the widest variety of sources to find so many facts that demonstrate the validity of this book's observations. Starling Childs and Brendan Hellweg supplied some of the other information that is scattered throughout the text. I cannot thank Paul and Iris Brest enough for convincing me that people would misunderstand what I had to say if I did not define what "downtown" consisted of, where it was located, and who was responsible for what happened there. This book's 96 illustrations are as important as the text, especially the maps created by Starling Childs of Citiesense, Dennis McClendon of Chicago Carto-Graphics, Ryan Salvatore, Benjamin Rubenstein, and Baolin Shen. Their work helped to convey what would have taken tomes of text to explain.

As my many photographs demonstrate, I traveled to downtowns across America to see for myself what was actually happening, as well as to discover what had been exaggerated in published articles and books. On all these visits local experts made sure that I would see places and activities that I might have otherwise overlooked. Many people contributed time, information, and thinking about the places discussed in the book. You all know who you are. I thank you, along with Bruce Alexander, Dan Biederman, David Brownlee, Jackson Cole, Jay Cross, Nick Dewald, Manny Diaz, Dan Doctoroff, Charlie Duff, Donald Elliott, Bob Ethington, Timur Galen, Philip and Nick Garvin, David Haltom, Philip Howard, Con Howe, Matt Jacobs, Meredith Kane, Paul Levy, David McGregor, Tom Morbitzer, Hunter Morrison, Max Musicant, Matt Nemerson, Rick Peiser, Liz Plater-Zyberk, Rosemary Scanlon, Carol Schatz, Jim Schroder, and David and Jed Walentas.

Chapter 1

What Is Downtown?

*D*owntown is a uniquely American word, born in early-19th-century New York City, when the city's population (confined to the area south of what is now Chambers Street) had just surpassed 200,000.[1] Those who lived north of Chambers Street began saying they were going *downtown* (meaning south) when they went to work, shop, or do business and *uptown* (meaning north) when they returned home.

As the largest and richest city in the country, New York became the standard by which other cities judged themselves. Thus, residents of other cities soon also began using the word *downtown* to refer to their business districts, although they may have been going east, west, or north rather than south. At that time their business districts, like lower Manhattan, were mixed-used concentrations of buildings that included many residences.

Over the ensuing decades a growing number of properties that had once been residential were replaced by businesses that could pay higher prices for busy downtown locations. Eventually the word *downtown* became synonymous with *business district*. In the mid-20th century, when residents of inner-city neighborhoods began moving to the suburbs, *Webster's New Collegiate Dictionary* still defined *downtown* as the business center of a town.[2]

The 21st-century downtown began to emerge in the 1990s when internet service began, deindustrialization accelerated, crime rates started to decline, and downtown business improvement districts (BIDs) began to proliferate. A BID is a section of a city in which the businesses and property owners form an entity to provide services (often thought to be inadequately provided by government), such as cleaning streets, collecting garbage, providing security, making streetscape enhancements and other capital improvements, and promoting the district, which it pays for from a special real estate tax surcharge collected by local government but transferred directly to the BID. BIDs are operated as government-chartered public–private partnerships administered by a professional staff supervised by a board of directors that often combines members elected from the district and relevant ex-officio government officials.[3]

Internet service, declining crime rates, and BID services altered the character of downtown retailing and opened opportunities for new business and property development that became the basis for action by individuals, institutions, and governments that generated downtown resurgence in some American downtowns, reversed downtown decline in others, and sometimes accelerated growth.

Retailing in 21st-Century Downtowns

Internet use is responsible for a major change in the amount of downtown building space devoted to retail sales. Total U.S. retail sales climbed from $1.8 trillion in 1992, of which $78 billion was sold by nonstore retailers (4 percent), to $4.85 trillion in 2016, of which $564 billion was sold by internet (approximately 12 percent).[4] Accordingly, one can assume that in 2016, 8 percent less building floor area space was needed for retailing. That change in land use is evident in the suburbs but less so in downtowns.

In 1990 there were more than 1,350 shopping malls in America containing 1.15 billion square feet of space.[5] By 2017 that number had dropped to 1,100 malls containing 96 billion square feet of space.[6] There were 6,985 retail store closures in 2017 in the United States.[7] The pace of store closures seems to be slowing down, however. Between January and September 2018, 4,480 stores closed, 21 percent less than the year before.[8] Nevertheless, we can expect further decline in the number of downtown stores, except in districts where the population (and therefore the number of retail customers) is significantly growing.

Some stores are closing because their customers no longer purchase the merchandise they once carried. In a world before cell phones, the internet, and digitized calendars, people used appointment books, ledgers, fountain pens, pocket calendars, and adding machines. They do not buy many of these items anymore. Moreover, if they are interested in some item, they will only stop in a store for a few seconds to take a smartphone snapshot and order the item online. Accordingly, there are now many fewer stationery stores in the United States. Even Staples closed 14 percent of its stores between 2014 and 2016.[9]

The decline in downtown retailing in the 21st century was much less pronounced than in suburban malls, because so many downtowns had acquired new residents during that period. During that period lower Manhattan gained 47,325 residents, downtown Los Angeles gained 21,701 residents, and downtown Philadelphia gained 9,708 residents.[10] These additional residents are customers for the new stores and restaurants opening in lower Manhattan, downtown LA, and other resurgent downtowns.

The same cannot be said about downtown retailing in cities that lost substantial populations over the past half century. Cleveland, which lost 518,000 residents between 1950 and 2010, lost all seven of its department stores. The world's second largest department store, Hudson's in Detroit, and Detroit's nine other downtown department stores are long gone, casualties of that city's 1.136 million population decline during the same period. Both cities would have to add more than 100,000 downtown residents to generate enough customers to justify the return of a department store. If that happens, however, there is no certainty that the additional population would be sufficient to overcome ever-increasing internet sales.

The disappearance of department stores in these cities is not just the result of their declining populations. Internet competition has reduced the number of department stores in the United States from 10,100 in 1999 to 8,800 in 2008.[11] Yet lower Manhattan, bereft of department stores throughout most of the 20th century, has acquired an extremely popular discount department store, Century 21. Philadelphia, on the other hand, has retained one of its six 1950 department stores and replaced three of them with large discount stores, one of which was a branch of the Century 21 flagship store in lower Manhattan.

The same national discount retailers that have become popular throughout the country thrive downtown. There were no Starbucks in New York City until 1994; as of 2002 there were 128.[12] The first Target to open in New York City appeared in Brooklyn in 2002. As of 2017 there were a dozen in different parts of NYC, along with 445 Dunkin' Donuts.[13]

Thus, by the 21st century *downtown* had become far more than a cluster of properties where business takes place. It has become a high-density concentration of business, retailing, entertainment, and institutional activity, combined with a large number of residences.

Three Downtown Trajectories

American downtowns are on three main trajectories. Uptown Houston, Atlanta's Buckhead, and downtowns like them have never stopped thriving. Others, such as downtown Detroit, have been in decline for half a century. Downtowns such as lower Manhattan and downtown Los Angeles, on the other hand, were once on the decline and are now resurgent.

The continuously thriving and resurgent downtowns have one thing in common: a large residential population. Struggling downtowns have small downtown populations. Thus, continually thriving Uptown Houston, the 18th largest downtown, has the fourth largest number of residents (167,000); resurgent Philadelphia, the eighth largest downtown, has the third largest residential population (190,000); and struggling Detroit, the 27th largest downtown, contains only 5,000 residents. Successful 21st-century American downtowns all have sizable residential populations.

In 1950, Uptown Houston was undeveloped rural land with a few emergent suburban subdivisions, that had been annexed to the city of Houston in 1949. Buckhead was a prestigious residential suburb with some service retailers. At that time, downtown Detroit was the thriving center of a city at its peak population of 1.85 million people. Lower Manhattan and downtown Los Angeles, on the other hand, were already declining and would continue to decline for another half century.

Today Uptown Houston contains 26 million square feet of office space, 34 hotels with more than 8,000 rooms, and more than 1,000 stores occupying more than 6 million square feet of retail space. More than 180,000 people live within a 3-mile radius of its main intersection, and 108,000 come to work there every day, nearly 100,000 more than in 1990.[14]

Post Oak Boulevard, Uptown Houston, 2016

In the nearly half century since the Galleria opened on Post Oak Boulevard, Uptown Houston has become the 18th largest downtown in America. (Alexander Garvin)

Buckhead, in Atlanta, may have expanded as rapidly as Uptown Houston, but it is a very different downtown. In 1950 it was a 1,594-acre high-end suburb with a population of 26,800 residents living in what the U.S. Census defined as the "urbanized area."[15] Two years later it was annexed by the City of Atlanta. Seven years after annexation, a major shopping center, Lenox Square Mall, opened on its main street. In 1969, a second shopping center, Phipps Plaza, opened down the street.

Today the core of Buckhead (as defined by its BID) includes more than 27 million square feet of office space, with 2 million overnight visitors every year staying in 23 hotels with more than 5,300 rooms; more than 200 stores occupying more than 6.2 million square feet of retail

Buckhead, Atlanta (helicopter aerial), 2007

Buckhead is now the nation's 20th largest downtown (2017). (Alexander Garvin)

space (including the 22-million-square-foot Lenox Square Mall and 10-million-square-foot Phipps Plaza) that attracts approximately 32 million customers annually; and 12,000 residents living in 8,500 dwelling units and 68,600 people coming to work there every day.[16]

Nothing like the mixed-use downtown that emerged around Post Oak Boulevard will occur in Buckhead. It is still a collection of separate automobile-centric, suburban destinations straining to become a mixed-use downtown. Its single-use buildings occupy blocks that people reach by driving to a drop-off location and parking in a garage or vast parking field. Shopping is just far enough away from apartment and office buildings that, rather than walk, occupants separate their day into single-use activities, often driving to a shopping destination rather than mingling with window shoppers on the sidewalk.

Retailing in downtown Detroit, on the other hand, is struggling to make a comeback. In 1950, it was the home of Hudson's, the second largest department store in the world (at 2.1 million square feet) and 10 other department stores. Today, smaller stores such as Bonobos and Warby Parker have opened on Woodward Avenue, but no department stores have survived. Its 12 hotels with 4,163 rooms had an average occupancy rate of 69 percent in 2016.[17] And its theater district, once second in size only to New York City's, now hosts only a handful of performances during a typical week. Only 70,000 people went downtown to work in 2016. Consequently, numerous multistory buildings were empty, and only 84 percent of 26 million square feet of net rentable space was occupied.[18] The major downtown attractions are the 41,000-seat Comerica Park, home of the Detroit Tigers since 2000, and Ford Field, a multiuse domed stadium, completed 2 years later, which has a maximum capacity of 80,000. Nevertheless, the downtown population has only climbed to just under 5,000, barely one-third of the number living in Buckhead, which doesn't come close to accommodating the number of residents found in Uptown Houston or downtown LA.[19]

Woodward Avenue, Detroit, 2017

Only 70,000 people come to work every day in downtown Detroit, the 27th largest downtown in the country. (Alexander Garvin)

By 1950, lower Manhattan, which in 1790 was the largest downtown in America, had dropped to number three (after Midtown Manhattan and the Loop in Chicago). However, it was a very different place, having become a single-function business district that went to sleep at 6 PM on Fridays and woke up again at 8 AM on Mondays. Fewer than a thousand people still lived there.[20] Nevertheless, in 1950 it still was an economic engine and continued to be one of the world's major financial centers. By 2016, however, lower Manhattan had become home for 61,000 people living in 31,000 apartments.[21] Every day 233,000 people came to work in 9,500 private businesses that occupied 88.5 million square feet of office space and 1,170 stores and restaurants. Many of the more than 14.8 million tourists who came there stayed in one of its 7,900 hotel rooms.[22]

Downtowns Are Forever Changing

Describing any downtown as it is today may be accurate now, but it will no longer be accurate the day after tomorrow. For example, turn-of-the-21st-century Americans could not have predicted that there would be thousands more private sector jobs in lower Manhattan than when terrorists destroyed the World Trade Center.

Most of the world's major downtowns are dense, mixed-use agglomerations of businesses and residences. Some downtowns, such as London and Tokyo, are also national politico-administrative centers. That was true of American downtowns when the United States was established—in 1790 its three largest cities, New York, Philadelphia, and Boston, were also politico-administrative centers—but it quickly changed.

Throughout the early 19th century, most people who worked downtown manufacturing goods, distributing products, or providing services had to live there. They had no choice. There were no trains, buses, or streetcars to take them anywhere else to shop, earn a living, or escape for the weekend. For them, as much as for visitors, available amenities were essential. At the end of the 19th century, electrified streetcars replaced horse-drawn omnibus lines. Streetcar service further enlarged most downtowns because residents and workers could now travel a greater distance to and from home, work, shopping, and entertainment within a short period of time. Thus, until the 20th century downtown America consisted of agglomerations of densely packed, mixed-use buildings where "diverse ethnic, economic, and social strains of urban life were bound together, working, spending, speculating, and investing."[23]

Elevator buildings transformed these and many other downtowns into single-function business districts, because developers could erect much larger buildings on sites that previously had been occupied by low-rise structures. They could collect more rent from these steel- and concrete-frame high-rise buildings than they could from low-rise wood-frame buildings without elevators. Moreover, the businesses that moved into elevator buildings could afford higher rents per square foot than

Inner Harbor, Baltimore, 1972

Inner Harbor, Baltimore, 2016

As a result of the redevelopment of the city's waterfront, downtown Baltimore, being redeveloped in 1972, had become America's 14th largest downtown by 2016. (Alexander Garvin)

paid by previous occupants of these sites. A few cities, such as New York, Chicago, and Philadelphia, were sufficiently constricted in the territory occupied by elevator buildings that their population densities supported high enough rents to justify building high-rise apartment districts on the fringes of downtown.

By the mid-20th century, mass-produced, inexpensive, privately owned automobiles had replaced most streetcars. Traveling within the same time period at higher speeds on broad interstate highways allowed residents to leave downtown and move to roomier, less expensive sites. They no longer needed to live close to locations where they worked, shopped, or went for recreation. Accordingly, large sections of downtown territory were abandoned for even cheaper land in the suburbs.

Not only was the use of private property changing, the public realm was changing as quickly. Stables had been ubiquitous and parking lots unknown in the 19th century. Once automobile ownership became widespread, downtown parking lots became a necessity, and by the 21st century most downtowns no longer included even a single stable.

It is too early to know what the impact on downtown America will be if autonomous vehicles (AVs) become the common means of conveyance. Some experts predict 80 percent fewer vehicles on the road; others say that if AVs become sufficiently easy and cheap, they will inundate existing streets.[24] Some urbanists predict that 90 percent of paved parking areas will be eliminated and that most in-city garages will no longer be needed; others point out that much of the space now used for on-street parking and sidewalks will be needed for AVs that stop to deliver packages and unload passengers. Traffic engineers tell us that a typical street, with only cars, can carry 1,900 people per hour and per lane. Buses on the same lane, with mixed traffic, can carry an additional 1,350 people. Bus rapid transit, with lanes exclusively for buses, can carry 2,700 people per hour. A light rail system (at three cars per trainset and a frequency of 15 trains an hour, or one every 4 minutes) can carry 8,100 people per hour, whereas a local train, such as Metro North, can carry 12,720 an hour. Finally, a subway lane, the most capital-intensive but efficient of all urban transit, can move 30,000 people an hour over a single track. AVs, still driving (autonomously!) along a normal roadway, are not going to replace downtown mass transit. They cannot carry enough people per hour. However, we can be sure that AVs will alter market demand for downtown locations and buildings, opening opportunities for further change.

Changes in communication technology, like changes in transportation technology, affected both private property and the public realm. Late-20th-century Western Union telegraph offices, for example, succumbed to competition from the internet. Similarly, by the second decade of the 21st century, few telephone booths were to be seen on city streets. Consequently, few small children could identify a telephone booth or explain its function.

Today, downtown New York, Philadelphia, and Boston are very different places than they were—not just because phone booths and telegraph offices have since disappeared. Downtowns are far larger and physically even more different from one another. Many of the activities that take place there today would have been unknown in 1790. New York has remained the largest city in America. Los Angeles and Chicago have supplanted Philadelphia and Boston as number two and three, and it is only a matter of time until Houston surpasses Chicago.

The Characteristics of Vibrant 21st-Century American Downtowns

Downtowns that have been thriving since their inception and those that became resurgent in the 21st century share several characteristics:

- Location with major warehousing, merchandising, and shipping activity
- Flourishing place of business
- Heterogenous residential district
- Major tourist destination
- Prosperous concentration of stores and restaurants
- Popular entertainment center
- Museums, libraries, hospitals, schools, and other institutions that serve the entire metropolitan region
- Public transportation system that makes downtown easily accessible for metropolitan area residents and international tourists while providing convenient, safe, affordable circulation when they get there
- Convenient and attractive public realm that includes streets, sidewalks, promenades, parks, and playgrounds that are open to anybody and provide something for everybody
- Concentration of trees and greenery that sustain a habitable environment
- District that public agencies (often with the help of the BID) keep safe, clean, and attractive

The single most important characteristic of any successful downtown is that it is a place where people do business. It is a place where goods and services intended for the surrounding area are sent for distribution and from which locally produced goods are exported around the world. Thus, by definition, downtowns are retail, wholesale, shipping, warehousing, and distribution centers.

Once there is a critical mass of merchandising, all sorts of other activities spring up that meet the needs and desires of people already downtown, both those who have come to trade and those who have settled there to serve them. Among its earliest businesses were those established to manufacture the products and provide the services for which people come downtown. By the 21st century, however, manufacturing had become a minor downtown activity. Between 1990 and 2017, it declined from 20 percent of the workforce to 8 percent in Los Angeles, 21 to 12 percent in Cleveland, and 11 to 4 percent in New York City.[25] By 2017, office work had become the most important urban business activity, representing 37 percent of the employment in Los Angeles, 35 percent in Cleveland, and 40 percent in New York City.[26]

Perhaps an even more important characteristic of vibrant 21st-century downtowns is the presence of thousands of residents who remain downtown when the office workers go home. Unlike the residents of 19th-century downtowns, who lived in low-rise, wooden buildings, 21st-century downtowners inhabit large apartment buildings, converted lofts and warehouses, and office buildings repurposed as high-rise residences. They settled for the same reasons as those in the 19th century, however, seeking new opportunities, working or looking for work, participating in a new economic venture, or enjoying the benefits of a thriving cultural center. These downtown residents are the critical mass of customers that support its huge variety of activities, everything from stores to restaurants and entertainment venues.

Many downtowns are host to thousands of tourists (both daytime visitors from the metropolitan region and vacationers who stay in downtown hotels). Not surprisingly, hotel occupancy and tourism have also been increasing in many downtowns. For example, the number of hotel rooms in lower Manhattan went from 2,300 in 2000 to 7,900 in 2017 and in Uptown Houston from 6,300 in 2000 to 8,000 in 2017 (1,000 more than in downtown Houston).[27] Whether local, national, or international, they represent billions of dollars of spending, intense street life, and employment for millions of people. Excluding places such as Orlando, Anaheim, and Las Vegas, which are major entertainment destinations, most of this activity takes place downtown. Tourist don't spend much time in the suburbs.

The stores, restaurants, and bars that operate downtown are used by the people who work downtown, visitors from the surrounding metropolitan area, national and international tourists, and residents. The same is true of libraries, museums, and other downtown institutions, as well as theaters, arenas, and stadiums. Many downtowns also include large convention centers that attract thousands of business tourists (during the days they are in operation). Some downtowns, such as those in Boston, New Haven, Philadelphia, and Baltimore, have major universities and hospitals. This complex mix of facilities is very different from the essentially residential surrounding suburbs, which is why so many suburban residents go downtown to shop, visit major institutions, and patronize entertainment venues.

To accommodate all those people, institutions, and activities, every downtown needs a suitable public realm of streets, squares, and parks. In the mid-20th century streets such as Michigan Avenue in Chicago and Market Street in Philadelphia, places such as Union Square in San Francisco and Market Square in Pittsburgh, and parks such as Balboa Park in San Diego and the parks along the Portland, Oregon riverfront provided all the excitement and activities needed by the people downtown. As a growing population began to move downtown at the end of the 20th and beginning of the 21st centuries, however, there was a need for a larger public realm that had been altered to provide room and be more convenient for the growing number of people downtown.

Denver, Minneapolis, and many other cities have experimented with removing cars from one or more shopping streets, adding benches, trees, and stylish street furniture, and introducing local bus service to attract more out-of-towners and to make downtown circulation more convenient for everybody. To be competitive they also needed improved access downtown from airports and the surrounding metropolitan area. Denver made the most ambitious and successful of such investments to bring people downtown and help them go to their desired destinations. It built an entirely new airport that opened in 1995, created a light rail system to connect the airport and its entire metropolitan area with a rebuilt downtown railroad station, and provided free bus service along its main downtown artery, 16th Street, connecting virtually every downtown destination. While making downtown more convenient, these investments also enhanced downtown livability. That is why more than 23,000 people now live in downtown Denver.[28]

Pittsburgh was one of the first cities to understand that a successful downtown had to sustain a livable environment. In 1943 it succeeded in

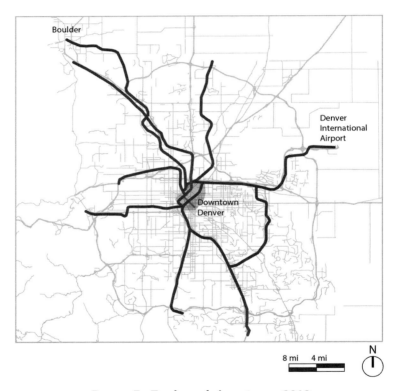

Denver FasTracks and airport map, 2018

Denver's FasTracks light rail system connects its international airport and the entire metropolitan region to the nation's 9th largest downtown. (Alexander Garvin)

getting the Pennsylvania State Legislature to pass laws that controlled smoke emission, established a public parking authority to build garages for the cars coming downtown, and created commissions to regulate and operate county traffic, transit, and waste disposal facilities and build new highways leading downtown.[29]

Some cities took quite different steps to sustain a livable downtown environment. Starting in 1996 New York City created the Green Streets Program to transform paved traffic triangles, which were not needed for regulating traffic, into parklets. Twenty-one years later there were 2,468 parklets where previously there had been asphalt.[30] In Chicago between 1996 and 2006, the city created 70 miles of planted median strips and installed 300,000 new trees.[31] By substantially increasing the amount of greenery, these two cities improved air quality, filtered stormwater, lowered ambient temperatures, increased the habitat for wildlife, and improved livability everywhere.

Many city departments do a first-rate job keeping streets and sidewalks clean, collecting and disposing of refuse, maintaining the flow of traffic, and controlling crime. Nevertheless, during the second half of the 20th century an increasing number of city governments reduced the proportions of their operating budgets devoted to providing downtown services. The resulting increase in filth, noise, and crime exacerbated the flight from downtown. In response, at the end of the century property owners and business owners banded together to form BIDs, which provided needed services for the entire district.

In some cases (Philadelphia's Center City BID, for example) they are legally incorporated and authorized to collect taxes directly from property owners without the city as an intermediary, thereby lessening local government leverage. The laws authorizing the creation of BIDs varied from state to state. By 2012, there were more than 1,400 BIDs in the United States and Canada, 67 in New York City alone.[32]

Predicting What Will Happen Downtown

The conventional wisdom about the fate of downtown has often been wrong. During the first half of the 20th century many experts believed that American cities would experience virtually continuous growth.

During much of the second half of the century they thought that cities were in an irreversible decline. Both erroneous beliefs were fostered by some of America's most thoughtful urbanists.

Seattle, 2010

Downtown Seattle experienced a brief period of decline in the 1960s and 1970s but has been experiencing resurgence for nearly four decades. (Alexander Garvin)

In 1910, Cass Gilbert and Frederick Law Olmsted Jr. predicted that New Haven, Connecticut would grow to a population of 400,000 by 1950. Ironically, this was the very year the city began a 50-year decline from its peak population of only 164,000.[33] Thirty-seven years after Gilbert and Olmsted Jr. made their prediction, Harland Bartholomew forecast that the population of St. Louis would climb to 900,000 in 1970. By that time, it had dropped to 622,000, had been falling for two consecutive decades, and continued to decline to one-third its previous size in 2010.[34]

In the second half of the 20th century many experts reached the opposite conclusion. Some thought downtowns were becoming obsolete. In 1982, the Brookings Institution even published a book titled *Urban Decline and the Future of American Cities*.[35] In their 1989 book

Downtown Inc.: How America Rebuilds Cities, Bernard Frieden and Lynne Sagalyn wrote that "forces beyond anyone's control were pushing" downtowns into "an economic back alley where they could die quietly."[36] Indeed, downtown Detroit lost 13,000 jobs between 1990 and 2017, while downtown Cleveland lost 24,000. Despite the common expectation of similar results throughout downtown America, during that period downtown Houston gained 30,000 jobs, downtown Atlanta gained 42,000, and center city Philadelphia gained 45,000.[37]

Those of us who want to keep our downtowns thriving and eliminate any reasons for decline must begin by learning to accurately predict the changes that will be happening downtown in the future. The rest of this book is about the forces that determine the territory and buildings that our downtowns occupy; the people and organizations that make changes to it; the ways in which changes in market demand, population, lifestyle, and technology will affect what they are engaged with; past mistakes that we need to avoid; the most recent best practices that will help us to succeed; and finally, my recommendations for actions we should be taking *now* to create vibrant downtowns for a new generation. Understanding all this will allow us to create vibrant downtowns for centuries to come.

Chapter 2

Where Is Downtown?

Downtowns are not finite objects, nor do they remain in place. They grow and shrink, spread and contract, and move around. The changing composition of their economic base induces those changes, as do their changing populations. Therefore, to understand how and why downtowns are ever-changing, one must first understand the basis of their locations and the ways in which a location is connected to the metropolitan area it serves.

Very few cities are centered around a single downtown. Downtown Philadelphia and downtown Boston have been at the center of the surrounding metropolitan region since their inception. In much of the rest of the country, however, there are multiple downtowns within a single city and more within its metropolitan areas. The city of Los Angeles (*not* including the separately chartered cities of Santa Monica, Beverly Hills, West Hollywood, Culver City, Glendale, and Pasadena), for example, includes more than a dozen downtowns, many of which, like Long Beach and Hollywood, are downtowns of major significance. There are currently three in Atlanta (downtown, midtown, and Buckhead), more than nine in New York City (lower Manhattan, Midtown, the Flatiron District, and Union Square in Manhattan; downtown and Dumbo in Brooklyn; and Long Island City, Flushing, and Jamaica in

Queens), two in Chicago (the Loop and North Michigan Avenue), and four in Houston (downtown, uptown, Greenway Plaza, and the Texas Medical Center).

Atlanta aerial rendering, 2018

Atlanta's three downtowns initially developed on the crest of Peachtree Street but began to mushroom after 1979 once the MARTA subway system had connected them with the airport. (Citiesense)

Long Island City aerial perspective, 2018

Long Island City became the first new 21st-century downtown in New York City once government redevelopment of the waterfront began and the territory around its major subway stations was rezoned. (Citiesense)

Downtowns are locations, clusters of properties, assemblages of buildings, sets of land uses; some parts are privately owned, the rest is commonly owned public realm. However, it is not just *any* location or cluster of properties. A main street in any small town has some of the features of downtown but is not big or diverse enough to be a true mixed-use, vibrant downtown.

Determining Its Location

Everybody has difficulty accurately defining the extent of downtown. The federal government used to determine the size and locations of American downtowns. But the last time the U.S. Census Bureau tabulated and reported statistics for specific downtowns (as opposed to whole cities and metropolitan areas) was 1984. While I was writing this book it became clear that downtowns could be compared only by using the territory served by a particular downtown business improvement district (BID), as identified by the International Downtown Association (IDA), or as reported on in real estate market reports. Consequently, throughout the book I provide statistics based on those definitions. Even so, using these sources can be problematic because of the many misconceptions of what defines the location of a downtown.

The IDA claims that "downtown" is everything within a half-mile or 1-mile radius of the center of a city. However, no downtown is a perfect circle, and many downtowns extend for much more or much less than a mile in every direction.

Defining *downtown* as everything within a specific BID is equally flawed, however. The BIDs in Chicago, San Francisco, Boston, and many other cities deal with only a small portion of those cities' downtowns. Although San Diego and Washington, DC have several BIDs, they do not cover the entire downtown either. Center City District Philadelphia, the Alliance for Downtown New York, and Downtown LA are among the BIDs that occupy territory that is generally considered to be downtown. Comparing what the BIDs and the IDA report as *downtown territory*, *population*, and *employment* underscores the difficulty of answering the question, "Where is downtown?"

As shown in Table 2.1, only one statistic appears to be available for every American downtown: office space (including government offices), measured in square feet. Moreover, as Table 2.2 illustrates, the amount of office space in a downtown is a particularly critical characteristic in defining that downtown. The largest concentration of office space in Atlanta is the 24 million square feet in Buckhead, far more than the 15 million square feet in downtown Atlanta, the 17 million square feet in downtown Detroit, the 18 million square feet in downtown Cincinnati, or the 21 million square feet in the Los Angeles Hollywood–Wilshire Corridor.

Table 2.1. Differing Definitions of Three Major U.S. Downtowns

City	BID Territory	IDA Territory	BID Employ-ment	IDA Employ-ment	BID Population	IDA Population[a]
Downtown LA	0.68 sq. mile	10.2 sq. miles	500,000	372,000	67,000	175,000
Lower Manhattan	0.44 sq. mile	2.6 sq. miles	276,000	527,000	61,000	173,000
Philadelphia CCD	0.90 sq. mile	7.2 sq. miles	308,000	288,000	66,000	170,000

BID = business improvement district; IDA = International Downtown Association.
[a]International Downtown Association and the Alliance for Downtown New York, Downtown LA, and Center City District (CCD) Philadelphia.

In some cases, downtowns have developed around large shopping facilities. Atlanta's Buckhead, now tied with downtown Sacramento as America's 19th largest downtown, evolved over several decades around its air-conditioned shopping malls. The same thing happened around the air-conditioned Galleria on Post Oak Boulevard in Uptown Houston, now the country's 18th largest downtown. Tysons Corner, Virginia, outside Washington, DC, also grew up around two air-conditioned malls: Tysons Corner Center and Tysons Galleria. By 2010 Tysons Corner, the nation's 21st largest downtown, contained numerous corporate headquarters and a residential population of 20,000, enough to be considered a real downtown.[1]

Table 2.2. 30 Largest U.S. Downtowns in 2017

Place	Downtown	Office Space (square feet)	Population
1	Midtown New York	243,000,000[a]	391,000[a]
2	Downtown Chicago	142,000,000[a]	86,000[a]
3	Lower Manhattan	82,000,000	61,000
4	Downtown Los Angeles	72,000,000	65,000
5	Downtown San Francisco	52,000,000[a]	40,000[a]
6	Downtown Houston	50,000,000	10,000
7	Civic Center San Francisco	42,000,000[a]	26,881[a]
8	Center City Philadelphia	41,000,000	190,000
9	Downtown Denver	38,000,000	23,000
10	Downtown Pittsburgh	35,000,000	14,000
11	Downtown Washington, DC	31,000,000[a]	63,000[a]
12	Downtown Minneapolis	29,000,000[a]	43,000
13	Downtown Dallas	28,000,000[a]	11,000
14	Downtown Baltimore	28,000,000	43,000
15	Downtown Charlotte	28,000,000	27,000
16	Downtown Seattle	27,000,000[a]	70,000
17	Downtown Portland	26,000,000	26,000[a]
18	Uptown Houston	26,000,000	167,000
19	Downtown Sacramento	24,000,000	21,000
20	Buckhead Atlanta	24,000,000	90,000
21	Downtown Tysons Corner	23,000,000	21,000[a]
22	Hollywood–Wilshire	21,000,000[a]	273,000[a]
23	Downtown Cleveland	19,000,000[a]	15,000
24	Downtown Jersey City	19,000,000[a]	48,000[a]
25	Downtown Cincinnati	18,000,000[a]	18,000
26	Downtown Newark	18,000,000[a]	4,000[a]
27	Downtown Detroit	17,000,000[a]	5,000
28	Downtown Atlanta	15,000,000	27,000
29	Downtown Miami	15,000,000[a]	89,000
30	Downtown Fort Worth	14,000,000	8,000

[a]Non–business improvement district source.

Each downtown is different in character and is evolving in different ways. As explained in Chapter 1, downtowns follow one of three trajectories: continuing to grow, struggling or declining, and resurgent. Recent investments in the public realm and transit are now providing each of them with second and third acts, however. Their further evolution, especially that of Uptown Houston, may well establish a new direction for downtown America.

Century City in Los Angeles, Greenway Plaza in Houston, and Atlantic Station in Atlanta are downtowns that were planned as mixed-use from the beginning. In each of these three cases, retail shopping is at the core of the development, which also includes hotels, corporate office buildings, thousands of residences, and ample parking.[2] Century City, which once had a large theater, still includes a hospital, medical offices, and a museum and will soon have a subway station. Greenway Plaza also includes multiple fitness facilities, three full-service banking centers, and conferencing facilities, and Atlantic Station contains a hotel, an exhibition center, and a variety of health facilities.

Where the Businesses Are

Some mid-20th-century Americans would have argued against the 19th-century opinion that downtown was "where manufacturers go to receive or send goods," pointing out that manufacturing was moving away from multistory downtown structures to single-story buildings with horizontal production lines. Others would have objected to the 19th-century opinion that downtowns had to include warehousing and shipping, explaining that we no longer shipped products in cartons and crates; we shipped cargo in large containers. They would have pointed out that multistory, downtown warehouses had been abandoned long ago and that piers and railyards had been replaced by huge sites on the outskirts of downtown that could accommodate large containers, numerous trucks, and the cranes that loaded the containers onto trucks. Still others would have explained that shipping by truck depended on interstate highways rather than traffic-laden downtown streets. Yet plenty of downtowns have thrived despite losing manufacturing plants, warehouses, and shipping facilities. Downtown

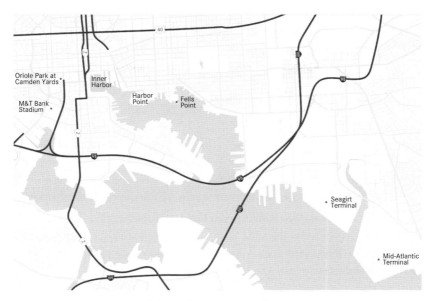

Map of the Baltimore waterfront, 2018

The Inner Harbor was opened for redevelopment once Baltimore's major shipping facilities moved to the Seagirt and Mid-Atlantic terminals. (Baolin Shen and Alexander Garvin)

Baltimore and Cleveland, for example, are resurgent despite losing such facilities.

Initially, downtown Baltimore grew around its port. By the 21st century, however, that port had moved from downtown 2 miles southwest to the Seagirt Marine and Mid-Atlantic terminals, both of which had plenty of room for cranes, containers, and truck parking. As a result, during the past half-century Baltimore demolished piers, rebuilt bulkheads, and relocated railroad and utility service; created sites for office towers, retail stores, hotels, convention facilities, sports stadiums, and museums; and reclaimed its waterfront for public use.[3]

Its centerpiece, where shipping had thrust the city into existence, remained in place. But as a result of redevelopment in the 1970s, it had been transformed into a tourist entertainment retail marketplace. However, its newest and trendiest extensions are centered at Harbor East and Harbor Point. They are the locations chosen by corporations

Inner Harbor from Harbor Point, Baltimore, 2017

Even before all the sites in the Inner Harbor had been developed, new construction shifted east along the water's edge to Harbor East, Harbor Point, and Fells Point. (Alexander Garvin)

opening offices or expanding in Baltimore, by hotels and restaurants seeking to profit from the increasing tourist traffic, and by high-end national retailers (such as J. Crew, Brooks Brothers, and Whole Foods) selling them consumer goods.

The location of downtown Baltimore may not have changed, but because of a half century of planning and redevelopment, the market that downtown serves and the amount of territory that it occupies has grown. Consequently, downtown Baltimore now extends southeast past Harbor Point to Fells Point and southwest to Oriole Park at Camden Yards and Otterbein.

Half a century ago, when the resuscitation of Baltimore's Inner Harbor began, the Cleveland waterfront was a disaster. The Cuyahoga River had been degraded by a century of industrial waste. The nadir was reached in June 1969, when the Cuyahoga River famously caught fire. Although this had happened numerous times before, this fire forced the city to finally take action to transform its liability into a major asset.[4]

Port activity in Cleveland, along Lake Erie, is only one-third the traffic of the port of Baltimore, the 13th largest port in the United States, with shipping cargo valued at $33.9 billion.[5] This figure reflects

Cuyahoga Riverfront from Heritage Park, Cleveland, 2017
The City of Cleveland cleaned up its waterfront brownfields, eliminated upland sources of pollution, and transformed large sections of the Cuyahoga Riverfront into attractive parkland. (Alexander Garvin)

the smaller role shipping plays in the local economy. Thus, waterfront business, despite its prominence, is far less important in Cleveland than in Baltimore.

Instead, Cleveland's riverfront has been reclaimed for parks and ferry landings. Facing them, once-abandoned lofts have become upscale residences and popular bars and restaurants. Its lakefront, on the other hand, includes First Energy Stadium, the Rock and Roll Hall of Fame, and Burke Lakefront Airport.

However, there is a fundamental difference in the role played by each of these two waterfronts. Cleveland's waterfront provides facilities for the nearby residential population. In addition to reviving demand for the area's historic row houses, Baltimore's acts as a regional magnet for the personnel of the many growing businesses that occupy its office buildings, tens of thousands of students going to the University of Maryland and Johns Hopkins, and tens of millions of tourists and suburban visitors who occupy hotels and patronize restaurants and stores, visiting everything from Camden Yards to the aquarium. Consequently, between 2009 and 2017, the number of downtown residents increased by 7 percent, the number of downtown jobs by 12 percent, and the number of downtown hotel rooms by 15 percent.[6]

Where the Stores Are

Mid-20th-century Americans would have objected to the notion that downtown was where you went shopping, pointing out that suburban shopping centers were replacing downtown stores and that almost nobody went shopping in major downtowns such as lower Manhattan and downtown Los Angeles. Many shopping facilities that were there at the start of the 20th century were gone by the end of the century (including all the department stores). The same was true of downtown Cleveland, downtown Detroit, and other struggling downtowns.

By 2018, that would have shocked most Angelinos. At that time there were scores of downtown retailers, including Macy's, Target, and the Grand Central Market (in 2018 home to 38 retailers), which had remained a popular shopping destination since it was established in 1917. Whereas shopping in downtown LA was resurgent, in other downtowns, such as Beverly Hills, Westwood, and Pasadena, shopping had never waned since those downtowns had begun to function.

The first department store in Los Angeles opened in 1896 on Broadway and was appropriately named Broadway. Next came the City of Paris, Hamburger's People's Store (later the May Company), and others. The city's movie palaces followed the department stores to Broadway. Between 1910 and 1931, they provided seating for 15,000 patrons. Like Broadway in Manhattan, they "screened Hollywood's latest fare, played host to star-studded premieres and were filled nightly with thousands of moviegoers."[7]

In 1929, when Bullocks department store opened its second location on Wilshire Boulevard, 2 miles west of its original 1907 downtown Broadway location, downtown Los Angeles began a slow decline.[8] Two years after Bullocks opened, the 2,200-seat Wiltern Theater opened 1 mile farther west on Wilshire Boulevard. By that time Hollywood Boulevard, 3 miles north, had become an equally important movie district. As Raymond Chandler explained, the city hated the idea that the movie business had moved to Hollywood, but it should have considered "itself damn lucky,"[9] because the movie business was still in Los Angeles, just not downtown.

Wilshire Boulevard, downtown Beverly Hills, 2013

Starting in the 1920s, commercial activity that had once dominated downtown LA shifted to a series of metropolitan subcenters, such as Wilshire Boulevard in Beverly Hills. (Alexander Garvin)

In 1929, 29.6 percent of all Los Angeles County retail sales took place downtown. Ten years later that figure had dropped to 17 percent.[10] Bullocks continued following its customers into the metropolitan region, opening stores in Westwood in 1932, in Pasadena in 1945, and at Fashion Square in Santa Ana in 1957–1958. Other department stores and movie theaters did the same. By 1940, there were new downtowns developing along the "Miracle Mile" (Wilshire Boulevard between La Brea and Fairfax avenues), in Hollywood, in Beverly Hills, in Westwood, and all the way to Santa Monica. The same flight of stores and theaters to the suburbs, in search of their former downtown customers, was taking place in Baltimore, Cleveland, Detroit, and cities across the country.

At first other businesses remained in downtown, but by the mid-20th century, like retailers, they sought their customers and personnel outside downtown. Because so many nonretailing activities did not move away from downtown until after World War II, many people deluded themselves into thinking that downtown was quite healthy.

In Los Angeles, hospitals and universities chose to locate beyond the traditional downtown, as did newcomers to the city. In 1945, 230,000 people lived in the San Fernando Valley. By 1950 that population had more than doubled and by 1960 had redoubled.[11] Greater Los Angeles was experiencing similar suburban growth. In 1953, 400 people a day were settling in the suburbs, rather than downtown as they had been doing during the previous 13 years.[12] The flight to the suburbs was not just a Los Angeles phenomenon. It had been happening across the country and had accelerated in the post–World War II period. The trend continued between 1975 and 1980, for example, when 453,000 New Yorkers moved to the suburbs while only 130,000 suburbanites settled in the city.[13]

The flight to the suburbs was not the only reason for the decline of downtown Los Angeles. Its older office buildings were not competitive with the new buildings opening in Beverly Hills and Westwood. The movie palaces on Broadway were beginning to succumb to competition from television. Many of them began closing their doors in the 1950s and 1960s, some converted to flea markets, churches, or other uses then in demand. The movie palaces that remained were expensive to maintain and more expensive to restore. Moreover, without its pervasive neon lights, Broadway was perceived as dangerous at night. By 1998, only two of the 37 original theaters were still showing films.[14]

Many other downtowns experienced the same departure of retail, wholesale, and shipping activities. Shuttering the great movie palaces was a more existential loss to a city that thought of itself as the world's film center, however. But like Detroit, Cleveland, and so many downtowns in the Rust Belt, downtown LA was becoming one more of the country's declining single-function business districts, with vacant and underused buildings. As Jane Jacobs had predicted, these downtowns were becoming "too exclusively devoted to one type of activity" and thus were in danger of becoming "has-beens."[15]

Traveling Downtown

Identifying a concentration of activity or buildings as "downtown" is not enough. To be a properly functioning downtown, it must be easily accessible from the metropolitan area and from the rest of the world. When you get there, it must be easy to move around and have a welcoming public realm that provides places for a wide range of activities. This requires arteries that handle traffic coming by boat, car, bus, truck, rail, streetcar, boxcar, or airplane traveling from places where there are people and goods that must go to and from downtown. In other words, downtown is a location whose businesses, retailers, institutions, entertainment venues, hotels, and restaurants are easily reachable from many points of origin and where people are able to circulate quickly and efficiently between successive destinations.

After World War II, cities across the nation invested huge sums (largely subsidized by the federal government with funds from the Federal Aid Highway Act of 1956) to increase downtown accessibility by automobile, truck, and bus. They also invested huge sums in acquiring property and building garages for the cars that came downtown by highway and parked downtown for the day. Political leaders were convinced that this would make it easier for the growing suburban population to get to downtown shopping and employment destinations. Ironically, the opposite occurred. Widespread use of trucks, buses, and cars using interstate highways accelerated the already-occurring flight of residents to the suburbs, followed by downtown retailers seeking to regain their customers and downtown businesses seeking a larger, closer labor pool.

The owners of the empty buildings they left behind continued to pay for building maintenance, insurance, and real estate taxes, without receiving rents to offset those expenditures. So they demolished them, paved the sites, and opened parking lots that occasionally produced enough parking fees to cover their expenses. The resulting plethora of parking lots only exacerbated downtown desolation.

It wasn't until the 1970s that different downtown leadership made major investments in public transportation, both to bring customers downtown and then to move them to their various destinations once they were downtown. As mentioned in the previous chapter, perhaps the most successful example is Denver.

As of 2017, Denver's 122-mile rapid transit system, the Regional Transportation District (RTD), often referred to as FasTracks (its funding program), includes 57 stations, linking downtown with the entire metropolitan area and its major international airport. FasTracks carries people more than 20 miles to downtown from eight of the 12 surrounding counties. These commuters, along with the 80,000 people who live downtown, the 48,000 students enrolled in various universities located downtown, and the more than 16 million overnight visitors staying in 95,000 hotel rooms in 35 downtown hotels, all patronize 4.2 million square feet of retailing and work in 35.3 million square feet of downtown office space.[16]

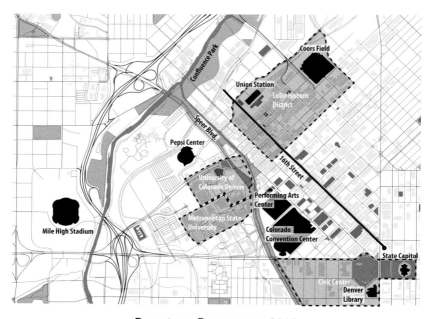

Downtown Denver map, 2017

Nearly every important destination in Denver is within walking distance of the 16th Street Pedestrian Mall. (Alexander Garvin)

The core of downtown Denver is the 16th Street Mall, a transitway that first opened in 1982. Nearly everything a visitor, office worker, or resident might want is within two blocks of 16th Street: most hotels, the State Capitol, the Performing Arts Center, the movie theaters and restaurants, the Colorado Convention Center, Union Station, the museums, the library, and the LoDo Historic District, and within four blocks Coors Field, Pepsi Center, the University of Colorado Denver, and Metropolitan State University of Denver. The proximity of all these destinations and the density of this downtown are possible because people can travel on a free bus going up and down the 1.4 miles of its main artery, 16th Street. Its traffic along 18 blocks, apart from the free bus, is exclusively pedestrian.[17] Moreover, this clustering of public destinations is no accident. Except for the State Capitol, a few hotels, and LoDo, all of it, including the 16th Street transitway, was built during the past half century.

16th Street Mall, Denver, 2011

A free bus that travels up and down 16th Street operates on 90-second headways. (Alexander Garvin)

The combination of the 16th Street Transitway and the RTD Light Rail System allows downtown Denver, albeit with a much larger market than Cleveland, to occupy a smaller district of 0.7 square mile with almost twice Cleveland's office space.

Attracting Residents Downtown

The flight of business to the suburbs resulted in a growing supply of multistory downtown buildings at the end of the 20th century. The lower price of these obsolete structures made them attractive candidates for conversion to residential use or for redevelopment as new buildings. Developers in lower Manhattan and downtown Los Angeles were able to make a profit converting or replacing them because of the growing demand for housing and the low residential vacancy rates in these cities. Successful downtown housing development was more difficult in a city with a growing downtown population, such as Denver or Minneapolis, and particularly difficult in a city such as Cleveland, which had experienced a substantial drop in employment and population. But in all three cities, as in so many others, the problem was the absence of services.

The relationship between the actual number of residents in an area and the number needed to support necessary services is a "chicken and egg" proposition. A critical mass of residents is needed to support retail services (e.g., grocery, drug and stationery stores), and a critical mass of children is needed to justify opening and operating a school. In the last decade of the 20th century an average drug store in a regional shopping center occupied a gross leasable area of 13,500 square feet and collected median sales of $347 per square foot.[18] Typical supermarkets occupied 50,000 square feet and needed between 3,000 and 40,000 customers, depending on their income.[19] Because residents need both drug stores and supermarkets, these numbers establish a minimum population for any healthy downtown residential community. Conversely, a critical mass of services in any neighborhood is needed to support any residential population.

In 1980, there were only 338 people living in the north loop district of Minneapolis, which was then a district of deteriorating buildings and declining businesses. Over the next decade 309 people moved in, among them artists who pioneered loft living. The cost of settling in these empty buildings was low because their owners did not have to pay debt service on large mortgages (they did not have any) or high taxes (which did not apply to such structures) and because, once they had installed necessary plumbing and appliances, they let the artists pay for and install partitions and finishes. This was truly affordable housing.

By 2000, the area contained 1,515 residents, still not enough for a self-sufficient residential community, but by 2010 there were 4,263 residents, an adequate number for a lively, mixed-use neighborhood.[20] Its buildings also provided a home for 9,500 jobs, a number that had been

North Loop (Warehouse District), Minneapolis, 2005

New residential construction in the North Loop (Warehouse District) of down-town Minneapolis. (Alexander Garvin)

increasing with the popularity and population of the neighborhood.[21] Increasing demand led to increasing rents and the inevitable gentrification. The rental tenants, who had pioneered loft living and could not afford to remain in the area, were replaced by occupants who demanded and received better fixtures and services for their higher rents. But condominium occupants either remained in a much-improved neighborhood or profited from selling their residences at the appreciated value.

Not only had the area's population increased over those decades, but residents' spendable income had increased as well. Accordingly, in 2013, a 38,000-square-foot Whole Foods opened in one of the new apartment buildings erected in the neighborhood. Two years later, Minneapolis's North Loop made it onto a list of "the 12 coolest neighborhoods in America."[22]

Similarly, the resurgence of downtown Denver also required a critical mass of downtown residents. In 1986, 6,500 people lived in its 3,200 apartments. By 2015 that had grown to nearly 23,000 residents in more than 14,000 apartments.[23] That year a King Soopers grocery store opened near Union Station in downtown Denver. The store was within walking distance of three of Denver's burgeoning residential neighborhoods: the Lower Downtown Historic District (LoDo), Ballpark, and Central

Platte Valley. Two years later it was joined nearby by a 50,000-square-foot Whole Foods.[24] By the time Whole Foods became downtown's second grocery store, those three neighborhoods had already attracted 14,000 of downtown Denver's 80,000 residents.[25] That was one reason why in 2017, *U.S. News & World Report* ranked Denver as America's second best place to live.[26]

Union Station, Denver, 2017
Once Union Station had been reconfigured and the yards rebuilt, new residential development boomed. (Alexander Garvin)

Attracting a critical mass of downtown residents was much more difficult in Cleveland. Its industrial and commercial structures began to empty out in the second half of the 20th century. The city lost one-quarter of its manufacturing jobs between 1958 and 1967.[27] Another 42 percent departed between 1983 and 2005.[28] Initially, very few of the leftover spaces were being adapted for residential use. The demand just was not there, as the empty downtown warehouses, office buildings, and stores demonstrated. Moreover, the city of Cleveland had lost 438,000 residents between 1970 and 2010, many of whom used to shop down-town, particularly at the now shuttered department stores.

The lost customers could not be replaced from the Cleveland met-ropolitan area, whose population remained static.[29] The price of living downtown may have been attractive for people who still lived in the

Warehouse District, downtown Cleveland, 2018

Cleveland's Warehouse District was one of the first areas in downtown Cleveland that was transformed into a popular residential neighborhood. (Andrew Sandweiss)

metropolitan area, but downtown Cleveland lacked the services needed by potential residential customers.

The city's first new residential district began to emerge in the late 20th century in the converted factories and lofts of its Warehouse District. Those conversions took off after a grocery store, Constantino's, opened on West 9th Street in 2005. At that time only 8,000 people lived downtown.[30] By 2017, the company operated downtown branches in Playhouse Square, in University Circle, and in two nearby suburbs.

It was easy to identify the location of downtown Cleveland at the turn of the 21st century. After all, a genuine downtown is where there are enough conveniently connected suppliers and consumers to attract a critical mass of businesses and a large enough number of residents to support all its daily needs. Together they create the 24-hour, mixed-use concentration of activity that we refer to as downtown.

By the 21st century, many other American downtowns were experiencing an influx of new residents. Between 2000 and 2017, for example, downtown Philadelphia, which already had 36,000 apartments, added another 1,200 apartments while gaining 72,600 jobs.[31] Downtown Minneapolis, which was home to 31,900 people in 2006, now includes 9,000 more residents.[32] Between 1990 and 2016 it also added 15.6 million square feet of office space and 4,400 hotel rooms.[33]

During the same period, downtown Detroit, which had already lost

Fifth Street light rail station, Minneapolis, 2017

Development of new housing has begun along the light rail corridor that begins at Target Field in downtown Minneapolis and connects the University of Minnesota, the airport, the Mall of America, and downtown St. Paul. (Alexander Garvin)

423,000 jobs in second half of the 20th century, lost another 8,300 jobs.[34] Its entire economy had changed. In 2017 there were only 20,000 manufacturing jobs in a city that had had 349,000 in 1950.[35] The 5,300 people who lived in the 4,000 downtown apartments did not move to Detroit in response to its declining job opportunities.[36]

The Impact of the Internet

The new residents of Minneapolis, Philadelphia, and countless other downtowns with growing economies moved in because of employment opportunities and a ready and growing supply of downtown housing. Both the new employment opportunities and the less expensive housing were products of computers and the internet.

Employment in information technology (IT) rose from 450,000 (0.6 percent of the U.S. labor force) in 1970 to 4.6 million (8.1 percent of the U.S. labor force) in 2016.[37] These changes would have been impossible without the growth in home and workplace computer use. By 2014, 85 percent of U.S. households had computers.

Today more than half of the workforce consists of people born after 1980. Most of them are "digital natives, collaborative, adept at multitasking and their attitudes and expectations will have a major impact on the work environment."[38] Personal computers and the internet allow them to work from anywhere: home, their own or somebody else's office, a hotel room, or an internet café. This is one reason the demand for office space has been declining and the number of freelance workers growing. The increase in collaborative tools has allowed different people in different locations to work on the same document, thereby reducing the need for meeting and conference rooms.

It does not take much imagination to understand that the internet has spawned all sorts of new tech industries, many of which have eagerly located downtown. It is less obvious that changes in space utilization caused by using computers and the internet have also spawned entirely new forms of business organization. Co-working facilities, such as WeWork, are just one example of what inventive businesses have done to profit from these changes. Combining technologies, workstations, and equipment that intercommunicate in a single building is now common. One example is Amalgamated Drawing Office in Greenpoint, Brooklyn. For a monthly fee of $600, members have access to "a staffed fabrication lab with tools including 3-D printers, a laser cutter and an etching press."[39]

The reverse is also true: Technological changes have made many older office buildings obsolete. In the past 20 years, developers have been purchasing them the same way they used to acquire lofts, warehouses, and multistory manufacturing for reuse as apartment buildings and hotels. Changes in technology (particularly computers and the internet) have substantially reduced the amount and character of space needed by most businesses, freeing up space in class B office structures, manufacturing lofts, and warehouses for reuse as apartment buildings. Initially, the cost of converting these quite different buildings was lower than the cost of acquiring land and building suburban one-family houses. The contemporaneous provision of new transit service rendered the cost of traveling to and from work, shopping, and leisure activities competitive with suburban alternatives.

Computer and internet use resulted in changes in office employment and a major reduction in the amount of space needed for filing, storage, and clerical activity. Accordingly, filing cabinets and filing clerks, typewriters and typists, and even address books are no longer needed, and neither is the space they occupied. In 1970 the typical U.S. office worker occupied between 500 and 700 square feet.[40] By 2017, that number had fallen to 151 square feet.[41]

As a result, firms needed less space per worker and could pay a higher price per square foot for the space they did occupy. However, the space they occupied had to be wired to accommodate the latest technology and provide ready access to the internet. The users of the office space were also changing. In 2018 employment in New York City's tech industries was estimated at 120,000 (an increase of 60 percent since 2008), while it had fallen to about 180,000 in Wall Street financial and investment services.[42] Naturally, obsolete class B office buildings with mid-20th-century wiring found it difficult to compete for tenants.

Computer and internet use has allowed small startup companies to operate within smaller offices and with much less clerical support. In response, a new form of business office emerged in 2006: co-working space.[43] Each business membership entitles the occupant to rent office space with on-demand access to high-speed internet, printers, meeting rooms, kitchens stocked with snacks and beverages, and often couches and other places in which to take a break from work.

As of 2016, there was a total of 27 million square feet of co-working space in the United States (0.7 percent of the entire U.S. inventory of office space).[44] Nevertheless, despite the hope that co-working facilities would alter downtown America, it represents less than 1 percent of the nation's office space—not enough to matter. Even where startup companies are thought to have played an important role, such as in lower Manhattan, co-working facilities occupied only 1.13 percent of downtown office space.[45] Besides, there are too few new startup companies in the United States to have a significant impact on all downtown America:

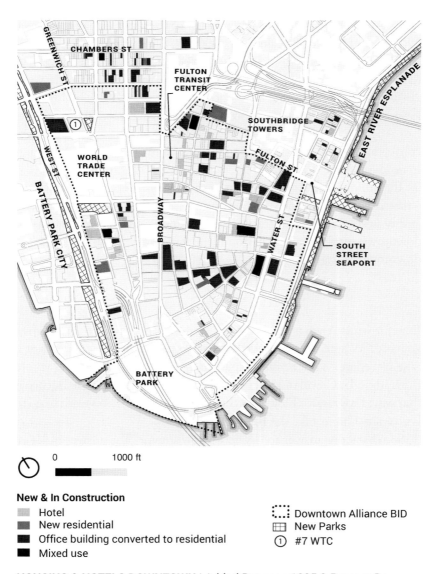

New & In Construction

▨ Hotel	⣀	Downtown Alliance BID
▨ New residential	⊞	New Parks
■ Office building converted to residential	①	#7 WTC
■ Mixed use		

HOUSING & HOTELS DOWNTOWN | Added Between 1995 & Present Day

Lower Manhattan map, 2018

For the past quarter century private developers have been converting lower Manhattan office buildings into apartment buildings and hotels, as well as investing in the construction of new apartment buildings and hotels. (Citiesense)

Between 2000 and 2015, the total number of startups fluctuated between 220,000 and 236,000 (peaking in 2006).[46]

When developers offer to purchase obsolete buildings for conversion to residential use, property owners are happy to sell. That is why, between 2001 and 2017, real estate developers converted 96 office buildings in lower Manhattan into 10,675 apartments.[47] Developers in downtown Los Angeles, Minneapolis, and Baltimore are currently profiting from converting their similarly large pool of obsolete class B office buildings to residential use.

The buildings that were converted to residential occupancy attracted a new downtown residential population (particularly Millennials and empty nesters). Thus, contrary to conventional wisdom, the increasing downtown residential population is the *result*, rather than the cause, of downtown resurgence.

It's a Moving Target

Downtown isn't what it used to be. In the Denver Metro Area, when you ask, "Where is downtown?" people reply, "Get on FasTracks, it'll take you there." When you ask people in Baltimore, they direct you to the harbor. In Cleveland, they are likely to reply, "Playhouse Square is that way; Progressive Field is in the other direction; if you want to go to University Circle, take the Redline."

So what's the answer to "Where's downtown?" The answer is, "It's a moving target."

Chapter 3

How and Why Downtown America Is Changing

America's suburban population increased dramatically between 1945, when suburban residents represented 13 percent of the population, and 1960, when suburbanites represented 33 percent of the country's population.[1] One reason for the shift was that many people were attracted by the availability of suburban residences that were larger and cheaper and included a yard. They could purchase a new house or desirable existing residence with a Federal Housing Administration (FHA)-insured, long-term, low-interest, self-amortizing mortgage. That was one reason that home ownership in America rose from 44 percent in 1940 to 62 percent in 1960.[2]

During this period of suburban growth, there were only two urban trajectories: growth and decline. Cities such as Dallas, Phoenix, and San Diego continued to grow despite suburban growth. This resulted in their downtowns occupying larger amounts of territory, developers continuing to build additional space for the new residents, businesses, and stores, and an expanding public realm to serve them.

Other cities, such as Detroit and St. Louis, began losing population, not just because of the attractiveness of less expensive suburban home ownership in areas made accessible by highway construction, financed largely by the Federal Aid Highway Act of 1956. In the 1960s urban crime had begun to rise and municipal services to decline.[3] Living in the suburbs was thought to be safer than in cities with growing crime problems.

By 1990 the 124,800,000 Americans who lived in the suburbs represented nearly half of the nation.[4] In addition to affordable housing, these new suburbanites were attracted by the greater variety and lower prices of goods offered by stores that had moved away from downtown to suburban shopping centers. Once there was a significant suburban population, businesses followed the new suburbanites because they wanted access to the growing pool of nearby residents, whom they thought of as potential employees.

The post–World War II flight of population, retail stores, and businesses to the suburbs resulted in substantial decreases in downtown populations (residents, workers, and retail customers) of many cities and caused a similar decline in demand for downtown property. Baltimore went from 859,000 people in 1940 to 621,000 in 2010 (a 28 percent decline). During the same period Cincinnati's population dropped from 504,000 to 299,000 (a 41 percent decline) and Newark's from 430,000 to 277,000 (a 36 percent decline).

Few people expected the third trajectory that appeared in the latter part of the 20th century. They did not anticipate that some cities that had been declining would start growing again. Between 1970 and 1980, New York City's population fell from 7.9 million to 7.1 million (a drop of just under 12 percent). Then, starting in 1980, it began to grow again, reaching a 1.1 million (16 percent) increase by 2010. The same shift occurred in Seattle, which experienced a drop of 63,000 (11 percent) between 1960 and 1980, when population growth resumed, resulting in an increase of 115,000 (23 percent) by 2010.

The 1990 census is a good point from which to measure changes to downtown America. It also is appropriate because the early 1990s is when widespread internet service began, deindustrialization accelerated, crime rates started to decline, and downtown business improvement districts (BIDs) began to proliferate, opening opportunities for new business and property development that became the basis for action by individuals, institutions, and governments that generated downtown resurgence in some American downtowns, reversed downtown decline in others, and sometimes accelerated growth.

What Stays Downtown

In answering the question "What stays downtown?," some mid-19th-century Americans would have said, "Receiving and sending goods." Others would have replied, "Shopping" or "Coming or going to the railroad station" or some other public facility. Many mid-20th-century Americans would have replied that activities had been moving elsewhere, whereas early-21st-century Americans would have had other reasons to object. Now, when I ask, "What stays downtown?" I get the answer, "I do. That's where I live."

From decade to decade, downtown activities change as they adjust to fluctuations in the size and character of both downtown and metropolitan populations, businesses, and institutions. For example, between 1970 and 2010, Cleveland's population dropped by nearly half a million people; many of its downtown office buildings went out of use, and all its downtown department stores closed. Religious institutions followed their parishioners into the suburbs. Downtown museums, hospitals, universities, and underused buildings remained in place, however.[5] After all, buildings are not torn down merely because the activities that took place there and building occupants move away.

The evolution of downtown Baltimore demonstrates that a decline in a city's population is not necessarily accompanied by the departure of downtown activities. Despite a loss of one-third of its population since 1950, Baltimore's downtown was able to expand because the city made significant investments that attracted additional businesses and residents that augmented downtown activity.

Deindustrialization

In the United States, employment in manufacturing plummeted from 17.8 million jobs (25 percent of the national economy) in 1970 to 12.3 million (8.6 percent of the national economy) in 2016.[6] However, the number of firms involved grew from 3.4 million in 1977 to about 5 million in 2014. Consequently, the average number of employees per firm fell from five people in 1970 to two people in 2014.

Despite the decline in employment, the value of manufacturing output soared between 1990 and 2017, going from $3.3 billion to $5.7

billion (in constant 2017 dollars), a 73 percent increase.[7] Growing reliance on automation and technology are among the explanations. This ability to produce more manufactured goods of greater value with fewer people has, in turn, resulted in a dramatic drop in demand for manufacturing space. Consequently, over the past half century, entire districts devoted to manufacturing have been abandoned.

Cities such as Pittsburgh, where 62,300 people (one-third of its workforce) had been employed in manufacturing in 1970, compensated for the loss of nearly 49,000 manufacturing jobs over the next 32 years with increases in other sectors of the economy, such as tech.[8] Consequently, the loss of manufacturing jobs did not prevent its downtown from prospering, in the process replacing blue collar employment with opportunities for a more skilled labor force.[9]

In Detroit, Buffalo, and St. Louis, where there was insufficient growth in other sectors of the economy, the impact was deleterious. Total employment between 1990 and 2016 dropped 64 percent in Detroit, 23 percent in Buffalo, and 10 percent in St. Louis.[10] Manufacturing in these and many other cities took place primarily in single-story buildings. Empty single-story manufacturing buildings are difficult to adapt for nonindustrial activities.

However, in downtowns such as Detroit and St. Louis, which are not experiencing resurgence, there are successful examples of the conversion of one- and two-story manufacturing buildings into restaurants, retailing, sports facilities, banks, garages, and even offices—but not housing, which has been one of the essential ingredients of vibrant 21st-century downtowns. Moreover, converting single-story manufacturing districts is particularly difficult, because that often involves major investment in decontaminating huge territories, reorganizing the infrastructure, and creating an entirely different street network. This explains the devastating impact of deindustrialization on some downtowns. Nevertheless, in single-story warehouse districts outside downtown Dallas, Los Angeles, and other thriving cities, it is a matter of time before new buildings used for other purposes will replace them.

Multistory manufacturing buildings present an entirely different situation. They can be both assets and liabilities. These structures were built to carry much heavier loads per square foot, have higher ceilings

Single-story industrial district just outside downtown Dallas, 2016
Initially factories moved out of multistory buildings in urban areas, where manufacturing was cumbersome, and moved into single-story suburban buildings
with easy truck access from nearby highways. As demand for space increases
in dense downtowns such as Dallas, the once-new one-story buildings will be
replaced by businesses that cannot find adequate space at a reasonable price
downtown. (Alexander Garvin)

(often high enough to insert an extra mezzanine level), and include
large plate glass windows that are not common in residential buildings.
These assets make them particularly attractive to occupants, especially
artists seeking unconventional living quarters and live–work spaces in
particular. More important, often potential tenants are willing to occupy
whole floors or portions of them without requiring the installation of
partitions, finishes, or much more than a bathroom and kitchen. Thus,
they can be used for residential purposes without spending the money
necessary to construct a brand-new apartment building. Consequently,
they can cost far less to occupy.

On the other hand, they may need expensive construction to comply with local building codes. Unlike office buildings, their large floor
plates may require cutting large openings in the center of the building
to provide adequate natural light and ventilation. They may also need
additional fire stairs to comply with fire code requirements specifying
minimum distances from apartment entrances. As a result, artists often
move in illegally, generating demand for legal conversions, which only
the wealthy can afford.

New York City was the first large city that dealt with the problem of
extremely expensive legal conversion of illegally occupied, multistory

SoHo, 1977

manufacturing buildings. However, it acted only when it became clear that SoHo, a district filled with architecturally important cast-iron buildings, was rapidly becoming a neighborhood of illegal residences. In 1971, the NYC Planning Commission altered the area's zoning to permit residential occupancy by artists.

Then, in 1975, the City Council altered the provisions of the city's J-51 Tax Exemption and Abatement Program (originally enacted in 1955 and named after the section number of the city's administrative code).[11] The J-51 Program granted building owners a 12-year real estate tax exemption for renovation that legalized residential occupancy and provided abatement from annual tax payments of 90 percent of those costs, taken in increments of 8⅓ percent for up to 20 years. This incentive spurred the conversion to residential use of a great many multistory lofts and warehouses. Finally, in 1976 the State Legislature altered the New York State Multiple Dwelling Law to permit "residential occupancy of

SoHo, 1998

The empty multistory buildings left behind by industries in places such as SoHo in New York City in the 1970s were initially occupied (often illegally) by artists, who found their large spaces with high ceilings desirable and affordable. Once these newcomers had transformed them into cool residences, boutiques moved in downstairs and wealthier households bought out the artists upstairs. In rapid succession SoHo, and districts like it, that had once been vacant became hot new neighborhoods of the end of the 20th century. (Alexander Garvin)

loft, commercial, or manufacturing buildings" if they complied with all residential occupancy requirements.[12]

Over time, similar provisions were extended to other districts and other cities with vacant and underused multistory loft and manufacturing buildings. These cities dealt with different legal and financial obstacles that applied to their situation. As a result, there are now residential loft districts in Chicago's River North and Printers Row districts, the

Third Ward in Milwaukee, Lowertown in St. Paul, Pioneer Square in Seattle, the Pearl District in Portland, the West End in Dallas, and cities across the country.[13]

Lowertown, St. Paul, Minnesota, 2017

The multistory lofts in the Lowertown section of St. Paul, Minnesota were converted from manufacturing to residential use. (Alexander Garvin)

The Advent of Container Shipping

While many buildings went out of use because of the reduction in the amount of space per worker used in manufacturing, others went out of use in response to changing international trading patterns, particularly local warehouse districts that were inappropriately located or ill-configured to cope with the shift from breakbulk shipping to freight movement in large containers of a standard size: 8 feet wide, 8 feet high, and 20 feet long. This change liberated large territories for downtown expansion as office, tourist, retail, residential, and park areas.[14]

In addition to the impact on employees of shipping companies, changes in freight handling affected people working for steamship, trucking, railroad, air carrying, warehousing, stevedoring, freight forwarding, tugboat, and a variety of other companies. The results of the emergence of cargo handling by container are particularly apparent at Fisherman's Wharf in San Francisco and on the Brooklyn waterfront.

Perhaps the most unexpected change to a freight, warehousing, and manufacturing district is its transformation into a tourist destination. That happened in San Francisco in the 1960s, when the city began to be outstripped by the Port of Oakland as the place that ships from all over the world brought and discharged cargo.

The piers along the Embarcadero and Fisherman's Wharf were not large enough to provide the space necessary for cranes to lift containers off ships, store them, and then lift them onto trucks that would take the cargo to manufacturing plants, increasingly located in suburban, single-story buildings that were easily accessible by highway. The properties across the street from these piers were in scattered ownership. It was very difficult to acquire and assemble enough territory for the dozens of container berths that constitute a major container port without displacing hundreds of businesses and spending sums that were not available to local government.

Container port, Boston, 2006

Shipping by container requires vast areas of open land, such as in the Boston Seaport, where the containers can be downloaded by cranes from cargo ships and railroad freight cars, preferably easily accessible by highway. (Alexander Garvin)

Even if spending enormous sums of money to assemble great numbers of privately owned properties had been possible, the time and complexity of driving through downtown San Francisco was simply not worth the effort. Moreover, extending rail lines through the city to create an intermodal rail freight complex was unthinkable. Instead, those facilities were created across San Francisco Bay in Oakland, where adequate territory could be purchased without significant displacement. It did not take long before Oakland surpassed San Francisco in shipping tonnage. By the 21st century the Port of Oakland had become the fifth busiest container port in the nation.[15]

Ghirardelli Square and Fisherman's Wharf, San Francisco, 2006

Urban manufacturing plants were left behind in districts such as Fisherman's Wharf in San Francisco that no longer were close to the areas from which they received raw materials and to which they shipped their finished products. Companies such as the Ghirardelli Chocolate Company moved out of downtown locations to be close to the warehousing and shipping facilities and were more accessible by highway. (Alexander Garvin)

When freight handling began to move away from the San Francisco waterfront, so did the manufacturers who depended on those freight facilities to supply the raw materials they needed for production purposes and later to distribute their products. The first large manufacturing firm to leave was the Ghirardelli Chocolate Company, which in the early 1960s moved to San Leandro, California, several miles south of the growing Oakland Container Port. Its factory was purchased by a developer who converted the property into a 54,000-square-foot urban marketplace on top of a 300-car garage. This new retail and restaurant facility became a contemporary tourist-oriented destination with views of the harbor and nostalgic "restored" buildings erected in the late 19th and early 20th centuries.[16]

The renovated Ghirardelli Square became a model for the adaptive reuse of the Del Monte Cannery down the street and soon for other buildings in Fisherman's Wharf that were also going out of use. They were replaced by tourist motels, seafood restaurants, and tourist attractions such as the Maritime National Historic Park and Ripley's Believe It or Not Museum. A similar district arose around Quincy Market and the piers and warehouses of Boston's North End and the warehouses in the Old Market District of Omaha, Lowertown in St. Paul, and Pioneer Square in Seattle.

A similar transference of port activities moved from Brooklyn to Port Newark. In the 1950s more than two dozen waterfront piers and 130 warehouses on the edge of downtown Brooklyn were taken out of service by the Port Authority of New York and New Jersey (PANYNJ). At the same time, PANYNJ invested in upgrading its 267-acre Port Newark, which had much better railroad and highway links to the rest of the country. In 1985, Port Newark was the world's busiest container port.[17] Even in 2016, it was the second busiest such facility in the United States, handling 3.6 million cargo containers, valued at nearly $200 billion.[18]

By the end of the 20th century, more than half of the piers in Brooklyn were vacant. Once the Port Authority announced that it would be closing piers 1 through 6, Mayor Michael Bloomberg and Governor George Pataki formed the Brooklyn Bridge Park Development Corporation to transform the piers into a 65-acre, 1.3-mile-long park, designed by landscape architect Michael Van Valkenburgh Associates.[19]

The piers have been adapted for use as athletic fields and playgrounds; a beach and marina; a meadow with native plants, flowers, and grasses; picnic facilities; snack bars; a pedestrian promenade; a passive landscaped park; a carousel; and an extremely busy weekend green market. In 2016, 135,000 visitors attended its concerts, movies, tours, fitness classes, and other activities.

Piers 1–6, site of Brooklyn Bridge Park, 2005

Piers 1–6 in Brooklyn were extremely active throughout World War II. They provided a colorful background for films depicting the world of blue-collar labor in movies such as *On the Waterfront*. These long-abandoned piers became an obvious spot to be transformed into the recreational facilities at New York's 21st-century Brooklyn Bridge Park. (Alexander Garvin)

Brooklyn Bridge Park, 2015

Like Chicago in the 19th and 20th centuries, New York in the 21st century is converting its underappreciated and underused waterfront into wonderful new parks such as Brooklyn Bridge Park. (Alexander Garvin)

Railyard Replacement

Railyards established to handle breakbulk cargo experienced a decline in use similar to the decline experienced at breakbulk piers. Because many of the railyards were located on the edge of downtowns, they constituted valuable real estate that could be profitably reused for other purposes. Chicago's big freight yards moved to the edge of town early in the 20th century, so the railroad property in the central city was used for the passenger stations and express shipment operations. After the Chicago Fair of 1893, some sections of passenger railyards opposite the downtown Loop were either replaced or platformed over to create Grant Park and major public institutions such as the Art Institute. The last section became the 24-acre Millennium Park in 2004, completing the 111-year redevelopment.

Often these railyards also accommodated waning passenger service. Freight movement in and out of yards leading to Dearborn Station, for example, had ended by the 1960s. Then, after 1971, the trains that provided intercontinental passenger service were relocated to Union Station. When commuter service was terminated 3 years later, 21 of Chicago's major businesses came together to form the Dearborn Park Corporation, which replaced 51 acres of the railyard with a residential complex that included 1,671 dwelling units.[20] Dearborn Park was built in two stages: phase I, completed in 1985, and phase II, completed in 1994.

Commuter rail service at nearby Central Station was terminated in 1972. Its 69-acre railyard was then expanded to 80 acres, which became a planned community of new townhouses, luxury condominiums, rental apartment buildings, parks, and retail stores. Work on Central Station began in 1989 and was halted by the subprime mortgage crisis at the end of the first decade of the 21st century, when financing construction of residential apartment buildings and purchase of condominiums within them became problematic. At that time two dozen buildings and townhouse clusters with some 4,200 apartments had been completed. Currently, an 800-unit apartment building is under construction, with a similar building planned next door. That will leave only one building site within the original 800-acre area, although the developer has discussed continuing the project onto air rights over Metra Electric's Weldon Yard.

Central Station, Chicago, 2012

In Chicago, Central Station and a great deal of other surplus transportation property has been reclaimed for new housing. (Alexander Garvin)

When these rail facilities went out of service, adjacent buildings were no longer needed as warehouses and factories because they were no longer able to receive raw materials or ship their finished products conveniently by rail. Consequently, these two projects, three blocks away from each other, have had a huge impact on their immediate surroundings. They generated billions of dollars of reinvestment in the loft district just south of the Loop and in dozens of blocks between

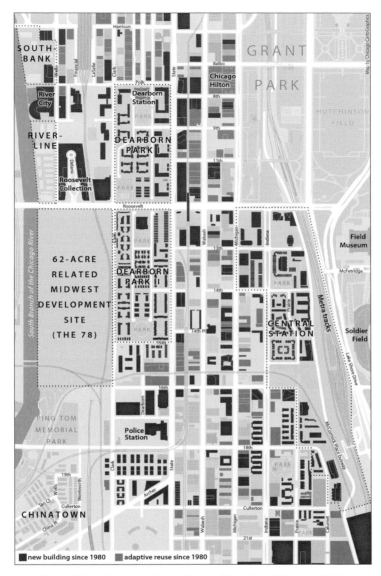

Map of Dearborn Park and Central Station, Chicago, 2018

Investment in the large-scale residential redevelopment of Dearborn Park and Central Station has generated widespread conversion of nonresidential property and new construction by private developers on nearby properties. (Dennis McClendon, Chicago Cartographics)

Roosevelt Avenue and McCormick Place, the city's convention center. As of 2017, about 100 apartment buildings (containing 20,000 units) and 1,800 townhouses had been built in the surrounding area, and some 75 loft buildings had been converted to residential use, adding another 6,000 units.

Increased Immigration

As explained in Chapter 4, the 43.2 million immigrants who lived in the United States in 2015 (13.4 percent of the population) are changing our downtowns. This was four times as many as the 9.7 million immigrants who in 1960 constituted 5.4 percent of the nation's population.[21] They are a major reason that 21st-century resurgent downtowns such as downtown Denver, Miami, and even Los Angeles had increasing downtown residential populations. These emerging downtown populations were a result of their increasing immigrant populations, not just increasing Millennial, empty nester, and "creative class" residents.[22]

In the parts of downtown with substantial immigrant populations, people with little money flock to the small stores, restaurants, and workshops, which provide them with jobs, services, and often locations where they start their own businesses. This has been the story of America, whether on Manhattan's Lower East Side in the latter half of the 19th century or in Cuban American sections of Miami in the latter half of the 20th century.

Currently, the imprint of immigration on our downtowns is particularly important. As Doug Saunders points out in his book *Arrival City*, we are now experiencing "the great and final shift of human populations out of rural agricultural life and into cities."[23] The buildings in downtown Los Angeles, Miami, Houston, or any other city with a very large proportion of immigrant residents do not reflect the final wave of immigration. Its impact is visible on streets lined with immigrant businesses.

The number of foreign-born residents has been climbing ever since the Immigration Act of 1965 went into effect, reaching 43.3 million in 2015. Consequently, immigrants have played a growing role in shaping the character of the cities in which they represent a large proportion of the population: Miami (53.3 percent), San Jose (38.9 percent), Los Angeles (38.2 percent), New York City (37.2 percent), and San Francisco (35.1 percent). (See Table 3.1.)

Table 3.1. Ten Cities with Large Immigrant Populations

City	Percentage Foreign Born
Miami	57.3%
San Jose	38.9%
Los Angeles	38.2%
New York City	37.2%
San Francisco	35.1%
Houston	28.5%
Boston	27.3%
San Diego	26.6%
Dallas	24.3%
Chicago	21.1%

Source: All data from the U.S. Census, 2015 (latest data).

Their impact is particularly vivid in Miami, where 2.25 million immigrants live in the metropolitan area and make up 65 percent of the labor force. At the start of the 21st century, 59 percent of the population of Miami-Dade County spoke Spanish at home.[24] In 2010, Latinos made up two-thirds of Miami-Dade County immigrants.[25] The dominant countries of origin included Cuba (34 percent), Colombia (5 percent), Mexico (2 percent), and Honduras (2 percent).[26]

A great many Miami businesses, stores, restaurants, and even streets cater to this large Latino population. They certainly add to the Latin flavor of these places. However, the build of downtown Miami is not much different from the rest of downtown America. Miami's prevalent balconies are more a reflection of the weather and the views of the water than the ethnicity, language, or national origin of their occupants.

Like Miami, the build of downtown San Jose, the city with the second largest immigrant population, does not reflect those residents. The build of those downtowns may not reflect the concentration of some immigrants in ethnic enclaves. On the other hand, their economy usually does.

32nd Street, Koreatown, Manhattan, 2018

Immigrant businesses, such as the Korean trading companies and financial institutions that cluster along 32nd Street in Manhattan, have transformed once-quiescent districts into lively, bustling downtown assets. (Alexander Garvin)

By 2014, San Jose had grown to 1 million residents, 38 percent of whom were immigrants. In 2014, there were more than 23,500 immigrant business owners in San Jose, 55 percent of the city's entrepreneurs.[27] Ethnically, it was much more diverse than Miami. Twenty percent were from Mexico, 16 percent from India, 14 percent from Vietnam, 11 percent from China, and 8 percent from the Philippines.[28] San Jose's Little

Saigon, for example, includes more Vietnamese-born residents than any other city outside Vietnam.[29] In all these downtowns, they play a dominant role in the economy.

The impact of immigrants on downtown also generates the color and lively sidewalk activity that is the product of street-front retailing. Doug Saunders describes it beautifully in his description of the impact of Latino immigrants on the northern section of the South Central neighborhood of Los Angeles, which gained notoriety in 1992 during the Rodney King riots.[30] He tells the story of a Salvadoran immigrant who came to the United States in the late 1990s, got a job in a Korean-owned sign-making business, scraped together enough money to rent a cheap store on one of the riot-damaged intersections in South Central, and started his own sign-making business. At that time, it was a neighborhood of poor African Americans and absentee landlords. Like the working-class White residents who had preceded them, they struggled to escape the area as fast as they could and move to the suburbs, providing the even poorer Latino newcomers with the opportunity to replace them, eventually purchase homes, and open small businesses. As in all immigrant enclaves, residents and business owners created a network of familiar faces that provided personal and economic support.

By the time he wrote *Arrival City*, Saunders could report that this Salvadoran immigrant had a thriving business, which employed his wife and two full-time assistants. The section of South Central where he had opened his business had become "a busy place, packed with small factories and shops, its sidewalks alive with constant activity."[31] The changes he and other Latinos had brought to this district on the edge of downtown Los Angeles were similar to changes immigrants have traditionally brought to American downtowns. Their function is to provide a destination where newcomers can start life over, prosper, and send their better-educated second generation to better neighborhoods, thereby providing room for another cycle of upward mobility.

In 2017, the substantial and growing immigrant contribution to America's economy and culture began to decline. The number of refugees resettled in the United States declined from 97,000 in 2016 to 33,000 in 2017, the steepest decline since the aftermath of 9/11.[32] This decline is a direct result of the policies of the Trump administration, which restricted Muslim immigration and capped refugee admissions for 2018 at 45,000, the lowest since Congress created the program to provide a haven for immigrants fleeing persecution in their country of origin in 1980.[33] Whether the decline in immigration to the United States will continue and whether it will have the same damaging effect on downtown America as the flight to the mid-20th-century suburbs remains to be seen.

Inexpensive Air Transportation

If deindustrialization led to decreases in employment and downtown spending, the increase in passenger flight and air freight has had the opposite effect: increasing downtown employment and spending. Memphis, for example, began its existence as a port on the Mississippi that by 1960 had grown into a city with a population of half a million people. In 1971, its future changed because a recent graduate of Yale College acquired an air freight company based across the Mississippi River in Little Rock, Arkansas. He renamed it Federal Express (now FedEx); moved it across the river to Memphis, which had an international airport that was rarely out of service because of bad weather; and began operations there 2 years later.[34] Today, FedEx operates in 220 countries and territories, completing 13 million shipments each business day.[35]

In 2009, Memphis was the location of five major freight rail lines, 11 interstate and U.S. designated highways, 490 trucking terminals, the nation's fourth largest inland water port, and the world's largest air cargo airport.[36] This combination makes Memphis, along with Chicago and Los Angeles, a natural location for handling international water, rail, and truck container cargo moving into, out of, and around the United States. Consequently, in 2007, 11 million tons of freight worth more than $23 was shipped into and out of the region's 193 warehouses and 136 industrial parks.[37]

Memphis' downtown, midtown, medical, and several popular residential districts are located within the 6 miles between its cargo handling facilities on the Mississippi River and the airport.[38] Without the freight handling business, the three downtown districts would be unable to

A sprawling section of downtown Memphis, 2006

Businesses in the Medical and Midtown districts of Memphis have prospered because of inexpensive shipping by air. (Alexander Garvin)

support the current level of employment or provide adequate demand for its residential neighborhoods.

As explained in Chapter 1, cities are forever changing. Despite handling 4.33 million tons of cargo and being the second busiest cargo airport in North America, Memphis International Airport has experienced a huge drop in passenger traffic.[39] In 2007, when it was the regional hub for Northwest Airlines, the airport handled 11 million passengers. A decade later, after Delta Airlines subsumed Northwest and transferred that airline's hub activity to Atlanta, passenger traffic dropped to 4 million.[40] Consequently, it is modernizing one of its three concourses and mothballing the other two.[41] This has not benefited downtown Memphis, but because of its continuing role as an air freight hub, $3 billion spending on conventions, sports, and tourism, and 35,000 tourist-related jobs, it is still thriving.[42]

When Delta shifted the Northwest Airlines hub to Atlanta, it only increased the importance of air travel to that city. Hartsfield–Jackson Airport had already become the world's busiest airport in 1998 (replacing Chicago's O'Hare).[43] In 2016, 104 million passengers passed through the airport.[44] One reason Atlanta's three downtowns experienced such extraordinary growth is that they were all connected to Hartsfield–Jackson Airport by MARTA and I-85.

The impact of inexpensive air travel was having a similar effect in other cities. While the nation's population nearly doubled, from 151.8 million in 1950 to 324.3 million in 2010, air travel increased 378 times, from 19 million miles to 7.2 billion miles.[45] Chicago, Los Angeles, Dallas–Fort Worth, and other cities whose airports became major international hubs profited from the increase in business. New York, Washington, DC, Miami, Las Vegas, and cities that were already major tourist destinations gained millions of new customers.

Expansion of Tourism and Leisure Services

The growth of the vacation industry as a result of less expensive air travel generated increased demand for hotel rooms and thus increased construction of additional hotels. In fact, tourism has become one of the nation's fastest-growing industries. As a result, the total number of foreign visitors soared from 39.3 million in 1995 to 75.6 million in 2016.[46] However, there was a 4 percent decline for the first 9 months of 2017 (at a time when international tourism worldwide was up by 7 percent).[47] It is not yet evident whether that decline will continue throughout the Trump administration. If it does, it will undoubtedly have a negative impact on downtown America.

Excluding three of the top cities that benefited from the pre-2017 surge (Orlando and Anaheim because of Disney resorts and Las Vegas

Downtown Denver, 2009

Tourism and leisure industries are thriving in downtown Denver and most growing downtowns. (Alexander Garvin)

because of gambling), the most popular destinations are predictable: New York, Chicago, and Atlanta (Table 3.2).[48] The next two are Los Angeles and Philadelphia, which explains why there are 5,300 hotel rooms in Buckhead. Unlike Buckhead's larger amount of office space, this is less than half the number of hotel rooms in downtown Atlanta.[49] In New York City, number two in quantity of hotel rooms after Orlando, tourism resulted in $42 billion in visitor spending in 2015 and $49 billion in 2017.[50] In Uptown Houston this figure is $3.2 billion for 2016,[51] and in Buckhead it is $243 million for 2017.[52]

Table 3.2. U.S. Tourism in 2017

Rank	City	Visitors
1	New York City	59,700,000
2	Chicago	54,100,000
3	Atlanta	51,000,000
4	Anaheim	48,200,000
5	Orlando	48,000,000
6	Los Angeles	47,300,000
7	Las Vegas	42,900,000
8	Philadelphia	42,000,000
9	San Diego	34,900,000
10	San Francisco	25,000,000

Source: "The Most Visited Cities in the US," Worldatlas.com website, June 26, 2018, https://www.worldatlas.com/articles/the-most-visited-cities-in-the-us.html

Tourists spend money on more than just hotels. They go shopping. They go to shows, restaurants, and museums. Most important, they enliven street life at night and during the day. Like residents of converted lofts, they provide the downtown with the cachet that attracts art galleries, interesting boutiques, and people spending money, who, in turn, attract more conventional retailers and national chains.

Employment in leisure and hospitality has grown from 4.8 million in 1970 to 15.6 million in 2016 (just under 11 percent of the national economy). In downtown Denver 16 percent of the workforce is involved with leisure and hospitality (45 percent above the national average).[53] These

Hilton Hotel, Post Oak Boulevard, Uptown Houston, 2015

In 2016 tourists spent $3.2 billion in Uptown Houston hotels and restaurants. (Alexander Garvin)

Third Ward, Milwaukee, 2012

Visitors from other parts of the metropolitan area flock to Milwaukee's Third Ward, the city's popular district of converted lofts, where they contribute to its retail sales and street life. (Alexander Garvin)

are among the reasons that total downtown employment in Denver has gone from 113,000 in 2000 to 130,000 in 2017.[54] With that 15 percent increase Denver outperformed the national economy, which increased only 9 percent.

Changing Household Needs

The nation's mid-20th-century population was quite different from that of contemporary America. The average life expectancy of an American in 1940 was 62 years; today it is 79 years.[55] In 1950, the percentage of people over 65 was 6.8 percent; by 2017 that number had more than doubled. During that time the average household income in constant dollars increased from $19,100/year to $59,000/year. The number of single-person households grew from 7.7 percent in 1940 to 27 percent in 2010.[56] Between 1950 and 2016 manufacturing employment dropped from 31 percent to 8.5 percent of the workforce, while those in professional and business services grew from 6.5 percent to 14 percent and those in education and medical services from 4.7 percent to 15.7 percent.

Shrinking household size is fueling the demand for additional apartments. In 1967, only 8 percent of Americans lived alone, a figure that rose to 28 percent by 2016. In Philadelphia, the average household size has contracted from 3.0 people in 1970 to 2.6 in 2015, meaning that for every 100 people, five additional housing units are needed today compared with 1970. Throughout Philadelphia, 55 percent of those living alone are renters. In most neighborhoods of Core Center City, household size averages just 1.6 people per unit.[57]

As a result, there are now large residential populations in what used to be single-function business districts. This residential population likes to meet and mingle with like-minded people in bars and restaurants, particularly at happy hour. Now, the entire downtown workforce no longer comes to work between 8 and 9 AM or leaves between 5 and 6 PM. This increasing downtown population has begun to demand that an increasing amount of territory be devoted to the public realm and that the public realm be adjusted to make it more user-friendly.

Changing Lifestyles

What city residents do when they are downtown has also changed. I roller-skated as a boy; rollerblading was unknown. But if I had been familiar with rollerblading, it never would have occurred to me that grownups would rollerblade. They do now.

Indeed, daily life has changed dramatically over the past three-quarters of a century, and those changes allowed various people to alter downtown America. Before 9/11 few Americans were concerned with protection from terrorism. Within a few months, insurance companies were requiring security checks and banks refused to renew mortgages for property that was not properly insured and protected from terrorist attack (even though nobody can specify what form the attack will take). Now, entering many office buildings in midtown and lower Manhattan requires passing through a metal detector. The desire for protection from terrorism is increasing the cost of doing business downtown and removing public access from the public realm, all of which increase the relative competitiveness of suburban office and retail districts. This is quite different from the cost of dealing with climate change and natural hazards, which affect both suburbs and cities in the same way.

Most residents of the United States, whether urban or suburban, live a more sedentary lifestyle and increasingly need additional opportunities for active recreation to compensate. As a result, there has been an increasing investment in bike paths, shared bikes, parks, health clubs, and gymnasiums.

Statistics on bicycle use tell the story. Between 2008 and 2017, the number of bike riders in the United States increased from 47 million to 66 million.[58] More people are riding their bicycles to work: 864,000 in 2016, a 40 percent increase over 10 years.[59] An increasing proportion of them are not using their own bicycles. The nation's first modern, theft-proof bikeshare system was launched in 2008 in Washington, DC, with 1,600 bicycles that were used for 320,000 bike share trips.[60] By 2016 the number of bicycles in 55 such systems throughout the United States had grown to 42,000, which made 28 million trips.[61] Bikesharing is having the greatest effect in the five cities that account for 85 percent of these trips: New York City, Washington, DC, Miami, Chicago, and Boston.

With increased bike and bikeshare usage, protected bike lanes have

Citibike interchange lower Manhattan, 2013

By 2016 there were 55 bikeshare systems in downtown America that generated 28 million bike trips. (Alexander Garvin)

become an increasingly important feature of downtowns across America (Table 3.3). Protected bike lanes are separated from both vehicular and pedestrian traffic by physical dividers (usually concrete curbs or planters). Between 1874 and 2011, there were only 78 protected bike lanes in America. As of the summer of 2016 there were 292 in 82 cities; by 2018 there were 420 protected bike lanes in 111 cities.[62]

New York City installed the nation's first bike lanes along 5 miles of Brooklyn's Ocean Parkway in 1894.[63] However, the city did not make a serious investment in protected bike lanes until 2007, when commissioner of transportation Janette Sadik-Khan initiated construction of a citywide system, since continued by her successors. By 2017 that system had grown to 338 miles of on-street bike lanes (65 miles of which were protected by physical barriers).[64]

Minneapolis has the nation's most impressive bikeway system, which has become an integral part of the finest park system in the country.[65] Its most outstanding feature is 51 miles of protected bikeways encircling the city, part of the Grand Rounds Scenic Byway, built in the 1990s and 2000s. Perhaps that is why 5 percent of the city's commuters use it as

Table 3.3. Miles of On-Street Bike Lanes in U.S. Cities in 2013

City	Miles of On-Street Bike Lanes	Bike Lanes per Square Mile
San Diego	620	2.6
Tucson	610	3.4
Los Angeles	463	1.3
San Jose	443	2.9
Philadelphia	426	4.3
Albuquerque	400	4.1
Fresno, CA	382	3.7
Phoenix	376	1.5
Mesa, AZ	360	4.2
New York City	338	2.7

Source: Niall McCarthy, "Which U.S. Cities Have the Most Bike Lanes?" Forbes, September 26, 2014, https://www.forbes.com/sites/niallmccarthy/2014/09/26/which-u-s-cities-have-the-most-bike-lanes-infographic/#7fbfbf217d7a

their main means of transportation, "a staggering figure for a country where a scant 0.6 percent of commuters bike to work every day."[66]

Atlanta is creating what is already the most lifestyle-responsive bike trail, the Atlanta BeltLine Inc. (ABI). In 2005, the city approved ABI as a way to create an alternative lifestyle by replacing the ring of freight railroad lines, which encircled the city about a mile and a half to 3 miles from the center of the city. It plans to create a very different public realm framework of bike paths, pedestrian trails, parks, and playgrounds. When it is completed, ABI will be an interconnected system of 20 new or expanded parks occupying 1,300 acres connected by 33 miles of multiuse trails and 22 miles of new transit lines. In 2012, the Eastside Trail became the first section of the BeltLine to open, and in the fall of 2017, the Westside Trail opened.

The BeltLine is already having a huge impact on Atlanta. At the start of the 21st century, Atlanta rivaled Los Angeles and Houston for the longest stretches of clogged highways, on which its residents spent increasing amounts of time traveling to and from sprawling agglomerations of single-family houses. By 2018, the BeltLine had become the place where residents of every ethnicity, income level, and social class encounter one another, skate, jog, sit on benches reading books, picnic,

Atlanta BeltLine, 2016

The BeltLine's network of bike paths, pedestrian trails, parks, and playgrounds has generated tens of thousands of permanent jobs and privately financed residential apartments. (Alexander Garvin)

or just wander.[67] The parks and trails that have already been built provide opportunities for recreational activities and increase the amount of time that nearby residents devote to exercise, supplying the changes in lifestyle demanded by 21st-century Americans.

Cities have found other inventive ways to increase the public realm as a way of providing recreational space for the increasing number of people spending time downtown. Philadelphia repurposed street and parking territory in front of City Hall as Dilworth Park, which reopened in 2014 as a water spray play area. In 2018 Philadelphia repurposed its Reading Railroad Viaduct into an elevated park with walking paths, much like the High Line in Manhattan and the Promenade Plantée in Paris. The City of Houston acquired 12 acres more than was needed for the George Brown Convention Center it was building. The site reopened in 2008 as a 12-acre park, designed by the landscape architecture firm of Hargreaves Associates, which includes promenades, gardens, playgrounds, dog runs, grassy knolls, and water features. Seattle, on the other hand, decided to provide the Seattle Art Museum with a site to display some of its sculpture. Consequently, it acquired a contaminated 9-acre site along the waterfront of Elliott Bay that had been used for fuel storage. Once the park opened in 2007, it became a popular recreational facility for children and adults.

Olympic Sculpture Park, Seattle, 2007
Like so many other contaminated waterfront sites, this fuel storage facility in Seattle was converted into an extremely popular park. (Alexander Garvin)

Recreational amenities tend to be scarce downtown because unlike suburbs, downtowns tend to be compact, high-density concentrations of multistory buildings. Consequently, developers of new multifamily residential buildings are adding recreational amenities to their projects. New York by Gehry, the 898-unit lower Manhattan apartment building and tallest residential tower in America, includes a 100,000-square-foot public elementary school and several floors of amenities, including a 3,300-square-foot fitness center, 50-foot swimming pool and sun deck, private training studio, movie screening room, spa suite with private treatment rooms, and children's playroom. Consequently, fewer tenants crowd into whatever amenities are available in the public realm.

Decreasing Criminal Activity

One reason people left many downtowns in the mid-20th century was the perception of increasing violence and crime. In 1963 when police dogs attacked civil rights protesters in Alabama, the United States saw what would be its lowest homicide rate for the next 50 years: 4.6 homicides for every 100,000 people. By 1980, the national homicide rate had reached its peak of 10 people per 100,000.[68] Most of this violence was occurring in cities, and people started to leave. The population of Washington, DC dropped from 764,000 in 1970 to 572,000 in 2000; during that period, Cincinnati's population dropped from 453,000 to 331,000, and Baltimore's dropped from 906,000 to 651,000.

The perception of urban violence remained, although the reality began to change at the end of the 20th century. Urban crime rates peaked in 1990, when New York and Philadelphia experienced homicide rates of 30.6 and 31.7 murders per 100,000 people, respectively.[69] By the 21st century, the change was dramatic. The number of murders reported in New York City fell from 2,245 in 1990 to just 300 in 2017.[70] The murder rates in Atlanta, Dallas, Los Angeles, and Washington, DC all fell by 60 to 80 percent.[71] Increasing prosperity, lower alcohol drinking levels, an aging population, growing rates of incarceration, and improved policing techniques are some of the reasons that are usually given for the decline in crime. In many downtowns, however, BID programs were partly responsible for the decline in crime.

Philadelphia's Center City District (CCD) initiated several such programs that continue today. Through a partnership with the Philadelphia Police Department, the CCD runs Alert Philadelphia, a program providing "immediate notification of emergencies to Center City businesses, employers, property owners, hospitals, residential groups, community leaders, law enforcers, first responders and private security representatives."[72]

Also, in conjunction with the Philadelphia Police Department, the CCD uses computer programs to create effective maps that outline "crime trends or patterns" to "make strategic deployment decisions." Perhaps the CCD's most effective crime deterrence tool is its Community Service Representatives. Clad in uniform, they are able to "administer first aid, provide directions, radio police or provide outreach to homeless individuals."[73]

In addition, the existence of a BID usually led people to move back to downtown residences, increasing the "eyes on the street" and further reducing downtown crime. Whatever the reasons, in the 21st century people began to perceive the decline in urban crime. As downtown violence decreased, fear of spending time there decreased, and people began to return downtown to live, shop, and do business.

The Evolving Downtown for a New Century

Deindustrialization, the advent of container shipping, and replacement of no-longer-used railyards reduced demand for large amounts of downtown territory, simultaneously reducing the price of acquiring those properties. Growing immigration, inexpensive air transportation, and expanding tourism increased demand for downtown locations and thus their value. Along with changing household needs and lifestyles and a decline in downtown crime, they created opportunities for transforming downtown America. The people and organizations who correctly identified these changes were able to acquire property, obtain the financing, convert old buildings, and develop new ones, thereby creating vibrant downtowns for a new century. The next chapter identifies who they are and how they are accomplishing those changes.

Chapter 4

People Who Are Changing Downtown

owntowns are changed by the people who live, work, and play in them along with the organizations they belong to and the public agencies that provide them with services. They include residents, workers, tourists, businesses (that are headquartered or operate downtown), retailers (local and national chains, as well as international companies), property owners, government agencies, cultural and educational institutions, hospitals, entertainment companies, sports clubs, restaurants, nonprofit institutions, interest groups, residents, and so on. The list is as extensive and complex as the downtowns themselves. So it is important to know who they are and how and why they keep changing downtown America.

What follows are brief accounts of what different people with very different objectives have done to change their downtowns. Their stories should convince everybody that actions by inspired and persistent activists can be quite successful in the change business.

Preservationists

There is a special group of downtowners that cherish the place, its buildings, its people, and the activities that take place there: preservationists.

They do their best to retain and enhance the historic buildings and districts they love so much. The earliest example of their efforts came between 1853 and 1858 when a group of women established the Mount Vernon Ladies Association, to purchase President Washington's home, Mount Vernon, and to ensure that the public would have access to this landmark.

Their work was the inspiration for the Association for the Preservation of Virginia Antiquities, established in 1889 to save The Powder Magazine in Williamsburg from being demolished.[1] The association went on to prevent the home of John Marshall, fourth chief justice of the U.S. Supreme Court, from being replaced by a new school. In 1956 it established one of the nation's first revolving funds to purchase historic properties and see that they were properly restored and transferred to caring owners.

That program preserved Church Hill in Richmond, named after the St. John's Church in which Patrick Henry proclaimed, "Give me liberty or give me death!" Over the next quarter century, Historic Richmond acquired more than 20 houses on Church Hill and wrote preservation requirements in their deeds before reselling them to residents who promised to cherish these buildings, sometimes helping them obtain rehabilitation mortgages from local banks. Similar downtown preservation organizations sprang up in Charleston, South Carolina, Annapolis, and other cities. In the 1960s, however, a single woman invested her own time and money to preserve an entire downtown historic district.

In 1954, when Dana Crawford, a 23-year-old recent graduate of Radcliffe, moved to Denver from her home in Salinas, Kansas, there were no threatened major landmarks in Denver, nor preservation organizations to protect them.[2] Her first job was in public relations, and her first assignment was working with William Zeckendorf, a well-known New York real estate developer who built some of the most important new buildings in Denver.[3] In the process, Crawford was bitten by the real estate bug, but unlike Zeckendorf and the downtown public officials focused on new construction, she wanted to restore the best of downtown Denver.

Crawford began by selecting a cluster of buildings on Larimer Street "where people with all kinds of backgrounds could get together and celebrate the city."[4] It was an area "lined with cheap liquor stores, seedy pawn shops, dilapidated hotels, and abandoned buildings."[5] Instead, she saw the 1400 block of Larimer Street as the site of historic 19th-century buildings that, if restored, could be used to generate the revival of Lower Downtown (LoDo).

Larimer Square, Denver, 2017

In the 1960s Larimer Square was essentially abandoned. Today it is one of the most popular destinations for metropolitan residents and tourists who visit Denver. (Alexander Garvin)

So she renamed the area Larimer Square, raised enough investment capital to gain control of all but two of its buildings, persuaded key investors to personally guarantee the bank mortgages to pay for their renovation, and even took out a second mortgage on her home to obtain all the funds needed to finance the project.

By 1957, Crawford had already renovated eight buildings in which retailers had opened stores or restaurants. Some of them didn't last, so she replaced them, opening several stores herself. While doing all this, she persuaded the city in 1974 to rezone a 20-block section of LoDo surrounding Larimer Square. The rezoning allowed warehousing and manufacturing to coexist with retail and residential use and led to the transformation of the area into one of Denver's most popular residential neighborhoods. In 1986, after she had demonstrated the potential of the area to attract retail customers and tourists, and made money from the project, she sold the package to the Hahn Company.

Crawford did not just focus on Larimore Square. She went on to purchase and renovate nine large loft buildings as residences and hotels scattered throughout LoDo and around Union Station (see Chapter 5). Her imprint on Denver is so significant that when the hotel in Union Station reopened in 2014, it was named in honor of this most effective downtown activist: the Crawford Hotel. Her story is the story of preservationists throughout the country who established the importance of historic structures as integral components of vibrant downtowns.

Real Estate Developers

It is difficult to outdo preservationist enthusiasm for retaining cherished sections of any downtown. However, many preservationists have difficulty raising the necessary money and, unlike Dana Crawford, rarely have the skills needed to rehabilitate downtown property or the gumption needed to take real risks.

During the decline many downtowns experienced in second half of the 20th century, clever businesses, property owners, and developers perceived the declines in demand for industrial, shipping, and rail facilities as opportunities to acquire property and replace existing uses at bargain prices. They acquired, at very low prices, underused and empty buildings once used for manufacturing, storage, or office work and converted them to residential use. In many cases, new or renovated buildings established on those sites could accommodate substantially larger markets, revealing that the developers expected a resurgence, which in many cases appeared faster than they expected.

The lofts and warehouses that were vacated when freight handling shifted from crates, barrels, and cartons to containers provided attractive, cheaper accommodations for artists. Many of these artists were pushed out later as building uses changed to galleries, boutiques, restaurants, and more expensive housing.

The activities of these pioneering downtown activists inspired countless others to initiate similar projects in other cities. Often, they took risks without fully understanding what they were doing.

Unlike preservationists, people in the real estate business, much as they may cherish the neighborhoods in which they invest, do so to make money. Although they rarely come to the table with a substantial amount of the necessary financing, they are willing to wait patiently for their return because they believe that real estate is about value appreciation, not rapid return on their investments.

David Walentas, founder of Two Trees Management, is unique among downtown developers. He virtually invented an entire new downtown on his own. Walentas began life without any money and grew up in a working-class family in Rochester, New York. After ROTC, college, and a variety of jobs in Austria and Japan, among other places, he moved to New York City in the late 1960s with the intention of going into real estate, a subject with which he was as unfamiliar with as he was with the neighborhoods and politics of the city.

Walentas learned on the job. He founded Two Trees with Jeff Byers, a wealthy partner who could provide some of the equity capital they needed. Starting in 1974, they acquired one building after another, finding investors, obtaining financing, hiring contractors to renovate apartments, collecting rents, and occasionally converting the rental buildings into cooperatives. The projects varied in size and location from a small apartment building on Manhattan's West Side to three garden apartment complexes in Queens with 1,248 apartments in 53 three-story buildings.[6]

The real estate market in New York took a downturn not long after Two Trees started investing. In 1977, Byers committed suicide. Nevertheless, Walentas kept on acquiring property. The most important of his initial investments were not the ones that made the most money. They were the empty loft buildings in SoHo and NoHo, which he successfully converted to residential use. Their success provided Walentas with the know-how he needed to acquire similar, largely empty buildings that had undergone decades of deindustrialization in a forgotten section of Brooklyn, then called Fulton Landing. Today, it has become famous as Dumbo (Down Under the Manhattan Bridge Overpass).

Initially, the businesses that occupied the warehouses and factories in this manufacturing district had been attracted by proximity to shipping facilities along the Brooklyn waterfront. They included appliance

Dumbo waterfront, Brooklyn, 2017

The Dumbo (Down Under the Manhattan Bridge Overpass) acronym was invented by the developers who converted abandoned lofts along the Brooklyn waterfront into one of the hottest districts for startup businesses and young professionals. (Alexander Garvin)

repair companies; factories making folding cardboard cartons, paint, and machinery; and firms packaging sugar, coffee, and other staples.[7]

Walentas started investing in Dumbo with the 250,000-square-foot Clock Tower Building. In 1981, he borrowed $12 million (largely from the Lauder family) to purchase from real estate magnate Harry Helmsley 2 million square feet in 13 buildings.[8] The buildings, which contained two-thirds of the office–industrial–artist–warehouse space in Dumbo were in a serious state of disrepair. Many of the businesses that occupied them had been failing or moving elsewhere. There were only 47 tenants left when Two Trees took over.[9]

Business tenants were slowly being replaced by pioneers seeking cheap accommodations. Artists unable to afford the increasing rents in SoHo moved to empty floors, which they used as studios. Others converted sections of lofts into residences. In many cases residential occupancy was illegal because the district was zoned for manufacturing. The 30 residential tenants in Two Trees Properties represented only one-fifth of the 150 then living in Dumbo.[10] Despite the increasing number of these younger pioneers, new residents were not flocking there in sufficient numbers to replace the waning business tenants. One reason there were so few residential tenants was that there were not enough stores to purchase basic supplies. Fewer than seven retail tenants occupied ground floor accommodations in all of Dumbo, only two or three of which were in Two Trees buildings.[11]

Revenues were not growing fast enough to cover expenses, expenses that were growing because of the extensive repairs, replacement, and restoration needed in each of the older buildings, plus investments that had to be made to transform abandoned streets into a safe, livable public realm. Walentas did everything possible to hang on: attracting additional investors, increasing borrowing, delaying tax payments, and deferring major capital improvements. Fortunately, he was able to keep afloat by renting a substantial block of space to New York State for occupancy by the Department of Labor.[12]

The turnaround began in 1998, when the City Planning Commission rezoned the area to permit mixed use that included residential occupancy. The man who managed that turnaround was David Walentas's son Jed, who had joined the firm a year earlier and gradually took over day-to-day operations. By that time, Dumbo included about 200 office–industrial– artist–warehouse tenants, 126 of whom were in Two Trees properties; and a dozen retailers occupying 30,000 square feet, more than 80 percent of whom were in Two Trees buildings. There also were more residences: 175 residential units in Two Trees properties and 150 loft occupants in the rest of Dumbo living in space without legal residential certificates of occupancy (referred to as interim multiple dwelling [IMD] tenants).[13]

Jed Walentas, David's son, was born in Manhattan in 1974, grew up among the lofts of SoHo, and went on to get his BA from the University of Pennsylvania, graduating in 1996. After Penn, he spent a year working in Donald Trump's real estate business.[14] His first assignment at Two Trees was the condominium conversion of the Clock Tower and establishment of offices for Two Trees in their building at 45 Main Street in Dumbo. Once he had completed both, Jed was ready to take on the further resurgence of Dumbo.

At that time, Two Trees faced several serious problems. It was under-capitalized and therefore depended on the success of its last project to provide money needed for the next one. Second, it needed to build Dumbo's reputation as an ever-improving neighborhood and thus had to spend more money on each venture than would have been necessary in an established district.[15] Because Two Trees, unlike many real estate developers, approached its property as long-term investments, Jed's strategy combined maintaining a mix of office and residential occupancy with quality execution: higher-quality design and construction than were common for out-of-use warehouses and lofts, prices that were slightly lower than in similar districts, devoted property managers, and attention to security, enhanced by ground floor retailers who provided eyes on the street and a warm working relationship with local police.[16]

The strategy worked because it amplified Dumbo's assets and provided a little extra something for the pioneers seeking space for their businesses or households. Unlike the city's often-sprawling deindustrialized districts, Dumbo was a walkable neighborhood, contained between the East River and the Brooklyn–Queens Expressway. It had easy access to the waterfront, the unique presence of the Manhattan and Brooklyn Bridges, and spectacular views of the lower Manhattan skyline, all of which were enhanced when the city transformed the abandoned piers into the Brooklyn Bridge Park (see Chapter 5). Year after year, Dumbo increased in popularity.

By 2018, Two Trees Dumbo properties consisted of 1.75 million square feet of office–industrial–artist–warehouse space occupied by 400 tenants, 1,100 rental and condominium apartments, and 150,000 square feet of retail space occupied by 50 stores and restaurants. Moreover, Two Trees' investments had generated widespread investment by many other developers.

The neighborhood then included 15,000 office workers, half of whom were under the age of 40, occupying 4.3 million square feet of space in businesses that included name-brand corporations and technology startups.[17] More than 5,000 residents lived in the district. Their median age was 36, and average household income was $200,000. Millions of visitors came to Brooklyn Bridge Park and Dumbo's theaters, galleries, and cultural attractions. All of them, workers, residents, and visitors, patronized the 120 stores and restaurants occupying a quarter of a million square feet, including national chains such as Equinox and Shake Shack, as well as local merchants such as Jacques Torres Chocolates and the Almondine Bakery.

Because of all the work Two Trees has done, the money it has spent, and the efforts of other real estate ventures during the previous 5 years, Dumbo has jumped north of the Manhattan Bridge to occupy territory that reaches the Vinegar Hill neighborhood to the north and expanded east of the Brooklyn–Queens Expressway into "Dumbo Heights." It has become a cutting-edge, mixed-use 21st-century downtown.

Like Larimer Square, Dumbo is the result of one person's vision. Like that historic Denver district, this cluster of 19th- and early-20th-century Brooklyn lofts triggered investment by property owners and developers—not just in once-empty old buildings but in new office and residential construction. The result is a mixed-use downtown that is far more intensely developed than the 100- to 150-year-old district that inspired the activists that created it.

Businesses

Downtown revival requires more than vision, a willingness to take risks, an ability to obtain financing, and skill at renovating structures. Buildings need occupants. Moreover, residential tenants, even a large number of them, are not enough to transform a popular neighborhood into a genuine downtown. Downtowns also need businesses that provide plenty of jobs and retail stores that supply area occupants with the necessities of daily life.

Occasionally, a businessperson comes along with the vision, determination, and money to tackle the revival of an entire downtown. Dan Gilbert is doing just that for downtown Detroit. It remains to be seen whether it will experience a revival similar to that of downtown LA or lower Manhattan. In 2014, Detroit's 5,000 residents, 107 stores, 188 restaurants, and more than 66,000 workers did not yet constitute a major downtown, like Philadelphia with 300,000 downtown workers, or even downtown Buckhead with its 12,000 residents.[18] But if the downtown revival succeeds it will be in no small part because of Gilbert's efforts.

Although Detroit's population began to decline from its peak of 1.85 million people in 1950, many people think the decline began with the race riots of July 1967. Others put the date as 1983, when Hudson's closed its downtown flagship 2.1-million-square-foot department store.

Whenever it started, the decline has been precipitous. In 2010, the U.S. Census reported that Detroit's population had dropped to 714,000 people, who occupied the same 139 square miles that had once been home to more than two and half times as many people. During those 60 years of political controversy and economic decline, the city's eight mayors (one of whom was convicted of racketeering, extortion, fraud, and two dozen other counts) were unable to make the same sorts of public investments that revived lower Manhattan and downtown LA.

Until Mike Duggan, the current mayor, took office in 2014, downtown activists such as Dan Gilbert had to operate independent of serious public action. However, like any businessman, Gilbert could invest his own money, obtain bank loans, purchase properties and businesses, and establish new commercial and manufacturing ventures. Moreover, he did so on a scale that was more extensive than what any activist in any city had achieved in recent memory.

Daniel Gilbert was born in Detroit in 1962 and entered the mortgage lending business 23 years later. Today he is the chairman of Quicken Loans (a company he founded), invests in numerous companies, owns more than 90 properties in downtown Detroit containing 15 million square feet, and possesses a fortune estimated by *Forbes* at $6 billion.[19] In 2010, Gilbert moved Quicken Loans headquarters to downtown Detroit. Today, 17,000 people, 70 percent of its staff, works downtown, making it the city's largest employer, minority employer, and taxpayer.[20]

In December 2017, Dan Gilbert announced that he would build the tallest building in Detroit, a 1.3-million-square-foot, 800-foot-high skyscraper, on the Woodward Avenue site that had once been occupied by Hudson's Department Store.[21] Among the other major empty buildings Gilbert plans to restore are the former 302,000-square-foot home of the Detroit Free Press, completed in 1925; the 38-story Art Deco David Stott Building, completed in 1929; and the 1.3-million-square-foot Book Tower, completed in 1926.

It is too early to know whether Gilbert will be able to restore Woodward Avenue or the rest of downtown Detroit to its former glory. Until recently, one had to be skeptical. Very few of Detroit's other downtown activists had the money to purchase even one small empty building or the skills needed to renovate it, much less obtain a bank mortgage.

Renovation at Woodward and Grand River avenues, Detroit, 2017
One of the many once-occupied office buildings in downtown Detroit that is being converted to residential use. (Alexander Garvin)

Gilbert succeeded with the assistance of a creative business improvement district (BID).

In 2014, the city established the Downtown Detroit Business Improvement Zone (BIZ), which covers 1.1 square miles enclosed by the Detroit River and the three highways that ring downtown. Like all BIDs it supplements services (primarily sanitation, security, and way-finding) provided by the city government and pays for them by levying an annual charge on 550 downtown business.[22] The BIZ has invested in major improvements to the public realm, including often-spectacular floral displays. Its work matches that of the best BIDs in the country. Together with Gilbert's investments, it could trigger a genuine resurgence for downtown Detroit.

Artists

One group of activists has generated downtown revival without purchasing property, investing capital, or knowing much about business: artists. However, they do possess the necessary vision, devote tremendous energy to renovating property, and are ready to take the necessary risks.

Often artists are the ones who initiate downtown resurgence. In New York City, for example, artists began occupying and converting empty industrial and commercial buildings into working studios in the late 1960s. At first that occupancy was illegal. When enough of them had moved into SoHo, a district of lofts and warehouses just north of the lower Manhattan financial district, they persuaded the NYC Planning Commission in 1971 to amend the Zoning Resolution to permit Joint Live–Work Quarters for artists. Two years later they convinced the Landmark Preservation Commission to declare it a historic district.[23]

Once occupancy had been legalized, they were followed by art galleries, retail boutiques, cafés, restaurants, and residents with enough money to convert whole floors into apartments. Eventually SoHo became too expensive for the artists. It was once again a mixed-use district, albeit one that was very different from its 19th-century predecessor. The same has been true of obsolete districts with obsolete and abandoned multistory warehouses and factories in downtowns across the country.

The mere presence of artists and architects can alter the character and perception of a waning downtown district. That is what happened in 2001 in an abandoned section of downtown LA when the Southern California Institute of Architecture moved from Santa Monica to the quarter-mile-long former Santa Fe Freight Depot (built in 1907). Its nearly 300 students and faculty have become a major arts anchor for downtown LA.

The Savannah College of Art and Design (SCAD) has had an even greater impact on Savannah's historic Victorian District, a neighborhood that 40 years ago was filled with lovely but abandoned "historic"

A mural on Traction Avenue in the Los Angeles Arts District, 2013

Artists gained a renewed interest in downtown LA when the Southern California Institute of Architecture moved there. (Alexander Garvin)

structures. SCAD began operation in a building on the edge of the neighborhood in 1978.[24] At that time SCAD included 71 students and 11 faculty and staff members. As of 2017, its 1,700 full-time and part-time staff (including 650 teachers) also operates programs for 13,000 students in Atlanta, Hong Kong, and Lacoste, France.[25]

In Savannah alone it occupies 70 renovated buildings throughout the city, from which it offers programs in 70 different subjects, ranging from advertising and architecture to visual effects and writing. SCAD attracts tens of thousands of visitors to its museums, galleries, and signature events. So many of the participants in the Savannah program now live in the Victorian District that the area has been thoroughly gentrified.

Jubilee Baltimore, under the leadership of Charles Duff, is having a similar effect by providing residences for artists. The first building included 69 apartments for artists, a gallery, and studio space. City Arts 2, its second project, was erected on a lot that had been vacant for years. It includes recreational space accessible to people from surrounding properties, 60 apartments plus a dance studio, multipurpose co-working space, a fitness center, and a lounge. The apartments in both projects are "affordable" (rented to artists whose incomes are less than 60 percent of area median income). The artists who live in these buildings are contributing to the revival under way in the surrounding Greenmount West neighborhood.

Perhaps the most unusual example of artists leading the revival of a downtown neighborhood took place in Pittsburgh in the last quarter of the 20th century. In the mid-1970s, the Mexican War Streets, a once charming mid-19th-century residential area directly across the Allegheny River from Pittsburgh's business district, had deteriorated to the point that the city government was planning to condemn its abandoned and dilapidated houses in order to build a complex of highway, retail, and housing projects. Barbara Luderowski, an artist who had recently moved there, purchased an abandoned mattress factory and transformed it into a museum and center for working artists. Over the next four decades, the museum supported the work of more than 600 artists-in-residence, sponsored dozens of exhibitions, coordinated the renovation of eight additional buildings, and provided a focus for dozens of others who acquired nearby abandoned and dilapidated houses, which they restored. Today the museum attracts more than 28,000 visitors and generates more than $5 million in spending by its employees and patrons.[26]

Immigrants

Boston, Philadelphia, New York, and almost every other 18th-century American downtown were filled with immigrants. Similarly, Detroit, St. Louis, Houston, and most downtowns that emerged in the 19th century were created by immigrants. The country of origin usually determined immigrant destinations. It was easier for Europeans to get to the East Coast, for Asians to go to the West Coast, for Caribbean and Latin Americans to travel to Florida, and for Mexicans and some Central Americans to migrate to Texas or California. Besides the character of their chosen destinations and the length and cost of travel, the other main differences between immigrant impacts were the result of the history and culture of their countries of origin.

After passage of the Immigration Act of 1924, which established an annual quota of new immigrants from every country, and until passage of the Immigration and Naturalization Act of 1965, the number of immigrants entering the United States was restricted to 350,000 per year. Consequently, the number of immigrants in the country dropped from 14.2 million (11.6 percent) in 1930 to 9.6 million (4.7 percent) in 1970. This decline in new arrivals along with the departure of future suburbanites contributed to the perception of urban decline.

During this interregnum immigrants were less likely to leave their mark downtown. Miami, however, is the one city where immigrants, between the 1924 and 1965 Acts, were fundamental to the emergence of an immigrant-reshaped downtown. Cubans in Miami set the pattern for later Latin arrivals, who could afford low-cost airfares to Florida from nearby countries.

Initial post–World War II migration to Miami was not necessarily for permanent settlement. Wealthy Cubans came for vacations or as home buyers seeking harbor from potential or actual unrest. Many purchased houses in Florida and other parts of the United States. Some came as refugees with capital to invest and entrepreneurial skills, sometimes believing they would return home once things got better. Others resettled permanently.

The first big wave of Cubans came when Fidel Castro overthrew the Batista regime. By 1965, 210,000 Cubans had settled in Miami; another 340,000 arrived over the next 8 years. They had a huge impact on Miami, whose population in 1970 had reached only 335,000. Those who did not rent or purchase homes in the city settled in surrounding Dade County, whose 1970 population had swelled to 1.27 million people.

One-family homes west of I-95 attracted many new Cuban Americans. They opened retail stores and other businesses along Southwest 8th Street, giving it the Spanish nickname Calle Ocho. In addition to the immigrants, Calle Ocho attracted tourists who came to purchase hand-rolled cigars, tortillas, and a variety of Cuban memorabilia. The section of Calle Ocho between Southwest 13th and 15th avenues became the social center of what became known as Little Havana.

Residents transformed 13th Avenue into what became known as the Cuban Memorial Plaza and Boulevard. They turned the southeastern corner of Calle Ocho and 15th Avenue into a popular place to play dominos, and the City of Miami turned into Maximo Gomez Mini-Park in 1976. It was soon commonly referred to as Parque Domino. By that time the Tower Movie Theater and many nearby bars and restaurants had extended community activity well into the night.

The second wave of immigration began in the aftermath of the 1980 riots in Cuba that resulted in a flotilla of boats leaving Mariel, Cuba, for Miami. After 159 days, some 125,000 additional Cubans had escaped to Florida.

The Cubans were followed by a third wave of refugees from unrest in Guatemala, Venezuela, and other Latin countries. They came because they felt comfortable speaking Spanish with other immigrants. Many of them, especially Nicaraguan Americans, moved into the homes on either side of Calle Ocho that had previously been occupied by Cuban Americans.

Calle Ocho, Little Havana, Miami, 2018
Cuban immigrants have provided Calle Ocho and the entire Little Havana district of Miami with its unique character and lively market. (Alexander Garvin)

Thousands of families from the first wave of immigrants had earned enough money to move to more expensive residences in suburban Dade County. By the early 21st century, their children became a fourth generation moving to Miami. In many cases they moved back to houses in Little Havana that their families still owned. Others were beguiled by the still-lovely homes that had been built in the 1920s and 1930s. Like the other three generations of immigrants, they left their mark on Little Havana. It remains to be seen whether the immigration policies of the

Trump administration will allow another generation of immigrants to further improve Miami.

21st-Century Newcomers

Many mid-20th-century downtowns could have been characterized by declining populations and businesses. The reverse is true of many 21st-century downtowns. Over the past two decades, they have begun to include a greater proportion of young people with high levels of income, education, and professional accomplishment. These new residents are now major occupants of many downtowns. Between 1990 and 2017, for example, the number of downtown residents living in lower Manhattan increased from nearly 14,000 to more than 61,000.[27] In Uptown Houston the resident population increased from 22,000 to 69,500.[28] These are enormous increases, especially considering that in 1950 only 800 people lived in lower Manhattan, and Uptown Houston was agricultural land just beginning to be converted into suburban subdivisions. Who are these people?

The newcomers are often erroneously thought to be the agents of change who are responsible for downtown resurgence. In fact, they were able to come downtown because an initial group of preservationists, developers, businesses, artists, immigrants, and other activist pioneers were responsible for creating the high-density, mixed-use districts that have become vibrant downtowns, not the later (often Millennial) newcomers.

In Los Angeles, as in many other downtowns, there are four sets of newcomers: Live, Work, Live–Work, and Tourist elements. The Live segment is characterized by young (the average age is 38), upwardly mobile professionals.[29] They tend to be employed in arts and entertainment, business, and professional, educational, and medical services. Many of them work downtown. They have moved into the places pioneered by preservationists, real estate developers, businesses, and artists.

Downtown LA's Work segment (those who work downtown but do not live there) tends to be older (the average age is 45). They are more likely to be employed in the business, professional, finance, insurance, real estate, and government fields, in positions such as professional or

Downtown Los Angeles, 2017

In the past two decades downtown LA has risen out of the ashes of a once busy district to become a prosperous, high-density, mixed-use destination for all of southern California. (Alexander Garvin)

senior staff or top-level executive or manager.[30] The average age of the Live–Work segment (those who both live and work downtown) is 37. These people tend to have higher incomes, have devoted more years to their education than typical suburbanites, and are more likely to be self-employed or an entrepreneur or business owner.

In cities such as New York, Miami, and Los Angeles, the Tourist segment plays a major role in the downtown economy. In 2016 more than 60 million tourists visited New York.[31] Lower Manhattan was host to nearly 15 million of them.[32] Eleven percent of city tourists, 6.6 million, stayed for an average of 5 days at one of the 6,600 lower Manhattan hotel rooms, spending an average of $488 at local shops and restaurants during their visit.[33] Annually, more than 10 million (21 percent) of the 47 million visitors to Los Angeles come to downtown LA annually.[34] They stay at its 8,000, soon to be nearly 11,000, hotel rooms.[35] Indeed, tourism is a large and growing sector of the economy of downtown America.

All these people come downtown for things they are interested in or need. Like the continually changing cities they go to, their desires and needs keep changing.

Public Action

The people who live in, work in, or visit downtowns are rarely responsible for altering the places that provide what they are seeking. It is downtown activists (property owners, real estate developers, preservationists, artists, immigrants, and all sorts of entrepreneurial pioneers) who create these places. Since there are many actions that even enterprising people cannot do on their own, they often band together, creating interest groups, citizen activist organizations, and public–private partnerships. When these entities also prove incapable of changing downtowns, people rely on existing institutions (particularly medical and educational establishments) or government, which often is the only actor that can obtain the necessary results. The next chapter is devoted to how such organizations are changing downtown America.

Chapter 5

Organizations That Are Changing Downtown

Downtown activists often do not have the money, power, or responsibility they need to make desired changes downtown. Consequently, they may create an independent organization, depend on an existing institution, or rely on government to achieve their objectives.

Business and property owners are the likeliest to create an independent organization to act on their behalf. In nearly every downtown they have done so to obtain services that either were withdrawn by local government or were not being provided by business improvement districts (BIDs) or economic development corporations. Citizens advocating improving public parks, a more sustainable environment, historic preservation, affordable housing, and other forms of public action have established conservancies and development corporations that are responsible for restoring deteriorating buildings and conserving, developing, maintaining, and managing of parts of the public realm that were suffering from government disinvestment.

Existing institutions are among least expected agents of change. Nevertheless, they have been taking an increasingly active role in changing downtowns. Over a 93-year period, 21 hospitals have taken responsibility for the Texas Medical Center, a 1,345-acre section of Houston.[1]

Similarly, the University of Pennsylvania and Yale University have made major investments and taken responsibility for large sections of Philadelphia and New Haven, respectively.

Despite the success of their ad hoc efforts, substantial improvements in the economy, infrastructure, and livability of any downtown are often beyond the capacity of such organizations. Major changes cannot be accomplished without the widespread and sustained citizen acquiescence for common action by government agencies. Moreover, they often cannot be accomplished in a day or even a year.

Specially Formed Organizations

At the end of the 19th century and the beginning of the 20th century there were already plenty of nonprofit organizations working to improve some aspect of downtown America, particularly urban design. Among the more prominent of them were the Municipal Art Society in NYC, the Municipal Arts Commission in Los Angeles, the Civic League in St. Louis, and perhaps most important, the committee formed by the merged Merchant's and Commercial Clubs of Chicago that commissioned Burnham and Bennett's 1909 *Plan of Chicago*.

Mid-20th-century efforts concentrated on economic development. Typical examples include the Allegheny Conference on Community Development, established by banker Paul Mellon and Mayor David Lawrence in 1944 to improve the economy and quality of life in Pittsburgh, and the Greater Baltimore Committee, formed in 1955 to advocate improvements to that city.

Late-20th-century efforts were directed at improving public services, sustaining a livable environment, and enhancing the public realm. They resulted in the creation of conservancies established to care for parks and other public facilities and, in particular, BIDs to improve security and sanitation.

Business Improvement Districts

After World War II, the increasing demand for neighborhood services challenged local governments to raise the money to pay for additional services, such as security and sanitation. Moreover, by the 1970s cities were experiencing a declining tax base as a result of suburbanization, deindustrialization, and, a decade later, reduction of federal revenue sharing. Because city councilmen depended on the votes of their constituents demanding these services, they appropriated the funds to pay for them, often by reducing spending elsewhere. The obvious places to cut were the increasingly single-function business districts with few resident voters.

Consequently, downtowns throughout the country began to experience littered streets and sidewalks, overflowing garbage cans, and increasing crime. Businesses and property owners responded by inventing the BID, described in Chapter 1.

By 2018, most downtowns had established BIDs. All of them are dedicated to the slogan that has become their cliché: "safe, clean, and attractive." To fulfill that mandate, most BIDs augment sidewalk cleaning, garbage collection, and security previously provided by municipal agencies. Some also provide wayfinding materials, tourist information, interpretive signs, decorative paving, distinctive street furniture, and artwork. Others program events and actively promote their own downtown business, locally and in other cities. Many BIDs vary in size; some are as small as a few blocks, and others occupy territory far beyond what is generally perceived as downtown. All of them maintain websites, some of which display carefully arranged statistics about their activities and the downtown in general.

BIDs are also responsible for generating a substantial amount of downtown employment. One of the earliest of them, the Bryant Park Corporation, was created in 1980. As its founding and current executive director, Daniel Biederman, likes to point out, at that time inadequate services were provided by two people employed by the City of New York. As of July 2018, the BID employed 142 people.[2] Most of those jobs were filled by low-income people who devoted their time to sanitation, security, maintenance, and visitor services.

The Uptown Houston BID has been making public realm improvements to the area since its inception in 1987.[3] In 2016, it began work on a complete reconstruction of its main street, Post Oak Boulevard, budgeted at $192.5 million. The entire artery will be widened to 136 feet, removing a great deal of asphalt while retaining six lanes of traffic. A new live oak–lined bus corridor will be created by eliminating the central portion of the roadway. The tree-lined sidewalks will be widened to 12 feet, further reducing the amount of paved roadway. Commuters traveling to work, office workers on their way to lunch or shopping, and tourists returning to their hotel will all be able to get on the bus to get to their destinations. A few properties along the roadway have been acquired to create additional strips of parkland. Thus, this grand new boulevard will not only be more pedestrian friendly, attract more retail customers, reduce automobile traffic, and improve circulation, it will also sustain a more livable environment and increase resilience.

Post Oak Boulevard, Uptown Houston (rendering)

Rendering of the new bus lane, widened street, and sidewalk, to be lined with new rows of live oak. (Uptown Houston)

I believe that by 2030, Post Oak Boulevard will be a shopping street rivaling Chicago's North Michigan Avenue and perhaps even Boulevard Haussmann in Paris. It will be a rare section of Houston where public action will have diminished the amount of asphalt (while retaining the same six flows of traffic) and added bigger storm detention boxes underground and larger inlets to improve drainage, thereby increasing the territory that can soak up excess water. A failure to make similar improvements to the public realm elsewhere in the Houston metropolitan area resulted in widespread flooding in 2017, during Hurricane Harvey.

Los Angeles business interests have been represented by its Central City Association (CCA) since 1924. In 1990, it hired lawyer Carol Schatz, who became the founder of the Downtown LA BID and downtown's greatest proponent. At that time the business district, which had been declining for decades, had been particularly hard hit by a recession. Schatz wanted to transform the organization into the sort of BID that had begun reviving downtowns in other cities. She organized support for state legislation authorizing the creation of a property-based BID and, in 1994, succeeded in getting approval from the California legislature. The next year she became CEO of the organization that was renamed the Downtown Center Business Improvement District (DTLA) in 1998. The first of its eight constituent BIDs was the 100-block Fashion District, established in 1996.[4] Over the next 18 years it became responsible for everything within the ring of highways around downtown: 360 prospering blocks, more than 3,200 properties, 295,000 jobs (as of 2013), one college, two hospitals, 19 arts and cultural institutions, more than 9,300 hotel rooms and 800 restaurants, and more than 22 million square feet of retailing.[5] The BID maintains a staff of 33 security officers, 40 maintenance workers, and 11 people to administer its activities. Its 2018 annual budget was $6.6 million.[6]

Since its creation in 1994, DTLA has taken responsibility for changing the perception of downtown LA from a declining business district into the thriving center of America's second largest city, promoting investment in downtown businesses and real estate, attracting customers, improving the streetscape, and providing long-missing services within the downtown freeway ring. Among Schatz's early efforts were a series of trips by pubic officials and business leaders to New York and other cities to attract new downtown investment. Another was a series of "open houses" to convince Angelinos that downtown was changing. During the downtown open houses, its parking lots became destinations from which thousands of people toured places that were becoming new attractions to which they would want to return.

Map of downtown LA, 2018

Investments in the Staples Arena, the Convention Center, the Museum of Contemporary Art, and additional subway service along with promotion and service provided by one of the nation's most successful BIDs have attracted new customers to downtown LA. (Baolin Paul Shen and Alexander Garvin)

The most important initiatives, however, were the additional sanitation and security services that kept downtown LA "safe, clean, and attractive." However, all these activities would have been for naught without substantial improvements to the downtown building stock. Consequently, DTLA promoted the effort to make much-needed changes in buildings and zoning codes that would enable the reuse and rehabilitation of downtown properties.

Philadelphia's Center City District (CCD) did many of the same things as DTLA but for a much more complex downtown with a far greater range of activities and institutions. It is responsible for what is generally thought to be downtown Philadelphia: 233 prospering blocks, more than 1,500 properties, 299,000 salaried jobs and 9,000 self-employed individuals occupying almost 41 million square feet of office space, 15 colleges and universities, five hospitals, 419 arts and cultural institutions, more than 11,000 hotel rooms, 1,050 retail establishments, and 464 full-service restaurants.[7]

The CCD is a quasi-public municipal authority with a staff of 231 full-time direct and contract employees, 24 seasonal employees, and a 2018 annual budget of $24.5 million, established to keep downtown Philadelphia "clean, safe, and attractive." It is managed by a 23-member private sector board of property owners and prominent business, real estate, neighborhood, civic, and healthcare leaders. Among the sanitation services the CCD provides are daily manual and mechanical sidewalk sweeping, high-pressure power washing twice a month, and regular graffiti removal. Its crime and safety prevention activities include enhanced police coverage, community service representatives who serve as the eyes and ears for the police and a source of visitor information, outreach services to the homeless, collaboration between a dozen agencies to improve the quality and usefulness of public spaces, and computerized mapping and analysis of criminal activity.

The CCD analyzes data and distributes information about the office, retail, and residential marketplace, maintains seven websites and multiple newsletters that promote the downtown, and produces a variety of public events designed to attract customers downtown. Its capital improvement program over the past two decades has resulted in the installation of "more than 2,220 pedestrian-scale light fixtures, 900 trees, 270 planters and hanging baskets, 1,300 pedestrian signs and maps, and transit and façade lighting for 24 large buildings."[8] In addition, it is responsible for the creation, management, and maintenance of five parks covering 8.25 acres.

Paul Levy, its founding CEO, has been the major force creating one of the most successful BIDs in the nation: improving its public realm, strengthening the transportation network, and opening five extraordinarily successful downtown parks, including Dilworth and Reading Viaduct Rail Parks.

Between 1990 and 2010, Philadelphia's population declined by 60,000 people, while downtown gained nearly 11,000 residents.[9] One reason is that in 1997, the city enacted a citywide real estate tax exemption program, which provided a 10-year exemption from any increase in real estate taxes because of conversion of vacant office or industrial buildings

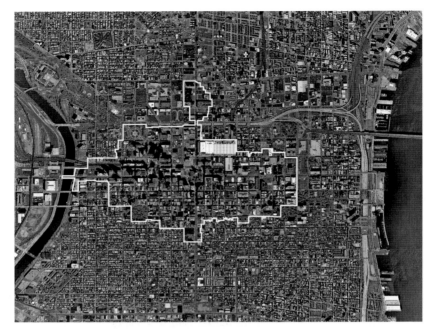

Center City BID, Philadelphia, 2018

Center City Philadelphia, which provides services to the entire downtown, is one of the nation's most innovative and effective BIDs. (Center City BID, Philadelphia)

to residential use. In 2000, the 10-year exemption was extended to new construction of all types. As a result, from 1998 to 2017, 9,811 new rental apartments, 7,239 new condominium apartments, and 3,866 single-family homes were erected in the CCD, and nearly 50 older office buildings and warehouses were converted into 4,298 apartments that had not previously been available for occupancy.[10] Altogether, at the end of 2017, downtown Philadelphia included 15,000 new and converted apartments (4,444 of which were single-family homes) that were not there when the CCD was established in 1991.[11]

One-family homes are particularly suited to the row house character of Philadelphia, in which there are two downtown neighborhoods with many blocks of particularly beautiful row houses, Rittenhouse Square and Society Hill. Between 1950 and 2000 the population of those two neighborhoods grew to 10,436 residents (a 75 percent increase), largely

Market Street in downtown Philadelphia, 2012

Between 2011 and 2018, with Market Street leading the way, downtown Philadelphia gained 40,000 jobs, 5,500 hotel rooms (nearly twice the number in existence in 1993), and 1.8 million additional square feet of office space (despite conversion of 5.5 million square feet of office space to residential use). (Alexander Garvin)

the result of renovation and construction of single-family row houses.[12] Together with the conversion and construction of 7,239 downtown condominium apartments, between 1998 and 2017 they reflect the national trend of increasing downtown home ownership. During that period New York City, for example, created nearly 40,000 new and converted condominium and cooperative apartments.[13]

The new residents of downtown Philadelphia are economically diverse (with empty nesters and twice its share of the region's 20- to 34-year-olds).[14] Not surprisingly, a far smaller percentage of them have children than the 27 percent rate for the city as a whole. One-third of downtown residents do not own automobiles (twice the citywide rate). Three-quarters of them have a bachelor's degree or higher (the citywide average is 25 percent). All of them were attracted by the CCD-enhanced environment: its walkability, convenient transit system, and easy access to restaurants and stores and its preexisting, outstanding cultural, educational, and medical institutions. By 2017 downtown Philadelphia was even more of a mixed-use district, in operation 24 hours a day, 7 days a week, than it had been a half century earlier.

Between 2010 and 2017 downtown Philadelphia had gained more than 40,000 jobs, 5,500 hotel rooms (nearly twice the number in existence in 1993), and 1.8 million square feet of office space, despite conversion of 5.5 million square feet of office space to residential use.[15]

Since its inception in 1991, the CCD has been the major factor spurring transformation of what was already a healthy, prosperous downtown in a city with a declining population into an even more prosperous downtown. As a result, downtown Philadelphia has continued to be the engine that helped the city add 66,000 residents who were not there in 2000.

Economic Development Agencies

There is a long tradition of public–private partnerships in Pittsburgh, Baltimore, and many other cities. It began in 1909 with the creation of the Pittsburgh Civic Commission. This coalition of civic elites and political leaders sponsored a 1910 report, *City Planning for Pittsburgh*, part of which was authored by Frederick Law Olmsted Jr. It called for riverfront, thoroughfare, and environmental improvements, many of which were carried out decades later as a result of the efforts of the Allegheny Conference on Community Development, a similar partnership composed of business, civic, and philanthropic leaders that seeks to work with political leaders to improve the quality of life throughout the metropolitan region.[16] As a result of planning by the Allegheny Conference, financing made available through the urban renewal program created by

Golden Triangle, Pittsburgh, 1900

Golden Triangle, Pittsburgh, 2012

Downtown Pittsburgh, an environmental disaster in the 1930s with serious economic problems in the 1960s, is becoming a model of downtown prosperity in the 21st century. (Alexander Garvin)

the Housing Act of 1949, and support from both business and political leaders, downtown Pittsburgh virtually reinvented itself.[17]

Similar but more modest organizations in Pittsburgh are now the primary entities working to improve the diversity and quality of downtown life and activities, economy, and culture. These include the nonprofit

Penn Avenue, Cultural District, Pittsburgh, 2012

Agnes Katz Plaza, Cultural District, Pittsburgh, 2012

The Pittsburgh Cultural Trust has transformed what had been a cluster of deteriorated multistory buildings into a lively arts district that attracts customers from all over the metropolitan area. (Alexander Garvin)

Pittsburgh Cultural Trust, Point Park University, the Andy Warhol Museum, and a variety of similar organizations.

The Pittsburgh Cultural Trust, created in 1984, is responsible for establishing a 14-block downtown Cultural District on the south bank of the Allegheny River. Initially the district contained blighted areas occupied by rundown performance halls, sex shops, X-rated movie houses, and numerous abandoned, deteriorating multistory lofts, but across the street from Heinz Hall a 1927 movie palace was renovated in 1971 to become the home of the Pittsburgh Symphony Orchestra.

The trust has restored the old theaters, built new performance venues, commissioned public art, and developed small parks and recreational facilities. It has also taken responsibility for management of art galleries in some of the buildings. The most prominent of these facilities include the Benedum Center for the Performing Arts (2,890 seats), Byham Theater (century-old, renovated vaudeville house with 1,300 seats), O'Reilly Theater (650-seat venue designed by Michael Graves), Harris Theater (a foreign and contemporary film house), and Agnes R. Katz Plaza, designed by landscape architect Daniel Kiley, featuring delightful "eye-ball benches" and a fountain by sculptor Louise Bourgeois. As a result, the Pittsburgh Cultural Trust now manages more than 1 million square feet of property. Today the Cultural District is home to thriving downtown theaters, concert halls, art galleries, restaurants, and bars, many of which were not there before the Cultural District was created. They attract 2 million visitors annually to 1,500 events that have an economic impact of $303 million.[18]

Downtown jumped across the Allegheny River initially because of the determined efforts of the city government to locate mass entertainment venues on the north side of the river. In addition to a lovely shoreline park, the area includes the Three Rivers Stadium, Carnegie Science Center, Heinz Field, PNC Park, the Andy Warhol Museum, the Children's Museum, and the National Aviary. In 1975, before many of these major investments were made, the Pittsburgh History and Landmarks Foundation was working to preserve the mid-19th-century structures farther inland in the district known as the Mexican War Streets.[19] The mattress factory in that area was converted into an arts center and museum, discussed earlier in chapter four. It is just one more example of

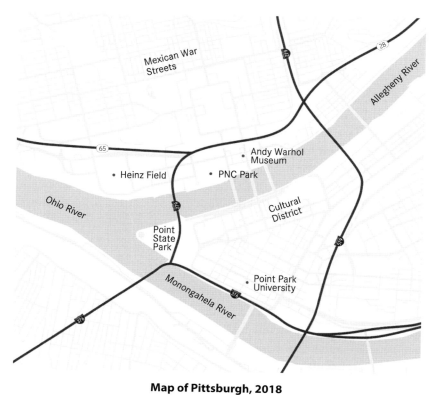

Map of Pittsburgh, 2018

Over the past 50 years, downtown Pittsburgh has jumped across the Allegheny River. (Baolin Paul Shen and Alexander Garvin)

the transformation of a single-function business district into a complex, mixed-use downtown with a great variety of places and activities that contribute to its vitality.

Point Park University, three blocks from the Monongahela River, includes a significant performing arts component in its downtown campus. Unlike these other institutions, however, it is moving some facilities in the opposite direction, away from the far side of Allegheny River into its downtown campus. The university is building a new theater downtown in order to integrate its theater programs with other downtown activities taking place in nearby Market Square.

In the 1950s, Baltimore business leaders created the Committee for

Allegheny River, Pittsburgh, 2012

Sports facilities, museums, and new businesses now line a riverfront park that was created at the end of the 20th century. (Alexander Garvin)

Downtown, Inc. and the Greater Baltimore Committee, Inc. specifically to deal with declining retail sales and tax assessments. Among the strategies they devised to "fix" downtown was the redevelopment of a 33-acre site that involved 216 properties in the middle of the business district. Once the project, known as Charles Center, was completed, there were 17,000 jobs where there had once been 12,000 and a 400 percent increase in real estate tax revenues.[20]

In the 1960s the business community took on the redevelopment of the increasingly obsolete Inner Harbor. James Rouse, who had been head of the Greater Baltimore Committee's executive board when Charles Center was conceived and was still deeply involved in downtown affairs, proposed centering Inner Harbor redevelopment around HarborPlace, a festival marketplace inspired by Quincy Market, a project he had just completed in Boston. The project ran into opposition from nearby merchants who feared competition, nearby neighbors who feared it would price them out of their neighborhoods, and open space advocates who did not want to commercialize the waterfront. Rouse sought the support of the city's many African Americans and their Ministerial Alliance in particular. The coalition of business people and the African American community was successful at winning support in a referendum. The project succeeded beyond everybody's wildest dreams. In its first year of operation, HarborPlace attracted more than 18 million visitors.[21]

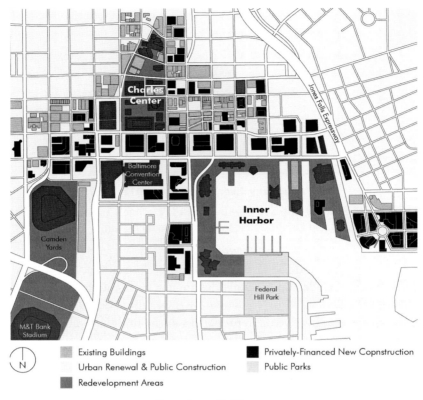

Existing Buildings
Urban Renewal & Public Construction
Redevelopment Areas
Privately-Financed New Copnstruction
Public Parks

Downtown Baltimore

By 2014, the redevelopment of Charles Center and the Inner Harbor, begun in the 1960s, had resulted in widespread and continuing private market development of properties throughout downtown Baltimore. (Alexander Garvin and Ryan Salvatore)

Baltimore's business community also took the lead in pressing for the location of a new convention center one block west of HarborPlace and two stadiums within walking distance of both Inner Harbor and Charles Center. All this publicly sponsored development triggered the construction of dozens of privately financed commercial buildings. It is no wonder that Baltimoreans believe that the business community is responsible for downtown.

Conservancies

Conservancies, like BIDs, are proposed when conditions have deteriorated significantly and government, for any number of reasons, is not able to correct the situation. That is what happened in 1980 when citizens of New York City established the Central Park Conservancy, in 1986 when St. Louis residents created Forest Park Forever, in 1989 when Atlanta residents founded the Piedmont Park Conservancy, and in countless other cities whose parks, like their downtowns, were in deep trouble because of the withdrawal of government services. These citizen groups created conservancies whose activities are managed by 501(c)(3) tax-exempt organizations funded by private donations. Shelby Farms Park, on the edge of downtown Memphis, is a particularly vivid example.

By the early 21st century, Shelby Farms Park, Memphis's largest park, was in deplorable condition and was deteriorating. Concerned citizens, who had formed Friends of Shelby Farms Park, decided to commission a comprehensive redevelopment plan for its 4,500 acres.[22] They hired my firm to run a design competition. I had never been to Memphis, so after spending 2 days learning about the city, its parks, and Shelby Farms Park in particular, I met with the group. However, they were unable to tell me what sort of park they wanted, so they began by having me prepare a program for a design competition. After 6 months, I shocked them by explaining that they were throwing their money away.

Shelby County, which owned the park, was not spending enough to take care of it. When the Friends of Shelby Farms Park said they would get the government to spend more money, I asked which policemen or teachers would be fired to provide that money and how taxes would be increased. Surely, they responded, there was another way to deal with the situation. I told them that other cities created park conservancies, which took responsibility for day-to-day management, maintenance, and capital investment, and also raised the money to pay for these services.

After substantial political maneuvering, they established the Shelby Farms Park Conservancy, negotiated a long-term lease with the county, sponsored an international design competition won by Field Operations (James Corner founding partner and CEO), raised tens of millions of dollars to pay for the first projects recommended in the plan, and took responsibility for the park. Today, the conservancy can proudly explain that it is one of the answers to the question, "Who is downtown?"

Shelby Farms Master Plan, Memphis, 2008

A privately supported conservancy sponsored a design competition in 2008, won by landscape architect James Corner (Field Operations) that became the basis of its restoration of downtown Memphis's 4,500-acre Shelby Farms Park. (James Corner)

Existing Institutions

Given widespread deindustrialization and the declining space needs of office workers, institutions have been playing an ever-larger role in the downtown economy. As Judith Rodin, president of the Rockefeller Foundation and president emerita of the University of Pennsylvania, points out, in the 20 largest cities in the United States, 35 percent of the people who work for private employers work for institutions of higher learning ("eds") and medical facilities ("meds"), "fueling the economy in their cities, as employers, as enormous consumers of goods and services," and as incubators of local business.[23] However, it is important to distinguish between the eds and meds that are integral to their downtowns and those, like the Houston Medical Center, that are essentially concentrations of single-function buildings serving major (institutional) businesses.

In Philadelphia, for example, in 2015 healthcare and educational institutions were the largest sector in the city's economy, accounting for 37 percent of all jobs.[24] In the fall of 2015, Philadelphia Center City's 15 institutions of higher education reported enrollment of more than 32,500 students. Immediately adjacent to downtown, Drexel University, University of Pennsylvania (Penn), University of the Sciences, and Temple University enrolled an additional 75,431, for a total student population of more than 107,000 (approximately 7 percent of the city's entire population) in or adjacent to downtown. Unlike many other 21st-century occupants of downtown institutions, students more often rent apartments, shop, patronize bars and restaurants, and enjoy the many amenities of Center City. They contribute mightily to Philadelphia's vitality.

Some meds, like the Texas Medical Center (TMC) in Houston, are virtually an independent downtown.[25] Its more than 50 institutions occupy 50 million square feet of buildings that cover a territory of 1,345 acres.[26] Its 106,000 employees provide medical services to 10 million patients every year. The TMC was founded in 1945, through a

Texas Medical Center, Houston, 2017

More than 100,000 Texas Medical Center employees provided services to 10 million patients in 2017. (Alexander Garvin)

combination of private donations, namely from banker M.D. Anderson, and the designation of 134 acres for a campus. The mission of the institution, which is run by the Texas Medical Center Corporation, was to cluster nonprofit health facilities to advance medical knowledge and care. It has stayed true to this mission by leasing land to various institutions for 99 years at $1 annually. For these institutions, it acts as an umbrella organization, providing infrastructure and organizational support but otherwise letting them function autonomously.

More than 8 million patients per year go to the 21 hospitals, eight specialty institutions, eight academic research institutions, four medical schools, seven nursing schools, three public health organizations, two pharmacy schools, and one dental school at the TMC.[27] This dense agglomeration of institutions and ancillary businesses is connected to center city downtown, Rice University the Museum District, and scattered residential neighborhoods by METRORail Red Line light rail service. However, the TMC itself includes almost nothing that is unrelated to medical services and thus, despite its high-density concentration of elevator buildings, operates as a single-use district rather than a genuine downtown.

Other meds, although located outside the center city, have contributed to giving a city an additional downtown, similar to Dumbo in Brooklyn or Buckhead in Atlanta. In Cleveland, Case Western Reserve University and six health science institutions and hospitals, along with the Cleveland Natural History Museum, the Museum of Contemporary Art, and Severance Hall (home of the Cleveland Orchestra), are at the core of Case University. By forming a nonprofit–business incubator, Case Western Reserve, Cleveland Clinic, and the University Hospitals have helped to launch three worker-owned cooperatives that employ nearly 250 people.[28]

Sometimes an existing institution perceives its future to be threatened by conditions in the surrounding downtown and is willing to find the means to reverse its decline. That is what occurred two decades ago when the University of Pennsylvania, under Judith Rodin's leadership, decided to take an active role in the revival of West Philadelphia and Yale decided to do what was needed in New Haven. Conditions in both cities were different, as were the roles they assumed to promote resurgence. Without their participation, however, that resurgence would have been unlikely.

Philadelphia's University City

University City, the West Philadelphia district that includes Drexel and the University of Pennsylvania, had been in serious decline since the 1950s, suffering from the same withdrawal of city services occurring in most downtowns. Trash-littered streets were becoming drug dealer hangouts. Rundown buildings were increasingly covered with graffiti. The area's public schools were in deplorable condition. In response, businesses were closing, and residents were moving away. These conditions kept students from applying to Penn. Parents even began threatening to transfer their children to other schools. The response came early but without much effect.

In 1959, the West Philadelphia Corporation was established by the University of Pennsylvania, Drexel Institute of Technology, several local hospitals, and neighborhood and civic organizations to provide support for local businesses, improve the local housing market, and improve building maintenance.[29] Nevertheless, the number of abandoned buildings and criminal activity continued to grow.

The situation spun out of control in September 1996, when University City experienced nearly 30 armed robberies, one of which involved a nearly fatal shooting of an undergraduate. That Halloween, a 38-year-old Penn biochemist was stabbed to death in an attempted robbery. In response, the university finally accepted the reality that if Penn did not take leadership of an effort to revitalize the neighborhood, nobody else would.

University president Judith Rodin "fired the University's commissioner of public safety, hired an experienced captain from the Philadelphia Police Department . . . [and initiated] a sophisticated, multi-pronged public safety plan."[30] The disparate efforts that were initiated became known as the West Philadelphia Initiatives. Working in concert with community activists, neighborhood residents, and community associations, university officials, faculty, and students developed five interrelated goals:

• Improve neighborhood safety, services, and capacities.
• Provide high-quality, diverse housing choices.

- Revive commercial activity.
- Accelerate economic development.
- Enhance local public school options.[31]

Although the interaction with the community and the agreed-upon goals were admirable, they were insufficient. Consequently, Rodin assigned all the university's administrative departments, the provosts, and the deans of its 12 schools to take an active part in the leadership and management of the West Philadelphia Initiatives. More important, she took responsibility for the program's direction and assigned day-to-day implementation to the university's executive vice president.[32]

The program they implemented included the following:

- Creation of the 40th Street Action Team to deal with real estate, security, housing, business activity, sidewalk repair, street trees, bike racks, and trash along this retail corridor
- Initiation of the U.C. Brite Program to light every building from curb to curb, from dusk to dawn
- Formation of the University City District, an entity involving the area's 11 key institutions, patterned after the city's CCD to keep the entire 2.2-square-mile neighborhood "safe, clean, and attractive," whose operating budget would be largely paid for by the university
- Rehabilitation of 9.1-acre Clark Park
- Establishment of LUCY (Loop throughout University City) shuttle service
- Opening of a new building in the district for the Division of Public Safety
- Investment by the university in housing development, rehabilitation, and subsidies for home ownership
- Assistance with local public school programs by the University Graduate School of Education
- Creation of the district's new Penn Alexander School

In each case, consultation with the community and agreed-upon goals were supplemented with direct action by entities established to achieve specific results, appropriations to pay for any necessary action, and designated personnel to execute the program. The results were dramatic.

After 20 years of clever and determined effort, the district includes 128 new buildings containing 14 million square feet, 9,000 additional residents, and 30,000 new jobs.[33] The crime rate is half of what it was 20 years ago.[34] In 2018 the University City District raised and spent about $10 million per year to keep the district clean, safe, and attractive. It is a dramatic example of the beneficial role an institution can play in transforming a troubled district into a resurgent downtown. Yale University, as a result of entirely different, less dramatic actions, has had an equally positive impact on downtown New Haven.

West Philadelphia, 2018

Two decades after eleven key institutions began working to keep the area "safe, clean, and attractive," thousands of students, workers, and residents patronized 113 thriving shopping and dining facilities. (Alexander Garvin)

Yale and New Haven

Thirty years ago, conditions in the territory surrounding Yale University, like those in Philadelphia's University City, were keeping some students from applying and causing some parents to think about transferring their children to other schools. Yale was the city's major employer, located right at the center of a small downtown in a city with a fraction of Philadelphia's population and businesses. Its current 14,000 staff and faculty constitute 11 percent of the city's population, and as the city's largest employer with 17.5 percent of its 80,000 jobs, anything the university did generated major consequences.[35] Yet neither Yale nor New Haven wanted to admit this essential relationship. So whenever Yale did anything that affected the city, it usually acted with maximum discretion, avoiding the high-visibility actions that were so important in Penn's program for West Philadelphia. Moreover, unlike Penn, which created a community-wide effort involving everything in the surrounding district, Yale restricted its effort to five investment strategies.

In dealing with its own property, Yale has adopted a conservative investment policy. Thus, beginning in 1993, when Yale began its $6 billion program to renovate the university's magnificent old buildings and build new facilities, many of the city's local businesses were the beneficiaries.

A second way that the university invests simultaneously in itself and in the city of New Haven is through programs that provide financing for local residents. The largest is its Homebuyer Program. Established in 1994, it provides permanent Yale University employees working 20 or more hours a week with up to $30,000, taken in annual installments over 10 years. Participants receive a $5,000 first-year bonus and an annual $2,500 grant for up to 10 years as long as they continue to own a home and live in New Haven and remain employed by Yale. As of 2017, more than 1,200 Yale faculty and staff had benefited from Yale's $31 million contribution toward $237 million in home purchases.[36]

Yale also provides $4 million per year to city residents who graduate from New Haven public schools and attend college in Connecticut. It pays $12 million per year in free medical care of New Haven residents; contributes to public park and streetscape improvements; supports Market New Haven, a nonprofit organization formed by the city, Yale, and the business community to publicize New Haven's renaissance; and co-sponsors the annual International Festival of Arts and Ideas.

Yale's third approach is to make strategic investments in surrounding property. Downtown New Haven had been in decline since the mid-20th century when the university established its Office of New Haven and State Affairs in 1998 and appointed Bruce Alexander its vice president and director. Alexander had spent 25 years as a senior executive at the Rouse Company, where he had managed retail and mixed-use properties throughout the United States. Thus, he was perfectly placed to revive the ailing retail activity on the periphery of Yale.

For decades, local customers had been driving to nearby suburban malls, rather than downtown New Haven, for their shopping. New Haven's population had declined from its peak of 164,000 in 1950 to 124,000 in 2000, when the city began growing again. The city's last department store closed in 1993. The retailers that remained downtown had as little appeal to Yale staff and students as they did to the people who worked downtown. Three retail concentrations on the edge of some sections of Yale's 345-acre campus were in particular need of revitalization: Broadway, which dominated vehicular traffic headed northwest to the suburbs; Whitney Avenue, which funneled traffic going northeast out of town; and Chapel Street, in the heart of downtown.

Broadway Retail, New Haven, 2017

By investing in properties on the edge of Yale and selecting tenants who had a synergistic ability to enhance the area, the university had helped to stimulate the growing resurgence of downtown New Haven by 2017. (Alexander Garvin)

Alexander, working on behalf of the university, purchased strategic properties in each concentration with the objective of creating an attractive customer base rather than quickly developing an income stream. He signed leases that required nighttime operation and sometimes waited several years to obtain the right retail tenant for particular locations, where they would attract spillover customers to other nearby stores. As a result of his efforts, in 2018, 110 stores and restaurants in Yale-owned property at these three locations were generating substantial rental revenues, attracting customers from all over the metropolitan region, paying real estate taxes to the city of New Haven, and, particularly important, providing a model for other developers to purchase nearby properties for rehabilitation and reuse or for new construction.[37]

Even before Yale targeted Chapel Street, Joel Schiavone, a local real estate developer, had begun to acquire many downtown properties, operating along Chapel Street south of the New Haven Green and across the street from Yale. Starting in the early 1980s, he struggled to keep them afloat, eventually losing them to foreclosure in 1993.[38] When the mayor requested that Yale take them over, the university was ready to buy them, because by then the price had decreased sufficiently. Thus, in 1999 Yale purchased eight formerly Schiavone-owned properties at bargain prices from their then-owner, the Federal Deposit Insurance Corporation, which had taken possession when the bank that had foreclosed on the mortgages collapsed.[39]

The fourth strategy consisted of economic development investments intended to attract budding new industries and promote local entrepreneurship. It began in 1981 when Yale began a cooperative effort with the City of New Haven to create Science Park within an 80-acre, predominantly vacant industrial complex adjacent to the Yale Science Hill campus. Since its inception, Science Park has attracted more than 30 startup businesses, high-technology firms, biotech companies, light manufacturing, and assembly industries to New Haven.

Yale's fifth economic development program includes the Yale Entrepreneurial Institute and the Center for Bioscience and Technology on George Street in downtown New Haven. The Yale Entrepreneurial Institute began in 2007 as a 10-week summer program for undergraduates and has expanded into an all-year program that provides programs and events throughout the year that serve the entrepreneurial interests of Yale students and the New Haven community. It offers assistance to budding entrepreneurs who are starting new ventures and up to $100,000 in startup funding to students and faculty launching promising new companies. The Center for Bioscience and Technology is a half-million-square-foot building of office and laboratory space with the advanced infrastructure that provides technical building services at a significant cost savings. The business provided by all three institutions is of real benefit to downtown New Haven.

Government

Local governments are still a part of the answer to the question, "Who is changing downtown?" Even in a city as vast and complex as New York, mayors such as La Guardia, Giuliani, and Bloomberg have been thought to be in charge. The same was true of both Mayor Daleys in Chicago and certainly Joseph Riley, who was mayor of Charleston, South Carolina, for 40 years. But even these leaders were not independent activists. Their roles were and are constrained by our decentralized democracy, with its commitment to the separation of powers, and by the many other players involved in any downtown. Furthermore, executing their policies and programs is likely to take more time that their individual terms of office.

The resurgence of lower Manhattan, for example, required ongoing and determined efforts over four decades by four mayoral administrations. It began under Mayor Koch, continued under Mayor Giuliani, and accelerated under Mayor Bloomberg. Without their efforts, lower Manhattan businesses and property owners would not have made the private investments that transformed this declining business district into a resurgent downtown.

Lower Manhattan had been in decline long before January 1978, when Edward I. Koch became mayor. At the end of World War II, lower Manhattan, which had recovered from the Great Depression, had begun a steady decline, similar to what was happening in many American downtowns.[40]

Because of fiscal mismanagement, the city almost went into bankruptcy in the mid-1970s. Spending in its capital budget dropped from $1.23 billion in 1971 to $695.5 million in 1978. As a result of years of disinvestment in its capital plant, the city's infrastructure everywhere, not just in lower Manhattan, was in deplorable condition. Consequently, in 1978 the City Planning Commission, in its charter-mandated assessment of capital needs, reported the following guidelines:

- Streets: The desirable rate for repaving streets is once every 20 or 25 years. At present the city is repaving streets at the rate of once every 200 years.
- Water mains: Engineers say a main should be replaced every 100 years. Today the replacement rate is every 296 years.
- Sewers: Engineers say a main should be replaced every 100 years. Right now, the replacement rate is every 300 years.
- Parks: The optimal rate of major repairs is 25 years per acre. The actual rate is every 900 years.[41]

Accordingly, the Koch administration initiated substantial increases in city capital spending. Moreover, as the city emerged from the fiscal crises of the mid-1970s and was able to increase borrowing, the administration continued to increase capital spending. By 1981, the administration had shifted its focus from disinvestment to identifying issues created by the city's economic revitalization. The next year, when it projected $34.7 billion in spending for 1983–1992, the city's fiscal crisis had been overcome.[42]

Because of years of similar disinvestment by the state-chartered Metropolitan Transportation Administration (MTA), the public transit situation was similarly dire. In 1978, the City Planning Commission reported that city buses and subway cars; the facilities for cleaning, maintaining, and repairing them; and track beds, rails, electric equipment, signals, and less visible underpinnings of the transit system had "been in service twenty-four hours a day since they were first constructed from forty to ninety years ago."[43] MTA administrator Richard Ravitch responded by assigning the NYC Planning Commission report, *A New Direction in Transit*, to the senior staff at the MTA. As a result, the MTA also instituted a major new capital investment program. Within 5 years the MTA capital plant and transit service were back to normal. (Cities tend to repeat their errors. The city's subway system was in similarly dire condition in 2018, after two decades of disinvestment by four gubernatorial administrations.)

Thus, by 1993, when Rudolph Giuliani was elected mayor, the physical plant of lower Manhattan was in relatively good condition. However, its privately owned real estate was in trouble. Businesses were moving to Midtown Manhattan, Jersey City, White Plains, and even downtown Brooklyn, leaving behind obsolete office space that was no longer needed. The Giuliani administration decided that the way to deal with the increasing stock of vacant office space was to convert it to residential use.

Thus, in 1995, it enacted the 421g tax exemption and abatement program for the conversion of lower Manhattan commercial buildings into multiple dwellings. The 421g program provided the necessary tax incentive: an exemption from any increase in real estate taxes for 12 years and a 14-year abatement of approximately 80 percent of the real estate taxes paid before conversion. These benefits applied to any buildings converted between 1995 and 2006.

Tax incentives, by themselves, were insufficient. To facilitate design flexibility for such conversions, Joe Rose, chairman of the New York City Planning Commission, proposed the creation of the Special Lower Manhattan Zoning District, which was approved by the Planning Commission and the City Council in 1998. Those tax and zoning changes remained in place when Michael Bloomberg became mayor in 2002. Thus, by 2006, when the tax incentives expired, 115 buildings had been converted from commercial use into 7,536 residential apartments.[44]

When Bloomberg took office, however, the environment of lower Manhattan was not entirely livable, and not just because of the aftermath of the 9/11 terrorist attack. Its public realm was deficient. Street traffic was congested, air quality was poor, and there weren't enough parks to attract families with children to live in recently converted or newly built apartments.

In 2002, when I was vice president of the Lower Manhattan Development Corporation, I was determined to reconnect the two ends of Greenwich Street, which had been severed by the original #7 World Trade Center, and restore the section of Fulton Street that had once connected Greenwich Street with what is now Battery Park City. A reconnected Greenwich Street would restore the artery that used to go from the Holland Tunnel to the Battery and would double lower

Albany Street, lower Manhattan, 2006

By 2006, privately financed new construction was beginning to occur through-out lower Manhattan. (Alexander Garvin)

Manhattan's capacity to handle the heavy north–south truck and bus traffic that passed through the area. It also would reunite the Tribeca neighborhood, north of the World Trade Center site, with the office district to its south. Unnecessary security measures continue to prevent the flow of traffic through the former World Trade Center site on Greenwich Street, as well as Fulton, Courtland, and Dey streets. Nevertheless, traffic in that section of lower Manhattan is less congested, and, more important, those streets can be reopened to traffic whenever city policy changes.

Underground improvements have also resulted in improved traffic flow. In the aftermath of 9/11, the city erected a $1.4-billion Fulton Subway Hub on Broadway. It provides underground pedestrian connections to and from all 15 subway lines that connect lower Manhattan with the rest of the city. In turn, that interchange has been connected to the PATH railroad system and beyond to Brookfield Place in Battery Park City. This has untangled the knot of subway connections that had confused New Yorkers and tourists for more than a century and is now used by 300,000 commuters every day, reducing pedestrian congestion on nearby streets.[45]

Fulton Subway Hub, lower Manhattan, 2018

The Fulton Subway Hub in lower Manhattan connects 11 subway lines with the PATH railroad station on the site of the World Trade Center. (Alexander Garvin)

There also are now major new open space and recreational resources in lower Manhattan. The National September 11 Memorial & Museum, which opens directly onto surrounding city streets, is occupied by a plaza, a museum, and two memorial pools. The plaza contains a grove of almost

400 white oak trees planted on paved territory with convenient public benches set aside for visitors and a large, decorative grassy areas fenced off from public use.

The block south of the memorial had been previously occupied by the 41-story Deutsche Bank Building and the four-story St. Nicholas Greek Orthodox Church. It now contains a replacement church and the 1-acre Liberty Park.

Silverstein Family Park, lower Manhattan, 2017

As part of the reconstruction of the World Trade Center, Greenwich Street again connects the Battery with the Tribeca District, just north, while passing through a brand-new privately owned park that is always open to the public. (Alexander Garvin)

To compensate the Silverstein Organization for land it had to give up to restore Greenwich Street, the City of New York agreed to give up equivalent territory between Vesey Street and the former southern face of the building. The new #7 World Trade Center did not need all the territory of the enlarged site. The 5,000-square-foot triangle not used for the new building is now Silverstein Family Park, which includes trees, greenery, shaded sitting areas, a fountain, and a red sculpture by Jeff Koons, called "balloon flower."[46]

Two major landscaped esplanades have been added to the east and

The new West Street Promenade, 2016

Lower Manhattan has an expanded and improved public realm that provides its occupants with new recreational resources. (Alexander Garvin)

west sides of lower Manhattan. They have been filled with people from the moment they opened. Both the West Street Promenade and the East River waterfront park were much more ambitious projects when they were proposed by Mayor Bloomberg in the 2002 *Vision for Lower Manhattan*, which presented his priorities for rebuilding. Nevertheless, they provide substantial additional parkland for the tens of thousands of people who moved to lower Manhattan after 9/11. The West Street Promenade was created by the New York State Highway Department by widening and relandscaping the portion of the Hudson River Greenway along West Street between Battery Park and Brookfield Place. It has become a promenade for everybody in Battery Park City, a link from the

East River Esplanade, lower Manhattan, 2014

For the first time in generations, New Yorkers can promenade along a new esplanade lining the East River in lower Manhattan. (Alexander Garvin)

Hudson River Park to Battery Park, and an essential part of the bikeway encircling Manhattan.

The Bloomberg administration spent more than $117 million creating a 2-mile-long waterfront park along the East River from the Battery Maritime Building to Pier 35, just north of the Manhattan Bridge. This facility, designed by landscape architect Ken Smith and SHoP Architects, combines the bikeway that encircles Manhattan Island with a landscaped esplanade and a double-decker park on Pier 15.[47] It is supplemented on the west side of the elevated FDR Drive with the wonderfully innovative Imagination Playground, designed by architect David Rockwell, which replaced a city-owned parking lot at Burling Slip.

It took the continuing efforts of the Koch, Giuliani, and Bloomberg administrations over four decades to make the capital investments that contributed to the resurgence of Lower Manhattan.

Change

Not all change is for the better. Nevertheless, plenty of changes are desperately needed to ensure the continued health of downtown. The next chapter examines what we can learn from the past to avoid making mistakes and identifies public and private initiatives that will increase downtown vibrancy and better adapt downtown to a new generation.

Chapter 6

Lessons for Any Downtown

M any 20th-century urban experts believed cities, and downtowns in particular, were obsolete. Their prescriptions for preventing them from withering away included redevelopment and reorganization in order to transform (presumably) obsolete downtowns into efficiently operating, modern districts; adding facilities designed to attract new customers whose spending would spill over into the rest of the city; or retrofitting the public realm to accommodate additional motor vehicles that would bring the goods, services, businesses, and people needed for continuing growth. However, each of these strategies was fundamentally flawed, because each one assumed that some particular end state would be the right means for achieving a properly functioning downtown.

A second group of experts, who dealt exclusively with a specific city, saw the future of downtown as a zero-sum game in which they were competing for business and people with other downtowns in the region. Their approach was to subsidize specific players directly, with tax rebates, direct grants, or below-market mortgage loans. However, if that subsidy continues in perpetuity, it cannot be a viable program for improving downtown. Rather, it is a program for purchasing, at taxpayer expense, the downtown presence of one particular set of residents, retailers, businesses, and activities that are deemed worthy of receiving subsidies.

Instead, urbanists should have been conceiving of ways to assist the downtown activists (described in Chapters 4 and 5), who are continuing to transform downtown America by attracting customers, improving services, altering the activities taking place in particular locations, erecting or converting buildings, changing land uses, opening businesses, and assisting the governments that are reducing the cost of doing business or living downtown.

The Mirage of Urban Redevelopment

Mid-20th-century urbanists, who believed that downtowns were dying because of an obsolete physical plant, were convinced that their revival could be achieved by clearing blighted areas and replacing them with modern, efficient business districts connected by superhighways to surrounding metropolitan areas. These urbanists thought that the redevelopment of downtown Pittsburgh was a perfect model. It involved eliminating air pollution, traffic congestion, flooding, and obsolete, underused railyards, factories, and warehouses that occupied prime downtown sites and, thereafter, replacing them with "the city of tomorrow."[1] They were correct about the need to reverse Pittsburgh's environmental degradation but failed to understand that the difficulties (e.g., air pollution from prevalent steel mills) faced by downtown Pittsburgh in the 1930s and 1940s were very different from the local problems that downtown Detroit (e.g., loss of more than half the population resulting in widespread property abandonment), Cleveland (e.g., river pollution), Los Angeles (widespread regional growth), and most other cities would face in the 1950s.

The techniques they devised were intended to be applicable anywhere: using the government's power of eminent domain to acquire private property, clearing obsolete buildings, and conveying the resulting sites to new owners who agreed to build and operate modern commercial and residential buildings. Accordingly, Congress passed the Housing Act of 1949, which offered to pay two-thirds of the cost of such city redevelopment projects. Over the next 24 years the federal government appropriated more than $12.7 billion to pay for urban renewal projects throughout the country.[2]

Supporters of this urban renewal program were correct in believing that neither business nor people would remain downtown unless it was easy for anybody in the metropolitan area to get there and circulate once they had arrived. It was thought that this required the reconfiguration of the public realm (especially streets and highways), government institutions, and the buildings occupying private property. However, they did not anticipate the cost or negative consequences of removing all the residents, businesses, and institutions that occupied those downtown sites or the damage to the city's cultural patrimony, especially since the sites selected for "slum clearance" were occupied predominantly by people of low income, particularly vulnerable to the negative effects of dislocation. Because it was nearly impossible for any real estate developer to assemble all the necessary sites, update the infrastructure, relocate site tenants, and demolish all obsolete structures, a local renewal agency was assigned that role.

Indeed, reconfiguring and improving circulation in what became known as Pittsburgh's Golden Triangle did attract new businesses and residents downtown. However, the departure of businesses from downtown Detroit, retail stores from downtown Los Angeles, and residents from downtown St. Louis was not caused by inappropriate block and lot patterns or poor vehicular circulation systems. Nevertheless, at considerable cost, these and hundreds of other cities engaged in downtown projects intended to redevelop entire sections of their downtowns.

The reason for so many downtown renewal projects was that the federal government paid nearly one thousand cities to engage in such redevelopment with appropriations from the Housing Act of 1949. Once these urban renewal projects had received federal approval, local governments used their power of eminent domain to condemn large sections of downtown, relocate the businesses and people occupying them, demolish everything, install "modern" infrastructure and circulation systems, and create large, "efficient" properties. These newly created properties were then resold to private companies for specific new projects at prices that reflected their value for the projected reuse. Government covered two-thirds of the difference between the cost of creating these sites and their market value.

Cleveland's Erieview Redevelopment Project is typical of the program. It cleared 30 acres of "a derelict neighborhood" lying "fallow and blighted ... cluttered with small makeshift parking lots ... dilapidated houses, warehouses, and workshops for light industry ... [so it could be] reclaimed and redeveloped to give the core of our city a vigorous, vibrant, pulsating heart."[3] In 1960, when Erieview was being considered, Cleveland (a city of 876,000 people) was the center of a metropolitan of nearly 2.1 million people.

Erieview Urban Renewal Project, Cleveland, 2012

As so many have explained, urban "renewal," such as Cleveland's Erieview, often turned out to be urban "removal." (Alexander Garvin)

The project that emerged consisted of 4.7 million square feet of office space, a 183,000-square-foot shopping mall, 5,500 apartments, a 600-room hotel, and parking for 6,900 cars. Erieview proved to be nothing more than a rearrangement of the deck chairs on the *Titanic*. Its gleaming modernist structures did not stop the continuing departure of businesses and people from downtown Cleveland, nor could they. By 2010 the city's population had dropped 56 percent, to 388,000, within a metropolitan area that had gained only 13,000 residents between 1970 and 2010. In fact, the vacancies in the deteriorating buildings in downtown Cleveland were unconnected to the modernity of its physical plant, which is why the new buildings did not fill up when they opened. The somewhat empty old and new commercial buildings throughout downtown Cleveland were the product of declining demand. Regional businesses and residents just did not want a downtown location. The action had shifted to the suburbs.

There was another reason, besides population decline, that some redevelopment projects failed to "renew" the rest of downtown. Constitution Plaza in Hartford, the World Trade Center in lower Manhattan, and the Renaissance Center in Detroit provided up-to-date facilities that were very much in demand and would not have been available otherwise. But they also attracted their cities' most profitable local businesses, which vacated obsolete commercial space that was no longer in demand, leaving behind empty class B office space, thereby weakening rather than "renewing" the rest of downtown.[4] Whenever this "comprehensive" approach to modernization ignored local market conditions, it was certain to cause the same unintended negative consequences that accelerated the decline of downtown Hartford, Detroit, and lower Manhattan.

Other urbanists believed that government ought to use the power of eminent domain primarily to assemble sites for quasi-public facilities that attracted additional customers to a location from which they would spill over for the benefit of other nearby business activity. In New York City, for example, Robert Moses, chairman of its Committee on Slum Clearance, used this technique to assemble a site for the Colosseum (a convention center) at 59th Street and Broadway and Lincoln Center (a performing arts center) four blocks north of it.[5] Together, they were responsible for bringing droves of people to the West Side of Manhattan. This success was infectious; cities around the country copied them. However, Moses understood that these were one-off projects, which at the Colosseum included 608 new apartments and at Lincoln Center included 4,260 new apartments. All his other redevelopment projects restricted the reuse to residential occupancy. Most other urban renewal projects concentrated on "economic development" rather than housing.

In Los Angeles, as explained later in this chapter, the cluster of cultural facilities it created on Bunker Hill, in the northwest corner of downtown, failed to generate genuine downtown resurgence because of inappropriately located highway construction. Los Angeles had a success similar to New York City's, however, with a new cluster of public attractions in the southwest corner of downtown. This second cluster involved the construction (in stages between 1971 and 1997) of 720,000 square feet of convention and exhibition space and 147,000 square feet of meeting space, the GRAMMY Museum, a 299-seat theater, and nearly 2 million square feet of parking; and the 20,000-seat Staples Center arena was added in 1999. The reason for its success was very different from that of Moses's Colosseum and Lincoln Center projects. LA's new "palaces for the people" attracted a huge market from an enormous metropolitan area, made accessible by one of the world's most extensive highway networks. For the first time in half a century, tens of thousands of ordinary Angelinos were attracted downtown to see one of their three sports teams, while businesses from around the world traveled to the convention center, and together they attracted tourists to downtown hotels.

St. Louis used this technique to assemble property for a convention center (The Dome at America's Center), a baseball field (Busch Stadium), and an auditorium (Peabody [formerly Kiel] Opera House). However, these facilities did not have the huge impact of Moses's West Side Story (large civic and cultural facilities built at a location made famous by Leonard Bernstein's musical) or the combination of attractions at the Convention Center and Staples Arena in Los Angeles. In St. Louis these projects were just far enough away from one another that people drove to one facility, attended an event, and drove home. Had they been clustered together, they might have provided a critical mass of downtown customer spending. Many other cities that invested in similar facilities intended to benefit the surrounding downtown attracted large numbers of people but achieved comparably meager spending outside that specific attraction.

We spent hundreds of billions of dollars that occasionally dealt with very real problems. In most cases, however, the money was wasted changing the physical layout of some sections of downtown, when that was not the cause of the economic and social problems facing that particular city. Worse yet, redevelopment in many cases caused devastating dislocation and harmed more than a few downtown businesses and residents. Going forward, downtown leaders considering redevelopment need to be sure that the problems they want to solve are not caused by an improper physical arrangement of private property and that the cost of dislocating area occupants and the damage it causes are worth the result.

Making It Easy to Get In and Out of Downtown

The advent of widespread automobile ownership and the accompanying suburbanization led the governments of the New York Metropolitan Area to invest in transportation facilities such as the Holland, Lincoln, and Queens–Midtown tunnels and the George Washington and Triborough bridges. They were intended to bring additional goods, services, businesses, and people that would help lower Manhattan and Midtown continue growing. Yet between 1930, three years after the Holland Tunnel opened, and 1940, when the Queens–Midtown Tunnel opened, population and employment in Manhattan hardly changed, largely because of economic decline during the Great Depression. The impact of the bridges and tunnels finally was felt a decade after the end of World War II. In 1924, before the opening of the Holland Tunnel, 2.34 million vehicles per day entered Manhattan. By 1956 that number had increased by nearly 1 million vehicles.[6]

If the redevelopment of downtown Pittsburgh was the model for the Urban Renewal Program, the bridges, tunnels, and parkways of New York City became the model for the Interstate Highway Program. Just as the Golden Triangle made sense in Pittsburgh, new bridges, tunnels, and parkways were appropriate to the New York Metropolitan Area. Thus, in part to supplement the urban renewal projects financed by the Housing Act of 1949, Congress enacted the National Interstate Defense and Highways Act of 1956, believing it would improve the flow of goods and people in and out of cities. Its goal was the creation of a 47,000-mile system of highways, bridges, and tunnels. Rather than paying for just two-thirds of its cost, Congress voted to cover 90 percent.

The reality was that relocation and demolition of property within the path of the new highways often damaged downtowns that were already troubled, especially when combined with nearby urban renewal projects financed by the Housing Act of 1949. In many downtowns demolition for highway construction accelerated the departure of retail, wholesale, and shipping activities. Those that remained in downtown LA, for example, remained in the adjacent Toy, Produce, and Fashion Districts. In many other cities, however, highway construction helped turn downtowns into single-function business districts with vacant and underused buildings.

Interstate Highway 110 in Los Angeles, for example, cut off down-town residents who lived in and around Bunker Hill, completing the transformation of a previously lively downtown into a bedraggled single-function business district. The once-fashionable mansions on Bunker Hill originally had been settled by doctors, lawyers, and merchants in the 1870s and 1880s. Once they left, the buildings began to deteriorate and were often converted into rooming houses. As Raymond Chandler explained in 1950, "You could find anything from down-in-the-heels ex-Greenwich-villagers to crooks on the lam, from ladies of anybody's evening to County relief clients. . . . It had been a nice place once, had Bunker Hill, and from the days of its niceness there still remained the funny little funicular railway, called Angel's Flight, which crawled up and down a yellow clay bank from Hill Street."[7]

Angel's Flight, Bunker Hill, Los Angeles, 1996

In 1996, before the resurgence of downtown LA, Angel's Flight was a quaint cen-turies-old relic from the days when Bunker Hill was an important part of a thriv-ing downtown. (Alexander Garvin)

All of downtown Los Angeles, not just Bunker Hill, continued to deteriorate. In 1959, John Rechy described downtown's Pershing Square as a place that was occupied by "scattered junkies, the small-time pushers, the queens, the sad panhandlers, the lonely, exiled nymphs haunting the entrance to the men's head."[8] This was only half a dozen years after Pershing Square had been torn apart to create a three-level, underground parking garage with a brand-new park on top.

The city's leadership began to deal with the problems of downtown Los Angeles the very year that Rechy sketched the problems in Pershing Square, by approving the redevelopment of the rest of Bunker Hill (133 acres).[9] The site was cleared of all its dilapidated, formerly "grand old houses with scrolled porches, parquetry floors, and immense sweeping banisters of white oak, mahogany and Circassian walnut."[10] The redevelopment project took more than three decades to complete, but unlike the combination of the Los Angeles Convention Center and Staples Center, it failed to generate genuine downtown resurgence, and there was no synergistic relationship among the structures erected on Bunker Hill.

Today Bunker Hill is the site of the 5,943-seat Los Angeles Music Center, the 2,265-seat Disney Concert Hall, MOCA, approximately 10 million square feet of offices in a self-contained enclave, 2,000 hotel rooms, 3,000 apartments, and nearly 600,000 square feet of retail stores and restaurants. It may have been "renewed," but the billions of dollars spent on Bunker Hill had little effect on the rest of downtown Los Angeles.

The completion of the interstate highway encircling downtown and its many extensions going everywhere in Los Angeles County also had little effect. They both only made it easy for Angelinos to drive to popular downtown destinations, do almost anything without going to the rest of downtown, and then return to their parked car to drive home on the freeway. Thus, for decades after the loop of Interstate Highways 10 and 110 encircled downtown Los Angeles, there was virtually no growth in downtown's population or job base. That changed at the start of the 21st century as a result of the work of the Downtown Los Angeles BID (see Chapter 5). The same results were evident after the interstate highway made it easier to leave downtown Detroit, St. Louis, Cleveland, and many other cities. However, their BIDs so far have been insufficient to reverse their decline.

Indeed, highway construction did make it easier to get in and out downtown—but not necessarily to its benefit. In cities such as Cleveland

and Los Angeles, where residents were moving to the suburbs, new highways made it easier for them to drive home at night and make their purchases closer to their suburban homes. First downtown lost those customers, then they lost the businesses that went after their suburban customers. Those highways also made it easier for workers to get downtown. In Midtown Manhattan in the 1920s, or more recently in downtown Pittsburgh, where employment opportunities were increasing, such transportation investments made sense. It is incumbent on downtown leaders to look carefully at what is happening and will be happening to the downtown customer and employment base before investing in highway construction.

Subsidizing Privately Owned Business

It is discriminatory to subsidize some businesses and residents without providing the same opportunity to everybody. If an entire district or building type goes out of use, leaving the area with abandoned properties that attract antisocial activity, the entire city ends up paying for remedial area services while generating substantially less revenue from those properties. In such cases, temporary, targeted subsidies may be enough to trigger a widespread and sustained private market reaction that will benefit the entire downtown.

Deindustrialization, for example, resulted in entire districts with vacant buildings. In such areas, the government rarely owns the properties and is unlikely to appropriate the money to buy them. Moreover, clearance, redevelopment, or even renovation of these districts by government agencies is neither appropriate nor effective. Subsidizing improvements carried out by existing property owners or developers who purchase empty buildings for that purpose can be mightily effective, however, especially when they result in resuscitating an entire district.

In the early 1970s, artists and other pioneers were attracted to empty lofts in SoHo, Tribeca, and other parts of lower Manhattan (see Chapter 2). Not only was their presence illegal under existing zoning, it violated fire and multiple dwelling codes. As a result of J-51 tax exemption and abatement (discussed in Chapter 3), nearly all empty buildings in those two sections of lower Manhattan had become legally occupied (expensive) residences, restaurants, and boutiques within a decade.[11] Twenty years later, they were all paying multiple times the real estate taxes they paid even decades earlier when they had been occupied by successful manufacturing companies.

Many downtowns at the end of the 20th century experienced the increasing obsolescence of older class B office buildings, whether because of inappropriately sized floor plates, inadequate wiring and internet service, changes in space utilization, or new business practices. As in the case of loft conversion, subsidizing new residential construction carried out by existing property owners or developers became a particularly effective tool in resuscitating dying business districts.

As described in Chapter 5, between 2000 and 2017, Philadelphia induced the construction of more than 17,000 new rental and condominium apartments by simply providing a 10-year exemption from any increase in real estate tax payments from sites that became new residential structures. Similar programs in Cleveland, St. Louis, Des Moines, and Portland, Oregon generated new and renovated housing. In other downtowns, governments provided subsidies to property owners who were experiencing widespread retail vacancies.

It is often difficult to know whether retail vacancies arise because of location, store appearance, retail know-how, high rents, or the inability of local retailers to deal with competition. However, empty shopping areas, like abandoned manufacturing and warehouse districts, can attract undesirable activities and require local governments to spend scarce city money on remedial services. A number of downtowns have been successful in reviving retailing by providing technical assistance, assigning additional personnel to the area, or establishing grant programs. In most instances, however, such programs (like other subsidies) are really gifts to the businesses that apply for them. They rarely benefit properties and business that are not located on the same retail corridor.

Raleigh, North Carolina, for example, provides matching grants to retail properties that make improvements and invest in façade treatment. Lower Manhattan provides commercial rent tax reductions. The downtown Houston BID provides direct grants to businesses that occupy ground floor retail space.

In Raleigh, the grants go to any retailer within the downtown Municipal Services District occupying ground floor space for the first time or seeking to expand its space by more than 30 percent. In these instances, the city matches 50 cents for every dollar spent, up to $5,000.[12] It is questionable whether this subsidy was needed for one of the fastest-growing cities in the nation, whose 2017 population of 460,000 had more than doubled over the last 25 years.[13]

In lower Manhattan, commercial tenants who locate in nonresidential pre-1975 buildings before 2021 and make improvements to their space are eligible for $2.50 per square foot real estate tax abatement for up to 5 years.[14] In addition, before June 30, 2020, profit-making businesses with an annual rent greater than $200,000 may receive an exemption for up to 5 years on the tax. Over the past 15 years, however, lower Manhattan has been the beneficiary of millions of square feet of newly converted office space, 18,000 new and converted apartments, and 6,000 new hotel rooms.[15] Their occupants, combined with everybody already in lower Manhattan, provided more than enough customers to justify opening additional retail stores, even without a subsidy.

Sometimes, the problem faced by local businesses is the unjustified unwillingness of banks, insurance companies, and other lenders to provide financing. This is especially true during economic downturns. Government assistance, targeted to districts and businesses with potentially increasing market demand, may provide enough marginal assistance to enable property owners and businesses to prosper until the downtown begins to wane and the area is again attracting new customers, thereby generating downtown resurgence. For example, Columbus, Ohio provides downtown businesses that apply for a low-interest loan up to $100,000 to cover property or heavy equipment purchases and a "working capital loan" of up to $199,000, when it is matched by another lending institution.[16] The big difference between the programs in Raleigh and those in Columbus is that loans, unlike grants, must be repaid.

Cities with vacant and underused properties should be copying programs such as those in Columbus, Raleigh, and New York that do not punish property and business owners for fixing up their buildings and, in fact, reward them with tax benefits for doing so.

Assisting Downtown America

Very few urbanists still recommend the radical redevelopment projects that were prevalent in the 1950s and 1960s. The infrastructure subsidies now being proposed are devoted largely to rehabilitation, repair, and maintenance—not new highway construction—and only occasionally additional mass transit. Stadiums and other megaprojects are still being proposed but in few places, largely because of local opposition or spending constraints. Tax rebates and direct subsidies remain popular, however, and at the right time, for the right purposes, and in the right places they will be effective.

There are many less expensive, more easily executed actions we can take to promote downtown America. Rather than engaging in cataclysmic redevelopment, building huge, extraordinarily expensive public facilities, or giving gifts (a.k.a. subsidies) to privately owned businesses, we should be devising actions that help the people and institutions who are changing downtowns (described in Chapters 4 and 5). The best way to do this is to engage in activities that attract existing customers and even increase downtown demand, from which people and institutions can profit from by changing land uses, renovating existing buildings, or erecting new structures. The more recent resurgence of many American downtowns has happened because of public action devised specifically to achieve one of these six objectives, all of which can be of benefit to any downtown at any time:

- Establishing a distinctive image that identifies the downtown as a special, particularly desirable place
- Providing easy access to and convenient circulation within downtown
- Creating a public realm with plenty of room for people to pursue the activities for which they go downtown
- Sustaining a livable downtown environment that will attract and keep people downtown
- Reducing the cost of doing business downtown
- Making it easy to alter land uses, remodel existing buildings, and build new facilities that meet the changing demands of downtown customers

As long as there is already adequate or growing market demand for the results, these strategies will help the downtown grow and expand. Without that market, however, they will fail. The following examples demonstrate when and how these strategies work and when they don't.

Establishing a Distinctive Image

Any company trying to market a product will spend as much time, money, and thought as needed to create an instantly recognizable and admirable brand. A downtown that wants to keep attracting residents, shoppers, businesses, and institutions must do the same. Sometimes that image evolves naturally. In Chicago, the array of office and apartment towers along Lake Michigan is unforgettable. In Philadelphia, the activity on Market Street has become an icon promoting that city's downtown shopping street.

Downtown leaders, trying to attract additional customers, often attempt to attract a market by creating a distinctive structure that will brand downtown. For example, the first significant post–World War II effort to retain businesses in lower Manhattan came in November 1955, when the Chase Manhattan Bank (under the leadership of David Rockefeller) announced it would consolidate its nine-building, 8,700-employee operations into two blocks bounded by Nassau, Liberty, William, and Pine streets. When it opened, the new Chase headquarters promoted the revival of lower Manhattan. Its construction encouraged other property owners to erect other new buildings. During the 15 years after 1960, when the new Chase Manhattan Bank Building was ready for occupancy, 47 buildings containing 39.1 million square feet of office space opened in lower Manhattan.[17] However, these buildings did little to enliven lower Manhattan, which continued to decline. Neither did the World Trade Center, the next iconic towers erected to promote the revival of lower Manhattan. By themselves, iconic structures do not generate downtown resurgence, just as flashy trademarks are insufficient to successfully market a new product. If market demand cannot support additional construction, there have to be changes in the local economy that generate increasing market demand.

Lake Shore Drive, Chicago, 2008

Chicago's best-known trademark is Lake Shore Drive. (Alexander Garvin)

Creating a memorable image for Post Oak Boulevard played an important part in catapulting Uptown Houston into its position as the 18th largest downtown in America (see Table 2.2 in Chapter 2). In 1993, 12 years after the City Post Oak Association, a public–private partnership, took responsibility for district "traffic operations, public maintenance and beautification, infrastructure improvement, economic development, marketing and communications," it hired industrial designer Henry Beer to reconceive the physical appearance of what was then a busy but typical automobile-oriented, commercial arterial.[18]

Beer devised dazzling stainless steel street furniture (steel arches erected at critical intersections, enormous stainless steel hanging rings

Post Oak Boulevard, Uptown Houston, 2016

Uptown Houston's stainless steel arches provide this downtown with a uniquely identifiable image, distinguishing it from the city's other downtowns. (Alexander Garvin)

with lettering that spells out the names of street intersections, and specially designed bus shelters, street lamps, traffic signals, and trash receptacles). They provided Post Oak Boulevard with a distinctive appearance that branded uptown as a very special, instantly recognizable place.

If a downtown is indistinguishable from the rest of the commercial landscape, as was the case in Uptown Houston 30 years ago, promoting that downtown requires an identifiable trademark such as stainless steel arches. Its leaders should be seeking something visually effective so that it can compete successfully within its metropolitan region.

Improving Access and Circulation

The more conveniently, inexpensively, and quickly people, goods, and the vehicles that carry them can get in, circulate within downtown, and leave, the easier and cheaper it will be for businesses, developers, and institutions to supply and enlarge market demand. Their ability to do so is not the product of highways that make it as easy to get into town as to leave. It is entirely a function of the transportation component of the downtown public realm: streets, sidewalks, utility systems, and vehicular operations, all of which are the responsibility of public agencies. Initially their effectiveness will be a product of their location, dimensions, and relationship with the market they serve. Thereafter, it will be affected by

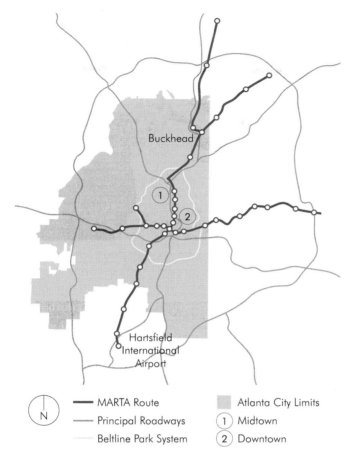

Atlanta's three downtowns

The MARTA subway system triggered the transformation of Midtown and Buck-head from suburban residential districts into the major downtowns they are today. (Alexander Garvin and Ryan Salvatore)

the quality and level of service, state of repair, and ongoing maintenance of the physical plant.

Downtown Atlanta, for example, expanded from the 1836 downtown railroad terminus, along various railroad rights-of-way, well into the 20th century. By the end of the 20th century, however, the railroad had been replaced by freeways I-75/I-85 and I-20 (completed in the early 1960s), subway service on the 77-mile, 38-station Metropolitan Atlanta Rapid Transit Authority (MARTA) (opened in 1979), and the transformation (after airline deregulation in 1978) of Hartsfield–Jackson International Airport into one of the nation's busiest hubs for air travel. MARTA connected the airport with downtown Atlanta, Midtown, and Buckhead, in the process triggering the transformation of Midtown and Buckhead from suburban centers into major downtowns. Yet despite the investment in MARTA, which gave Atlanta three downtowns rather than just one, the number of commuters who drove alone increased from 61 percent in 1990 to almost 70 percent in 2014, while the number of commuters carpooling dropped from 20 percent to just under 11 percent and mass transit ridership fell from just under 11.6 percent to 6.7 percent.[19]

Service matters as much as the capital plant. The level of service depends as much on the condition of the infrastructure and its ongoing maintenance as it does on staff, labor contracts, scheduling, and management. When downtown New Orleans was inaccessible in 2005, it was not only because of the flooding caused by Hurricane Katrina, it was because the location of the streets and highways and the capacity of drainage network approved by the Army Corps of Engineers and created by local government had not been designed to handle the situation and because of the absence of a robust public transit system. Downtown Des Moines was inaccessible after the blizzard of 2017 because the local sanitation department was not prepared to remove the massive amounts of snow dumped downtown by the blizzard. These examples provide rationales for government to provide the services needed to maintain the flow of goods, services, and people throughout downtown, despite environmental conditions.

The importance to downtown vitality of investing in the creation, expansion, and maintenance of transportation is vividly illustrated by the growth of downtown Denver over the past six decades. Without its expanding highway, light, and commuter rail networks leading to an enhanced Union Station and the new Denver International Airport and the creation of a pedestrianized 16th Street served by a free bus, downtown Denver could not have accommodated 21,600 new jobs and nearly 20,000 additional residents (see Chapter 2).[20]

Cleveland's $200 million investment in bus rapid transit on Euclid Avenue is an equally dramatic example. The city had been struggling for several decades to trigger downtown resurgence. The one place it is clearly occurring is along 6.8 miles of Euclid Avenue, a corridor that starts at Public Square, a few blocks from Progressive Field (baseball stadium) and Quicken Loans Arena (a sports and entertainment facility). The route continues past Playhouse Square and on to Cleveland State and Case Western Reserve Universities, the Cleveland Museum of Art, the Museum of Contemporary Art, Severance Hall, and the city's major hospitals, connecting nearly all of the city's major destinations. The bus rapid transit line not only supplies market demand, it creates accessible locations along Euclid Avenue, where new retail stores are opening and housing renovation and construction are taking place. Since 2008, this transportation corridor has been the focus of much of downtown Cleveland's growth beyond the thriving Historic Warehouse District along the Cuyahoga River.

At the end of September 2017, I traveled to Detroit to observe its much-discussed downtown revival (see Chapter 1). To get an overview of downtown, at 9:30 AM on a Friday, I got on the 13-station, 2.9-mile-long elevated Downtown People Mover, a heavy rail line that encircles downtown. Planning for this transit loop had begun in the early 1970s. Engineers projected at least 67,000 daily passengers.[21] At that time Detroit had a population of more than 1.5 million people. The People Mover was intended to help them circulate within downtown after they had driven there and parked their cars. The People Mover proved to be an expensive mistake. After four decades of population loss, as I quickly discovered, the estimate of 67,000 daily riders was a fantasy.

The day I rode the Detroit People Mover, its population had dropped to less than 673,000 residents, approximately 5,300 of whom lived downtown and 66,000 of whom worked there.[22] It took 20 minutes to cover the entire route, during which time I was able to get a wonderful aerial image of much of what was going on. During that circuit, only three people got on or off, two of whom were policemen. It was a loud statement on the much-vaunted downtown revival and a sad comment on the effectiveness of a transit line that had been in operation since 1987. The four passengers using the system during those 20 minutes were nowhere near the number of customers that had been planned for or would have been needed to spur a genuine downtown revival. Transit systems, like identifiable trademarks, need a large enough market to generate genuine downtown change.

Making a mass transit investment like MARTA or the Detroit People Mover will certainly benefit its users. But for a downtown to justify an expenditure on the resulting inexpensive access and circulation, it must be of benefit to more than just the riders. Neither MARTA nor the Detroit People Mover reduced dependence on automobile commuting. Although the People Mover did nothing that changed Detroit, MARTA has transformed two suburban residential districts (Midtown and Buckhead) into new and thriving downtowns and improved access to and from them and downtown Atlanta to its international airport, contributing to the airport's role as the busiest in the nation. Thus, before investing in a transit system, every city should examine how and where it will improve its downtowns and its airports.

Enlarging and Enhancing the Public Realm

The transportation network is only one part of the infrastructure that makes a city's downtown, such as Denver's, so successful. It brings residents, retail customers, and office workers downtown. When they get there, however, it is the public realm that provides them access to the places they use when doing the things for which they have come downtown. The 16th Street Transit Mall is Denver's centerpiece from which people make their way to these places. But it is only one component of a public realm that has been vastly expanded and improved over the past half century—a public realm that enabled downtown to accommodate nearly 20,000 additional people and 22,000 jobs since 1990.

Any downtown that is growing will have to expand and improve the public realm so that it can accommodate an increase in people and activity. New York City has been particularly effective in doing this without acquiring additional property by reconfiguring territory used by pedestrians, moving vehicles, and parking. In each instance the number of people downtown increased substantially and, with them, safety and retail spending. Some of the most effective examples are along Broadway in Manhattan.

Everywhere that Broadway crosses a north–south avenue of the Manhattan Grid, a public square has emerged. The intersection of Broadway and Eighth Avenue at 59th Street connects Central Park with the Midtown business district to the south and the Upper West Side residential district to the north. In 1892 the intersection was renamed Columbus Circle, in honor of the 400th anniversary of Christopher Columbus's "discovery" of America. Two years later a 70-foot-high column topped with a sculpture of the famous Italian explorer was erected at its center. Neither the Circle nor the traffic islands between the arteries that passed through the area could really be called a public square, however.

Columbus Circle, 2006

A traffic roundabout such as Manhattan's Columbus Circle can be recaptured for active recreational use by children and adults. (Alexander Garvin)

In 2005, the city transformed this traffic roundabout into a 148,000-square-foot circular public realm designed by the landscape architecture firm Olin Partnership, with trees, benches, planting, and fountains by WET, a design firm responsible for numerous fountains around the world. It was only then that New York City finally had transformed this small portion of its public realm into a site worthy of the title *public square*.

Two years later, when Janette Sadik-Khan became the city's transportation commissioner, the city took the more ambitious step of transforming its entire network ("6,300 miles of streets, 12,000 miles of sidewalks, more than 1 million street signs, 12,700 intersections with traffic signals, 315,000 streetlights, and 789 bridges") into a public realm that could handle the additional 1 million residents that the city expected by 2030.[23] She initiated the Sustainable Streets program to "cut traffic fatalities in half, introduce a system of dedicated bus and bicycle lanes, install more efficient lighting, and reclaim arterial streets for pedestrian use."

If the transformation of Columbus Circle where Broadway crosses Eighth Avenue was dramatic, the results were even more so at Times Square, where Broadway crosses Seventh Avenue. Working with the Times Square Alliance and its president, Tim Tompkins, the Department of Transportation removed all vehicular traffic from Broadway between 42nd and 47th streets and rerouted the traffic southward along Seventh Avenue. The roadway was repaved, with new lighting and seating installed, to create a continuous pedestrian realm. Now 80 percent fewer people are walking in the roadway. Between 2004 and 2009, the first 5 years during which these five blocks of Broadway were closed, the average number of traffic crashes with injuries fell 14 percent.[24] The number of people there on a typical summer Saturday between 8 AM and noon increased from 48,600 in 2002 to 142,300 people in 2012, a 293 percent increase.[25] Nearly quadrupling the number of people in the area over 10 years probably caused the 48 percent decline in reported criminal incidents for the area.[26]

Most cities are not as inventive as New York or Denver in improving both the pedestrian environment and vehicular circulation. In Los Angeles (with the nation's largest city sidewalk system), half of its 11,000 miles of sidewalk are in disrepair, because for most of the past half century the city has spent less than 1 percent of its transportation budget on sidewalks, crosswalks, and signals.[27] It was not until 2015 that Los Angeles finally committed to serious spending on pedestrian improvements and sidewalk repairs, but only as the result of a $1.4 billion settlement in *Willets v. City of Los Angeles*, the largest disability access class action settlement in U.S. history.[28]

Because the country has become less dependent on fossil fuel–generated electric power, gasoline-consuming motor vehicles have

Times Square, 2009

Even busy streets such as Broadway in Times Square can be recaptured for pedestrian use. (Alexander Garvin)

become the major contributor to climate change in the United States.[29] Thus, if downtowns are to enhance the public realm, downtowns must take actions that sustain a habitable environment.

During most of the 20th century our public realm had been determined by highway engineers. Today, our public officials should be examining how to alter vehicular and pedestrian use for the benefit of the public at large. That way squares (while continuing to carry huge amounts of traffic) can also become territory for recreational and pedestrian use.

Sustaining a Habitable Environment

People who lived in 19th-century downtowns with major industrial production breathed polluted air, drank unsanitary water, and used streets filled with household refuse, horse manure, and waste that did not make it to the often-absent sewer systems. It is now more than a century since any but a tiny number of American downtowns has experienced even one of these problems. However, there are actions that can be and are being taken to improve their habitability. The improvements to access and circulation described earlier in this chapter are reducing air pollution and noise. Personal safety has been increased by enlarging and enhancing the public realm, as has the amount of time downtown occupants devote to exercise and thus to improving public health. Nevertheless, there are still places that need remediation. Equally important, there is much we can do to continue increasing downtown resilience.

Trees are the most effective and underestimated downtown occupants that improve air quality while reducing noise, absorbing runoff, and stabilizing ambient temperature. Many cities, not just those with ample parkland, include substantial amounts of private property with tree cover. For example, tree canopy covers 35 percent of the total land area of Washington, DC, 33 percent of St. Paul, and 32 percent of Minneapolis.[30]

Many cities devote substantial resources to planting trees, shrubs, and greenery. Between 1996 and 2006, Chicago planted 300,000 street trees and added 70 miles of median strip planters.[31] Los Angeles planted 407,000 street trees between 2007 and 2013. In 2007, New York City initiated a program that resulted in planting an additional 1 million trees over a 10-year period.[32] In addition, between 1997 and 2013 New York City transformed more than 2,500 paved traffic triangles that were not essential to vehicular flow into 169 acres of parklets.[33]

Although trees make a substantial difference, the most effective way to improve the habitability of a city is with parkland. New York City, Boston, and San Francisco have set aside approximately 20 percent of their territory for parkland. Because they contain so much parkland, these cities can accommodate intense waves of added use, as well as continuing changes to the climate, economy, or population. The amount of public parkland in most cities continues to grow, with New York City in the forefront. Among its most significant additions are the 550 acres of the 4.5-mile-long Hudson River Park (established in 1992), 85 acres of the 1.3-mile-long Brooklyn Bridge Park (established in 2002), and 2,200 acres of Staten Island's Fresh Creek Park (in development since 2008).

An easy way of creating new parkland is by acquiring more land than is needed for a popular project and reusing the surplus as parkland. Georges Eugene Haussmann in 19th-century Paris and Robert Moses in 20th-century New York City and on Long Island were particularly imaginative and successful in using this technique, a recent example of which is the creation of Discovery Green in downtown Houston.[34]

Discovery Green is a 11.8-acre park designed by Hargreaves Associates, opened in 2008 in conjunction with Houston's George R. Brown Convention Center. It tied together three major hotels, the Astros' Minute Maid Baseball Park, the Toyota Center Basketball Arena, new apartment buildings, and stores in the surrounding district. In addition to splendid new trees and other plantings, Discovery Green includes a 2-acre lawn, a lake, a fountain, 1 acre of floral gardens, a jogging trail, bocce courts, bandstands, performance areas, food stands, two restaurants, three major works of art (including a sculpture by Jean Dubuffet), two dog runs, playgrounds, a putting green, and recreational areas for people of every age, built on top of a 630-car underground garage. As a result of these investments in the public realm, there are now scores of people using a section of downtown that was devoid of pedestrians at the start of the 21st century.

Denver's approach has been far more complex and perhaps even more successful. As explained earlier, it began in 1982 with the transformation of 16th Street into a transitway with a free bus connecting all the major downtown destinations. The bus itself was later connected to the entire metropolitan area by the FasTracks regional light rail system and to the Union Station transit hub, which also provided heavy rail service to Denver International Airport.

This investment in transit was matched by the transformation of polluted waterways into parkland. Denver began reconsidering, replanning,

Discovery Green, Houston, 2017

Leftover property from construction of Houston's Convention Center has become a popular public park, now known as Discovery Green. (Alexander Garvin)

restoring, and enlarging its creek parks in response to major flooding in 1965. Nine years later the Greenway Foundation was established to engage the public and gain support for improvements to the Cherry Creek and South Platte River Corridors. The first results were the transformation of the place where these two waterways came together, an area surrounded by underused 19th-century warehouses and manufacturing lofts.

The site was transformed into Confluence Park, a combination of a kayak run, walking trails, performance sites, and river overlooks that has been continuously improved ever since, most significantly in a $9 million renovation completed in 2016. The Greenway Foundation continued with efforts to restore and enlarge the 12-mile downtown portion of Cherry Creek, which ran along Speer Boulevard.

Next came the commitment to restore and expand the 10.5-mile stretch of the South Platte River, which ran through Denver. In 1996 Mayor Wellington Webb established the South Platte River Corridor Council to coordinate planning, community outreach, fundraising, and

Confluence Park, Denver, 2000

Denver has spent decades reclaiming its waterways for recreational use. (Alexander Garvin)

development of the park corridor. The results include two extensions of Confluence Park along the south side of the South Platte River: 20-acre Commons Park and 35-acre City of Cuernavaca Park. They provided the setting for playgrounds that attract a variety of local children, grassy natural amphitheaters that are used for outdoor performances throughout the year, and jogging trails that are popular with Millennials. Perhaps even more important, the parkland increases the attractiveness of surrounding sites as real estate development opportunities, which is why developers have erected dozens of market rate apartment buildings facing these parks. This new housing, along with the already existing residential properties in LoDo, have helped downtown Denver become a vibrant, high-density, mixed-use downtown with increasingly marketable residential districts. Simultaneously, its constantly improving park system, pedestrianized and cycling-friendly environment, and extensive transit system are improving downtown habitability.

Cities as different from one another as Houston, Denver, and Chicago have been investing in increasing the amount of territory they devote to plant and animal life, in the process improving the habitability of the overall environment. By copying their most effective techniques we can do the same while also attracting additional business and residents.

Commons Park, Denver, 2017

Denver's new parkland attracts customers for whom developers build new residential buildings. (Alexander Garvin)

Reducing the Cost of Doing Business

The largest amount of money spent on doing business in any city is spent by the city government. In 2017–2018 that spending in the 10 largest American cities ranged from $82.2 billion in New York City, whose population that year was estimated by the U.S. Census at 8.55 million, to $1.2 billion in San Jose, whose estimated population was 1.03 million. The average amount spent by these 10 cities was $2,822 per capita. Only two cities exceeded that average: New York, with a whopping $9,614, and Chicago, with $3,153.

One reason for the different amounts of government spending per capita in different cities is that the components of any city's budget vary. For example, New York budgets more than $8 billion for its Health & Hospitals Corporation, whereas Phoenix budgets nothing for hospitals. Chicago's parks are not city funded but paid for by the Forest Preserves of Cook County (a quasi-government agency established by the Forest Preserve Act, enacted by the Illinois legislature in 1905), which is responsible for 69,000 acres of county parkland, not just the 7,600 acres in the city of Chicago.

Nevertheless, government agencies spend too much money in most cities, not just in New York and Chicago, or even Phoenix, which only spends $1,320 per capita. The reasons for the high costs is that government operations involve many activities that are unnecessarily complex; are required to be done by several city agencies rather than just one; are vestiges of another era, whose requirements are now irrelevant but have not been removed from the city charter, the existing body of law, or agency procedures; involve multiple agency actions, without having any single entity responsible for seeing that they are carried out within a specified period of time; or require action by city residents or businesses that make it more expensive than is necessary to live or work in that city.

I am not inveighing against government. I believe government has an important role to play in preventing harm and encouraging desirable activity. As Peggy Noonan explains, "We're all human; business leaders will make decisions that are good for the company or shareholders or themselves, but not necessarily good for the town, state, country. So, regulation has an important role: It helps you be a good citizen and gives cover to you when you are one. But excessive regulation ... kills progress, growth, jobs, good ideas and products."[35] A few examples are in order.

During the 20th century some cities enacted laws requiring restaurants to serve water to all their customers. That added costs to running restaurants and coffee shops. Then, during water shortages, some of these cities repealed the legislation. Whether those cities required serving water or not, they had to appropriate funds to pay for inspectors to verify that the laws were being obeyed. The same is true of legislation involving smoking. Again, some cities enacted regulations requiring that there be ashtrays in all building lobbies and in front of elevators in the upstairs corridors. Then, when it became city policy to restrict smoking, they passed laws forbidding ashtrays in those locations. Building inspectors thereafter issued violations and required that they be removed, even if they had been built into walls.

Most cities have a confusing tangle of off-street parking requirements that add to congestion and pollution, making life in the city more expensive. They require any developer who puts up a new building to provide a minimum number of parking spaces. These rules vary depending on the city, the allowable uses on the property, and the location of the building.

Over time, however, parking has become an expensive problem: Developers must devote money and space to parking lots and garages or avoid building within the city. This limits the supply of housing, retail, and office space, creating higher rents for residents and businesses and higher prices for consumer goods.

Often, zoning laws reduce parking requirements for federally supported public housing projects occupied by people of very low income, because the government correctly assumes these residents cannot afford to own and operate private automobiles. However, no city that I know of adjusted these requirements when federal housing subsidies shifted to private sector buildings that received mortgage subsidies or low-income housing tax credits but were not fully occupied by people of low income or built by government housing authorities. Thus, affordable housing developers must provide parking, which their target market cannot use, forgo construction in those sections of the city, or change their mission and construct fewer apartments for higher-income tenants.

In every car-dependent city, the parking requirement is unnecessary because developers must include parking in order to make sure they can sell or rent what they build. However, developers in areas with accessible public transit and available parking should be given the flexibility to adapt to local conditions.

Eliminating parking requirements in areas with convenient transit service will reduce traffic congestion and pollution, and it will free hundreds of acres of land for new housing, stores, and offices. It will allow all developers to build more affordable housing and encourage more convenient, transit-friendly retail and commercial destinations. The result will be cleaner air, cheaper housing, and more opportunities for working families and small businesses.

Every city can eliminate regulations that are no longer relevant, expensive to comply with, and expensive to administer. Very few cities regularly review and eliminate unnecessary regulations. Nevertheless, this must be done on a regular basis. Downtown organizations, whether BIDs, resident associations, industry coalitions, or chambers of commerce, ought to maintain committees whose sole responsibility is to find ways to reduce the cost of living and doing business downtown.

Making It Easy to Use Private Property

The simplest way to make it easy for owners to use their property is for local government to establish explicit requirements for any action, provide automatic approvals for as-of-right action, simplify and consolidate the permit approval process, and designate a single agency as responsible for all required actions. One way to reduce the unnecessary time and expense involved in living and working downtown is to provide one-stop service from a single agency. (A specific recommendation of this sort in included in Chapter 8.) That agency would be responsible for and have the authority to obtain approvals from all agencies. Such one-stop service would dramatically reduce the time and money spent by citizens and businesses alike. For example, Germany has adopted this approach by designating a single administrative agency with responsibility for all administrative decisions by the relevant national and local agencies.[36]

A second way is to set a time limit for action. For example, any project going through NYC's Uniform Land Use Review Process is subject to a 2-month period during which the City Planning Commission may hold public hearings, commission project analyses, and request the applicant to supply material. At the end of the 2 months, if the agency has not acted, the project is deemed approved and automatically moves to the City Council for another 2-month review, at the end of which, if no action has been taken, it is deemed approved.

In his extraordinary book revealing how laws and regulations are "suffocating" America, *The Death of Common Sense*, Philip K. Howard argues that government "understanding of the situation has been replaced by legal absolutism" involving "a system of final rules . . . yes or no, legal or illegal, proper procedure or Return to Go."[37] Rather than compliance with a fixed result, he calls for intelligent exercise of judgment. He is correct, of course, except that one cannot staff an entire 325,000-person government, like New York City's, entirely with people who have good judgment. Governments need to operate with procedures that anybody can understand and follow, leaving only a few particularly important actions to people with judgment.

One easy way to reduce the cost of doing business downtown is to evaluate the cost to citizens, businesses, and institutions doing so. If the private cost of any government action or regulation were explicitly measured on an annual basis and if it required reauthorization every 5 years, we would be eliminating unnecessarily expensive programs and regulations on a regular basis.

Taking Necessary Action

Any one of these actions will make life downtown easier and more pleasant. However, creating vibrant downtowns for a new generation requires combining them in a manner that will continue to attract people, businesses, and institutions. The next chapter describes the combination of such actions taken in five cities, where they are responsible for the emergence of the 21st-century downtowns that are harbingers of the future.

Chapter 7

Emerging 21st-Century Downtowns

In the past two decades, New York, Dallas, Los Angeles, Cincinnati, and Boston have initiated projects that demonstrate effective strategies for creating vibrant 21st-century downtowns. Their activities provide a model for activists seeking to improve their own downtowns. Each venture responded to changes in demand by enabling development of vacant and underused properties, providing public transit to a growing market, identifying developers to transform such properties into attractions for that market, providing more accessible financing, investing in the improvements to the public realm, creating new cultural institutions and improving existing institutions, and encouraging development of new and rehabilitated housing and retail stores. It is worth looking at each project in greater depth to understand what worked and what didn't.

For more than a century the Hudson Yards (New York City's huge open-air railyards, behind Pennsylvania Station, between Tenth Avenue and the Hudson River) remained vacant despite being on the western edge of the biggest and most prosperous downtown in America. The site of Klyde Warren Park in Dallas was filled with speeding motor vehicles before it became a destination for thousands of people from all over Dallas. Downtown Los Angeles was the center of one of the fastest-growing counties in the nation, yet it had been in continuous decline from the end of World War I until the end of the 20th century because no property owner could afford to convert its once-occupied office buildings and stores into housing while also complying with zoning, building code, and earthquake protection regulations. Businesses and residents alike avoided the Over-the-Rhine (OTR) section of downtown Cincinnati because it had become notorious for the criminal activities that took place in hundreds of empty, deteriorating buildings throughout the neighborhood. The Boston Seaport, which had been the city's economic engine in the 19th and early 20th centuries, was no longer used intensively for waterborne trade by the turn of the 21st century. As a result, it consisted largely of vacant and underused parking lots and warehouses that were of little use to local businesses. The transformations of these five areas illustrate innovative approaches that can be used throughout the country to create vibrant downtowns for a new generation.

Transforming a Desirable Location into a Desired Destination

The Hudson Yards are an excellent demonstration of how to transform a desirable location into a desired destination by providing transit access, walkability, and an attractive public realm.

Beginning in 1910, when Pennsylvania Station opened on Seventh Avenue between 30th and 33rd streets, the idea of expanding Midtown Manhattan westward seemed obvious. The Regional Plan Association commissioned elaborate plans for building over Hudson Yards as part of its multivolume Regional Plan of 1929.[1] By 1932, when the Independent (IND) Subway opened its Eighth Avenue line, building on the railyards seemed even more inevitable, especially because there was a huge market west of Eighth Avenue, but without subway service. Despite its excellent location and a huge potential market, however, without transit service there was no inexpensive way to attract that market. The huge expenditures that would have been needed to do so were unimaginable during the Great Depression and World War II. So the site remained empty.

In the early 1970s, the Lindsay administration proposed building between 2,800 and 4,100 apartments on the site.[2] Creating that many new apartments without relocating anything seemed obvious. This time the city's fiscal crisis precluded initiating this sort of megaproject. For a brief period in the mid-1970s, Donald Trump, who had purchased an option on the site from its owner, the New York State Metropolitan Transportation Authority (MTA), proposed building a convention center there. He also failed to put together a deal before losing control of the site.

Once the Koch administration successfully maneuvered the State of New York into building the 1.8-million-square-foot Jacob Javits Convention Center (completed in 1986) over the section of railyards west of Eleventh Avenue between 34th and 38th streets, construction over the Hudson Yards again seemed inevitable. Nevertheless, developing

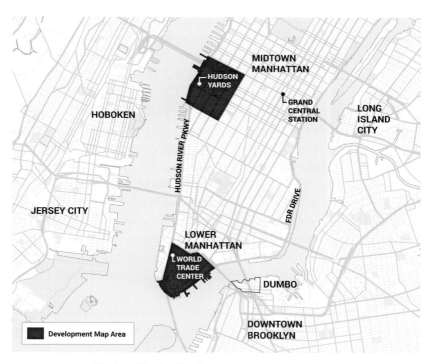

Hudson Yards, Manhattan context map, 2018

Extending the No. 7 subway to the Far West Side made possible the construction of the Hudson Yards, which in combination with the HighLine, Hudson River Park, Convention Center, and Garment Center is extending Midtown Manhattan to the Hudson River. (Citiesense)

the Hudson Yards continued to be an enticing fantasy until it became a desired location for a potential NYC Olympics.

In 1996, Daniel Doctoroff, who would become deputy mayor for economic development and rebuilding (2002–2008) in the Bloomberg administration, hired me to devise a plan to bring the 2008 Summer Olympics to New York City. We planned to use the Javits Convention Center for eight sports played on mats and for a 600,000-square-foot press center; to build a 1.3-million-square-foot broadcast center, a replacement for Madison Square Garden on the southern side of the Yards; erect an 80,000-seat Olympic Stadium on the western side; and use the remaining 8.5 acres for a grand Olympic Square.

In the early days of the Giuliani administration, City Planning Commission chairman Joseph B. Rose had advocated extending the Midtown office district to this vacant territory. He understood that for the development to take place, the site needed to be accessible by public transportation, and he believed that the rail lines passing through the site could provide the necessary access.

When I approached him to present our plan to hold the Olympics in New York City with the Hudson Yards as a major component, he encouraged me to proceed because it would provide yet another reason to extend Midtown westward. He went on to suggest creating a new station using the Long Island Rail Road to bring athletes to the area. He recognized that a temporary station used by Olympic athletes could be transformed into a permanent railroad station after the games, thereby providing the public transportation access necessary to open the area to Midtown expansion. Unfortunately, the U.S. Olympic Committee decided not to compete for 2008, and our planning effort was terminated.

When the dream of a NYC Olympics was revived for 2012, the city finally invested in the one item that had kept the location from being developed: access via public transportation.

Build It, So They Can Come

Most people ridicule the proposition "Build it and they will come" because they misunderstand what is being said. Indeed, a highway to nowhere attracts nobody. Where there is a large market, however, providing it with access to a previously inconvenient location will attract substantial interest. It will also induce property owners and developers to build new facilities to accommodate that market. That is exactly what happened when New York City extended the No. 7 subway line from Times Square westward to the Jacob Javits Convention Center and the Hudson Yards.[3] The Dallas Area Rapid Transit (DART) light rail system, which began transit services in 1984, and the M-Line Trolley, which went into operation 5 years later, had the same effect on the territory surrounding Klyde Warren Park in Dallas, as did the Silver Line bus rapid transit when it connected the Boston Seaport with Logan Airport. Although the establishment of the Downtown LA Business Improvement District (discussed in Chapter 5) probably had more to do with the resurgence of the area than any other factor, without Los Angeles Metro Rail, which began operation in 1990 and today connects 93 stations, the construction and renovation of downtown buildings would probably not have been as widespread.

In 1999, NYC resumed its efforts to become the site of Summer Olympics, this time for the 2012 Games. The support of Planning Commission Chairman Rose and the Giuliani administration encouraged us to continue pursuing the Hudson Yards as a major location for the Olympics. As we got deeper in the planning, several problems emerged. At one of our first weekly meetings, I announced dejectedly that our Olympic Plan did not work. Doctoroff, astonished, asked why not. I replied, "We cannot get the spectators to the Convention Center and Olympic Stadium unless we extend No. 7 subway service from Times Square." He believed subway access was essential and asked me to propose how we could pay for it. I told him I would have an answer at our meeting the next week.

At our next meeting, I showed three pictures: the railyard behind Grand Central Terminal in 1902, before the current station was built; the same location the year the current terminal was completed, with streets bridging over the empty yards extending north to 50th Street; and a drawing showing all the buildings that had been erected over the railyards by 1930. I did not have to say a word. Doctoroff immediately understood that their real estate tax payments, like the taxes from the buildings that would be built on the Hudson Yards, could cover the capital costs of platforming and extending the No. 7 subway.

We commissioned Parsons Brinckerhoff to study alternative routes for the No. 7 extension and two railroad terminals, all ending at the Hudson Yards (including the Long Island Rail Road route recommended by Chairman Rose and one for the Empire Line coming down from Albany, which would be located midway between Tenth and Eleventh avenues). The new terminals would not only reduce the number of trains coming into Penn Station, they would also provide direct access to the proposed new No. 7 subway station. The property for the Empire

**The reconstruction of Hudson Yards as proposed by
NYC2012, 2000**

The redevelopment of West Midtown proposed that net operating proceeds from the 2012 Olympic Games cover a large part of the cost of extending the No. 7 subway, expanding the Javits Convention Center, erecting an Olympic Stadium, building a 1.3-million-square-foot broadcast tower (to be converted later to commercial offices), replacing Madison Square Garden, creating new railroad stations for the Empire Rail Road Line and the Long Island Rail Road, opening a new boulevard between 10th and 11th avenues, and creating an 8.5-acre Olympic Square over the Hudson Yards. (Alexander Garvin)

Line extension was all either vacant or underused low-rise manufacturing sites. Inspired by Park Avenue, we imagined this station as an underground terminus for the Empire Line, with a broad boulevard above, lined by midblock, high-rise corporate headquarters.

When Michael Bloomberg was elected mayor in November 2001, he asked Doctoroff to become deputy mayor. Based on a West Midtown Framework Plan that had been completed by the Department of City Planning in December 2001 and our work for the proposed 2012 Olympics, the new administration initially proposed rezoning everything west of Eighth Avenue between 28th and 42nd streets so that it would become a high-density, mixed-use district.[4] The rezoning would enable developers to satisfy the Midtown Manhattan demand for millions of square feet of additional office, retail, and housing.

The Bloomberg administration decided that extending the No. 7 subway underneath Eighth Avenue (rather than under 41st Street), rerouting the Empire Line and building a terminal between 10th and 11th avenues, and creating a Long Island Rail Road terminal at the Hudson Yards was too expensive to be seriously considered.[5] Instead, the north–south Park Avenue–like boulevard with the terminal beneath became a much lower-cost, at-grade diagonal park–boulevard.

The MTA would agree to extend the No. 7 only if the city covered most of its cost and if the ultimate developer of the Hudson Yards paid them for the right to build over the MTA-owned railroad tracks. Doctoroff proposed that the city create a tax increment district (see the discussion of tax increment financing in Chapter 8) and issue bonds whose debt service would be paid from the additional real estate taxes generated by all the new construction. Consequently, the city government established a nonprofit local development corporation, the Hudson Yards Infrastructure Corporation.[6] Based on its estimate of the increase in real estate taxes induced by development on the Hudson Yards and the rezoned property west of Eighth Avenue, the city was willing to pledge $2 billion in bond revenues to pay for the No 7 subway extension. Consequently, the cheaper 41st Street route was selected, without any stop between Times Square and 34th Street.

Development of the Hudson Yards has been an unusually complex and difficult task, far more complex that any of the other four downtown expansions discussed in this chapter. However, each of them created a transportation line that transformed a desirable *location* into an accessible *destination*.

Downtown Dallas, like so many other downtowns, was circumscribed and defined by an interstate highway ring completed in the mid-1960s. These highway rings separated downtown from the rest of the city and sometimes blighted adjacent territory. In Dallas, for example, the Hispanic and Black neighborhoods north of the Woodall Rodgers Freeway, which later become known as Uptown, went into decline after the highway was completed in 1964.[7]

Dallas map, 2018

Klyde Warren Park tied together Turtle Creek and Uptown with the central section of downtown Dallas. (Baolin Paul Shen and Alexander Garvin)

At that time, the northern section of Uptown was already an upscale, single-family residential neighborhood surrounding Turtle Creek. Much of the underused territory between the freeway and Turtle Creek soon became a desirable location for real estate development. The process began in 1984 with the designation of State Thomas, a Victorian neighborhood north of the freeway, as a historic district. The proponents of its preservation wanted to spur its evolution into a pedestrian-friendly, culture-oriented older neighborhood that would echo the pedestrian-friendly, culture-oriented Arts District being built from scratch south of the freeway.

Two years later, when the Crescent (a 10-acre, 1.1-million-square-foot hotel, office, and retail complex designed by Philip Johnson and John Burgee) opened, it accelerated the transition of Uptown into the pedestrian-oriented mixed-use district that would become typical of successful 21st-century downtowns. That transition was impeded by the Woodall Rogers Freeway, which separated the area from the downtown Dallas Arts District and the rest of the business district, as well as by the limited services provided to the area by local government.

Thus, the question that needed an answer was how to connect these downtown destinations with the rest of the city and its increasingly popular close-in residential districts. Streets and highways alone could not do the job. Consequently, in 1984 Dallas decided to create the DART light rail system, which would do the rest of the job.[8] Today, this 93-mile-long light rail system is the longest in the United States. Its 64 stations carry 97,000 passengers on an average weekday.[9] Particularly important to Uptown and the Arts District, DART was supplemented by the M-Line Trolley, a free 4.6-mile heritage streetcar system with 41 stops that began operation in 1989, starting in the Arts District and running across the Woodall Rogers Freeway and through Uptown.[10]

Transit access played a similar, if less important role in transforming downtown Los Angeles from a desirable *location* into a *destination* inexpensively accessible by means other than the city's frequently clogged freeways. Subway service connecting downtown with the rest of the city was initiated in 1991 and by 2018 extended 106 miles, connecting 93 stations and serving 360,000 passengers on an average weekday.[11]

Its Expo Line, which reached Santa Monica in 2016, extended service all the way to the Pacific Ocean.

The leaders of Cincinnati were convinced that for OTR to become a popular destination, it needed to be connected to the rest of downtown and its sports stadiums by light rail. The Cincinnati Bell Connector streetcar system, first proposed in 2007, opened in 2016. Its two north–south routes, one block away from each other, run parallel to one another, connecting OTR with the business district and the city's waterfront attractions (two stadiums, a park, and a museum) at the south. However, streetcars were not needed to spur development in OTR. The revival of OTR was already well under way before the system opened.

The critical act took place in 2003, 13 years *before* the Cincinnati Bell Connector opened, when the city created the Cincinnati Center City Development Corporation (3CDC), an entirely new nonprofit

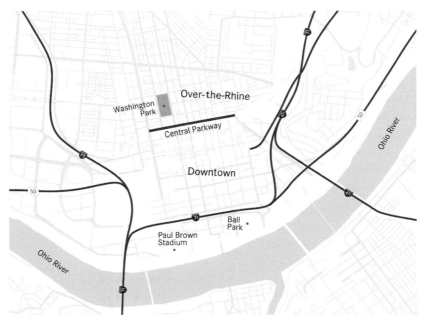

Cincinnati map, 2018

Over-the-Rhine is the northern extension of downtown Cincinnati. (Baolin Paul Shen and Alexander Garvin)

organization to manage downtown revival in the three major sections of downtown (the waterfront, the business district, and OTR). The 3CDC targeted liquor stores first. It believed that a high proportion of people using alcohol were likely to engage in antisocial and criminal activity. Thus, 3CDC began its activities in OTR by purchasing buildings that rented the ground floor to liquor stores, which they closed. "Crime dropped 36 percent from 2004 to 2008 as they pushed the stores out."[12]

The 3CDC devoted most of its time, money, and energy to acquiring empty buildings and vacant lots, cleaning them up, and holding them until they were ripe for development. By the time the streetcar began operation, 3CDC had "either invested or agreed to invest over $1.1 billion in downtown's Central Business District (CBD) and OTR, resulting in 155 buildings restored, 52 new buildings constructed, 15 acres of restored civic space, 1,457 residential units, 156 hotel rooms, 320 shelter beds, [and] 908,849 square feet of commercial space."[13]

Although transit was not crucial to OTR, it was critical to the revival of the Boston Seaport. Like other major cities, Boston built highways that were intended to bring business downtown from suburbs clustered around Route 128 (I-95). Instead, those highways succeeded in attracting business to Route 128 and away from downtown. Worse yet, its primary downtown highway, the elevated Central Artery (I-93), separated its decaying waterfront from the rest of downtown, accelerating its decline.

Like cities with similar transportation and redevelopment projects, the Boston transportation projects failed to prevent the loss of 227,000 residents (28 percent) between 1950 and 1990. But unlike nearby Hartford and Bridgeport or more distant St. Louis and Detroit, however, Boston added 25,000 jobs (5 percent) during the same period.[14] In fact, at the end of the 20th century Boston began growing again, adding 181,000 jobs between 1990 and 2015.[15]

Because there were no large sites still available in either the Financial District or the Back Bay, and most other desirable sites had been redeveloped with subsidies from the federal urban renewal program, the city had to decide how and where to channel its growth. The obvious place to expand was east of the Central Artery (I-93) among the parking lots and empty buildings in the Seaport. However, that expansion was blocked

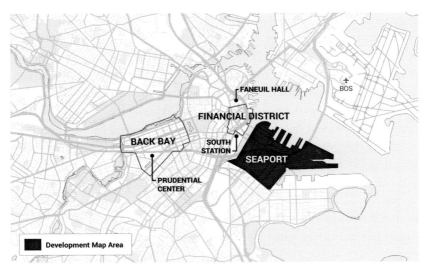

Downtown Boston Context map, 2018

The Seaport was the natural place for the expansion of downtown Boston. (Citiesense)

by the elevated Central Artery that was still impeding development in the Faneuil Hall–Waterfront Renewal Area. Consequently, in the early 1980s the city began planning for its replacement with an underground tunnel. This nearly $15-billion project, commonly called the Big Dig, was funded by Congress in 1987.[16] Construction began in 1991.

As part of the Big Dig, the Boston Massachusetts Bay Transportation Authority initiated development of the nearly 14-mile-long Silver Line, a bus rapid transit line that operates within a dedicated, and partially subterranean, right-of-way connecting Logan Airport with the rest of the city.[17] The system began operation in 2002. Two years later the three Seaport stations opened and connected the district to the rest of the city.

Empowering Developers to Get the Job Done and Pay for It

There was no lack of developers to invest in downtown Los Angeles. However, very few of them were willing to consider purchasing downtown vacant and underused buildings because government regulations made the cost prohibitive. In Cincinnati they were unwilling to risk investing in what was perceived as the nation's worst downtown slum. Consequently, in 2003 the city created a development entity that was specifically designed to manage its revival: the Cincinnati Center City Development Corporation. When Dallas leaders decided to transform the territory within its highway ring into something beyond a nine-to-five business district, it did so by creating a series of entities that could raise private sector money and provide services in its unique but troubled downtown districts. Developing the Boston Seaport and New York's Hudson Yards also required government institutions that could overcome the difficulties involved in acquiring huge amounts of privately owned property, complying with government regulations, and obtaining the enormous sums of money needed to redevelop those districts.

Los Angeles and Cincinnati had the easiest way to proceed. If they could eliminate the problems involved in renovating buildings, private developers would do the rest. By the 21st century, the success of loft conversion in New York City, Chicago, Cleveland, and elsewhere had transformed deteriorating, empty buildings into an asset that could trigger resurgence. That observation was shared by a growing constituency of Angelinos that included advocates of historic preservation, such as the Los Angeles Conservancy; artists who, as they had in New York City and Chicago, pioneered living and working in lofts; movie fans, who wanted to save the lavish film palaces that were often at the base of or next to deteriorating or vacant office buildings; civic organizations, such as the Central City Association; innovative developers such as Ira Yellin and Tom Gilmore, who were trying to renovate distinctive downtown landmarks; and thoughtful public officials such as Con Howe, the Los Angeles director of planning (1992–2005).

During a visit to Dallas in 1996, Howe toured a nondescript downtown office building that had been converted into apartments. Surely, he thought, the much larger, more glamorous office buildings throughout downtown LA provided an even more promising opportunity for conversion.[18] He also understood that such conversion would be difficult: LA office buildings could be converted to residential use only by going through the expensive, time-consuming process of obtaining variances from suburban-oriented zoning requirements or by complying with expensive provisions of the building and zoning codes and environmental review requirements. Neither was cost effective, except for very special buildings that represented a tiny fraction of empty and underused downtown commercial property.

So many of these buildings had been producing little or no income for so long that they could be acquired for low prices. Not only did the properties cost far below the price of land in much of Los Angeles, but nobody would bid on them because the codes and the cost of conversion were prohibitive. Unlike sites for new development, nothing needed to be spent on creating the building structure or exterior shell. Loft-style conversion often left existing utilities in place or kept them exposed, erected minimal partitions, and invested in only basic kitchen and bathroom equipment.

Thus, after conversion they could be rented or sold at low prices. The people who moved in were there partly because they were attracted to the bohemian character of the apartments and partly because life downtown was beginning to become quite lively.

Howe became an advocate for "unzoning," shepherding agency support and public approval for the Adaptive Reuse Ordinance in 1999. The ordinance allowed commercial buildings erected before 1974 to be

Broadway, Los Angeles, 2015

After decades of underuse and vacancies, the grand old buildings on Broadway in downtown LA are experiencing a renaissance. (Alexander Garvin)

reused as residences as-of-right without complying with zoning, building, and fire code requirements, specifically by:

- Not complying with lot line, yard, setback, and height requirements imposed by zoning
- Not adding more parking spaces than were already there (no matter how many more would have been required by zoning)
- Not limiting the number of units to what zoning required
- Not forbidding the insertion of mezzanines that complied with the building code
- Not obtaining environmental clearance under the California Environmental Quality Act [19]

As soon as the Adaptive Reuse Ordinance had been enacted, the problem of finding developers evaporated; they began looking for properties to convert. By 2018, 89 buildings with 10,278 apartments had been converted in downtown Los Angeles.[20] Downtown LA is once again a mixed-use district, buzzing with life 24 hours a day. The ordinance has been so successful that Oakland, Long Beach, Glendale, and other California communities have adopted regulations similar to the provisions of the Adaptive Reuse Ordinance.

In Cincinnati, there were plenty of developers who had the skills, money, and legal authority to renovate buildings. None of them would go anywhere near OTR, which was widely believed to be the nation's most dangerous downtown residential neighborhood. The police reported that in OTR, an area with 7,500 residents, there were 1,452 incidents of rape, murder, and robbery in just the first 8 months of 1996.[21] City leaders decided to deal with the situation by enacting management reforms and creating a nonprofit agency established to revive OTR.

OTR is a 362-acre neighborhood that was initially settled by 19th-century German immigrants who moved into handsome brick Italianate, Greek Revival, and Queen Anne buildings in the mid-19th century.[22] It reached its peak population of nearly 44,500 residents in 1900. At first, it was separated from the rest of downtown Cincinnati by a section of the narrow Miami and Erie Canal. That barrier was platformed over in 1928 to create a major new city artery, Central Parkway.

In the 20th century, migrants from impoverished areas of Appalachia and low-income African Americans began to replace German American residents. By 1960, OTR had lost one-third of its population. Twenty years later, the population had dropped to 11,914, and then it declined still further to 7,422 by 2000.[23] At that time there were 5,261 housing units in OTR, one-third of which were vacant.[24] New arrivals to OTR were not just poor, they brought a range of social problems with them.

Vine Street, Over-the-Rhine, Cincinnati, 1996

By the end of the 20th century, continuing building deterioration, population decline, and criminal activity had given Over-the-Rhine the reputation of being the worst residential slum in a major downtown. (Alexander Garvin)

Various institutions were established to provide OTR residents with much-needed services. The most important of them were the Drop Inn Center (DIC) Shelter for Homeless Adults and the magnet Cincinnati Public School for the Creative and Performing Arts, both established in 1973, and the Race Street Tenant Organization Cooperative, a low-income housing cooperative founded in 1977, which provided sustainable, high-quality housing for tenants below the poverty line. These and other OTR community-based organizations were considered by downtown interests as a source of the antisocial activity that was preventing the resurgence of downtown Cincinnati. Neighborhood activists opposed efforts by downtown interests to promote market-rate development, insisting that they had a right to maintain OTR as an area for lower-income residents.

Nevertheless, civic activists were determined to change the situation. In 1994, property owners established Downtown Cincinnati Incorporated (DCI), a nonprofit organization similar to the business improvement districts (BIDs) appearing across the country. DCI promoted downtown office, retail, restaurant, convention, and hotel development; enabled new arts, culture, and entertainment facilities to emerge; improved downtown access and parking; and supplied stakeholder services intended keep the district safe and clean.[25]

Next, the city began experimenting with legislation to deconcentrate poverty, drug use, and crime. With support from DCI, in 1995 the city enacted a series of ordinances to regulate panhandling, all of which were abandoned because they were determined by the courts to violate rights guaranteed by the Constitution. However, they did reduce the visible presence of panhandling and homeless people.[26]

In 1996 Cincinnati passed a Drug Exclusion Ordinance that restricted "undesirable people" from being in exclusion zones (defined as "areas designated by the city council ... where the number of arrests ... [has been] significantly higher than for other similarly situated/sized areas of the city").[27] This law also was deemed unconstitutional, while similarly reducing the presence of addicts. Both laws had been enacted to reduce the influx of people into the center of the business district from nearby areas of concentrated poverty.

Conditions in OTR were not entirely bleak. The southeastern corner, nearest to the business district, had begun to change in the early 1990s. Edgy bars and clubs that attracted young people from all parts of the metropolitan area had begun to open on Main Street. They were followed by young entrepreneurs attracted by cheap rents who "moved into the upper floors, creating a nascent tech start-up scene soon dubbed the Digital Rhine."[28] By 2000, *Cincinnati Magazine* reported that two young entrepreneurs had acquired a narrow five-story warehouse that they rented to just under a dozen digital-age companies and predicted that the number would climb to 30 by the end of the year.[29]

Nevertheless, OTR exploded in 2001 with the shooting of an

unarmed, 19-year-old Black man by a White police officer. African Americans (approximately 70 percent of the OTR population), already infuriated by many such incidents, initiated four nights of civil unrest. Angry bands pulled motorists from their cars, looted stores, and set fires. Riot police occupied OTR, firing tear gas and rubber bullets. Damage sustained during the riots totaled $3.6 million.[30] The riots convinced Cincinnati's leaders that the revitalization of the business district would not succeed without also altering conditions in OTR.

Mayor Charles Luken sought and obtained the support of the city's major corporations, particularly Procter & Gamble, to initiate major management reforms and continue innovative efforts to reduce the presence of people considered "undesirable," and he persuaded them to contribute the huge sums of money needed to pay for these efforts. At the mayor's request, the Cincinnati Business Committee, an organization of chief executives of major business enterprises of greater Cincinnati established in 1977, provided 3CDC with $17 million in startup capital. Procter & Gamble and other corporations provided $50 million to purchase property. The city provided tax incentives and federal programs for many 3CDC activities.

As happened in so many BIDs, 3CDC (which was not a BID) replaced failing or nonexistent city agency efforts to make the neighborhood "safe, clean, and attractive." These included litter, leaf, debris, graffiti, sticker, trash, and snow removal; landscape and flower pot maintenance; paving repair; and vacant lot care. Similarly, it devoted substantial money and effort to improving streetscapes and creating great civic spaces.[31]

However, its great success is a result of its property development activity, which involved purchasing and land banking properties that were available at low prices; developing real estate at a cost that allowed a reasonable return on the investment; creating and managing great civic spaces and streetscapes while also preserving the historic structures that enclose them; developing public parks on behalf of the city, fostering investment in the Cincinnati Bell light rail system that connected the waterfront and the business district with OTR; and encouraging the establishment and operation of arts institutions.

At first, 3CDC efforts were centered on Vine Street, just north of

Central Parkway. This section of OTR was closest to the business district and had begun to attract bars, restaurants, and clubs. It was beginning to be known as the Gateway Quarter. The 3CDC purchased buildings in the area and converted them into residential condominiums with ground floor retail and restaurant space that was rented to pioneering entrepreneurs.

Vine Street at 13th Street, in Over-the-Rhine, looking south at the office towers in the business district, Cincinnati, 2018

By purchasing buildings, redoing the sidewalks, providing streetlights, installing new utilities, and renovating parks, the Cincinnati Community Development Corporation transformed a slum into a vibrant and healthy residential district. (Alexander Garvin)

Year by year, the 3CDC gradually moved beyond the Gateway Quarter, purchasing more buildings, redoing the sidewalks, and providing streetlights and new utilities. Its second locus of development was Washington Park, two blocks west of Vine Street. As with the Gateway Quarter, 3CDC wanted to move homeless residents to other, "more appropriate" facilities where they would be more likely to become "self-sufficient, stable, productive citizens," in the process freeing up territory for renovation, redevelopment, and new business development.

Unlike all the previous planning initiatives that proposed goals and objectives but implemented nothing, 3CDC was charged with providing local services and engaging in business activity, real estate development, and property management—genuine entrepreneurial activity. The big innovation was to devote substantial sums of money to real estate development, the same approach (operating as a quasi-public institution) that had been used for private gain by Dana Crawford in Denver, Two Trees in Brooklyn, and Dan Gilbert in Detroit (see Chapter 4).

Two decades later, the *Wall Street Journal* reported that "almost 15 years and over $1.1 billion later, Over-the-Rhine [had become] a mecca for trendy restaurants, loft apartments, cafes with home-cured meats and artisan doughnut shops. Modern condominiums have gone up and public spaces, including two parks and a neighborhood pool, have been revived."[32] The story of OTR illustrates a particularly effective way of transforming a residential lemon into high-density, mixed-use downtown lemonade.

In Dallas the process began in 1975 with the designation of 30 blocks in its West End as a historic district characterized by midsize, red-brick warehouses, which became a tourist-oriented complex of bars, restaurants, and retail stores, with office and loft residences above the ground floor.[33] Eight years later the city began the creation of a 17-block Arts District at the northern end of downtown that would eventually include new buildings for the Dallas Museum of Fine Art, a symphony center, an opera house, major sculpture and Asian art collections, and a high school for the visual and performing arts.[34] However, both districts appealed to very specific audiences without having much impact on the rest of the city.

Dallas had a number of quasi-public entities that had been formed to foster downtown development. In 1993 a combination of businesses, office properties, and residences formed the Uptown Public Improvement District (UPID), similar in its activities to other downtown BIDs (see Chapters 1 and 5). The UPID covers territory north of the Woodall Rodgers Freeway and, south of the freeway, the Dallas Arts District Public Improvement District (PID). Together, both PIDs spend $2.4 million annually on capital and landscape improvements, security, sanitation, transportation services, and marketing. None of these institutions had the skills needed to transform the Woodall Rodgers Freeway, a noisy, pollution-spewing, below-grade obstacle to area development, into a downtown attraction. Consequently, Dallas created a new public–private partnership, the Woodall Rodgers Park Foundation, to develop, manage, program, and operate Klyde Warren Park. The foundation was formed in 2004, began work on the deck 5 years later, and opened the park in 2012.

In 2004, the city's Real Estate Council provided a million-dollar grant to fund feasibility studies and provide staff support during the incubator stage. Texas Capital Bank founder Jody Grant heard about the project and joined the cause with a million-dollar personal donation and a million-dollar donation from the bank. In 2005, Jody Grant, Linda Owen, president of the Dallas Real Estate Council, and Mayor Laura Miller formed the Woodall Rodgers Park Foundation, the organization that led the project from design to completion. Many city and civic leaders contributed to the park throughout the process.

Klyde Warren Park, 2016

Klyde Warren Park attracts thousands of people of every age, ethnicity, and income from all over the Dallas metropolitan area. (Alexander Garvin)

Eventually, this $110-million project was funded through a public–private partnership. Public support included $20 million in bond funds from the City of Dallas, $20 million in highway funds from the state, and $16.7 million in stimulus funds. The balance of funding is through individual donors directly to the Woodall Rodgers Park Foundation.

In 2012, 1,200 feet of the freeway was capped with 5-acre Klyde Warren Park, designed by the Office of James Burnett Landscape

Architecture and built by the Woodall Rodger Park Foundation, which continues to manage and program the park.

The freeway had been in use since 1964. Its continuing use required 16½ feet of clearance. The platform above is a concrete sandwich deep enough to contain infrastructure and enough earth to grow trees.[35] The park that was created on the platform provides something for everybody: a children's play area, a white-tablecloth restaurant, a reading room, a game room with Ping-Pong tables, a great lawn for 5,000 people, a performance pavilion, a dog park, a botanical garden, a jogging trail, an interactive fountain plaza, a pedestrian promenade, ample seating, and other amenities. Food trucks, offering a variety of ethnic and artisanal fare, line its south side, facing the Arts District. More than 1,300 free events are programmed throughout the year, including dance parties, yoga lessons, poetry readings, simulcasts, and almost anything else you can think of. It should be no surprise that Klyde Warren Park is filled with people of every age, sex, and ethnicity at all times of the day and night. Nor is it a surprise that people going to the park spill over and enliven the Arts District to the south.

Boston's Thomas Menino (mayor from 1993 to 2014) understood that reviving the Seaport required: reconnecting downtown Boston with its historical waterfront and amazing array of vacant and underused sites for development projects; large sums to pay for property acquisition; tremendous relocation difficulties; and institutions with the ability to overcome regulatory problems. He assigned the project to the Boston Redevelopment Authority, which prepared a preliminary plan for the expansion of downtown Boston into the Seaport and the Boston Convention and Exhibition Center, created in 1997 by the Massachusetts State Legislature. Together they acquired 60 acres for the Convention Center and developed the rest of the plan for the Seaport.[36]

Moreover, investment in the Seaport had already begun. In 1990, Commonwealth Pier (previously the World Trade Center) was converted into an exhibition space and office for Fidelity Investments. By 2018 it included 163,000 square feet of exhibition space, 41,000 square feet of flexible meeting spaces, three grand ballrooms, and a 5,600-square-foot amphitheater.[37]

The John Joseph Moakley U.S. Courthouse (designed by Harry Cobb of Pei, Cobb Freed & Partners Architects), built on the edge of Fan Pier across Fort Point Channel from Rowes Wharf, was completed in 1999. This $197 million, 675,000-square-foot federal project includes administrative offices and 27 courtrooms and opened in 1998.[38] Identifying a successful developer for the Hudson Yards was far more complicated and took even more time.

Boston Seaport, aerial photo, 1995

In 1995, the Boston Seaport consisted of vacant property, parking lots, and underused, obsolete buildings. (Google Earth)

For almost a decade, New Yorkers had expected NYC2012, the private, nonprofit entity created to bring the Olympics to the city, to develop the Hudson Yards as part of its role in developing and operating a 2012 Olympics. When the rezoning of the Hudson Yards was approved in January 2005, the administration still hoped to win the 2012 Olympics, build the stadium, extend the subway, and spur development of 28 million square feet of office space, 12,600 apartments, 1.5 million square feet of hotel space, and 700,000 square feet of retailing.[39] Doing this much construction over a functioning railyard with trains coming and going at all times of the day and night is extraordinarily expensive, and the logistics are extremely complex.

Six months later, when NYC lost the 2012 Olympics to London, the proposed stadium was abandoned. Finding another developer with the resources to develop the Hudson Yards was more than possible in NYC because so many large development corporations were headquartered there. The problem for the city was to create the conditions (in addition to providing mass transit access) that made their participation possible, particularly when so many trains were coming and going from Penn Station.

Initially, because the cost and complexity of building the platform were so high, the city assumed that the MTA would not receive payment for its property from the developer.[40] Instead, its compensation was expected to come from selling development rights not used on the site itself. For that reason, the Eastern Railyard was rezoned with a floor area ratio (FAR) of 19, of which 11 FAR could be built on site and 8 FAR were available to the MTA to sell to developers of other sites in the district.

A new plan for the Hudson Yards evolved, one that eliminated the stadium, and extended the East Hudson Yards westward all the way to the West Side Highway and the newly developing Hudson River Park. The West Yards would be rezoned for 5.7 million square feet of mixed-use development and 1,300 affordable housing units.[41] The new version also reconceived property development all the way east to Pennsylvania Station and linked everything to the developing High Line Park.

In 2007, based on this new plan, the city and the MTA announced a competition for 12.7 million square feet of mixed-use development on the combined 26-acre site. Five finalists were selected.[42] In March 2008, Tishman Speyer won the bid, agreeing pay $1 billion to lease the site from the MTA for 99 years. The deal collapsed 2 months later.

That December the MTA awarded the project to the Related Companies, which had financial backing from Goldman Sachs. It agreed to pay $1 billion for the same 99-year lease and the right to lease/purchase the airspace development rights over the entire Hudson Yards. The lease/purchase arrangement enabled the MTA to use its exemption from state and local sales taxes (8.875 percent) on construction

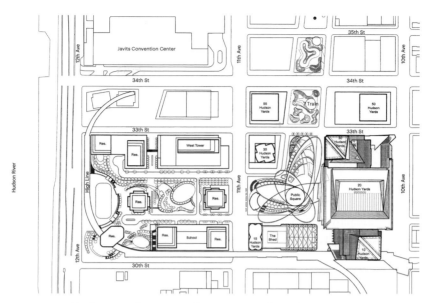

Hudson Yards Master Plan, No. 7, and High Line, 2018

In 2024, when construction is completed, the Hudson Yards will include more than 18 million square feet of commercial and residential space, more than 100 shops, 4,000 apartments, "The Shed" (a center for artistic invention), "The Vessel" (an iconic sculptural monument), a hotel, a 750-seat public school, and 14 acres of public open space. (KPF)

materials for a building erected on MTA-owned property and thereby to collect millions of dollars in payment in lieu of sales taxes from the developer.

The 21st-Century High-Density, Mixed-Use Downtown

Each of these downtown districts combines office space, residences, stores, cultural facilities, and new and renovated parks. However, they are not a reversion to the apartments and businesses above retail ground floors that were characteristic of 19th-century America. OTR resembles such a place but is quite different in that it includes parks, schools, performance venues, and internet-related businesses that are quite contemporary. By its very nature Klyde Warren Park does not include offices, housing, and institutions. They are across the street, and when combined with the facilities in the park they form a mixed-use destination for everybody in metropolitan Dallas. In Boston and Los Angeles, high-density and mixed-used development evolved by accretion. The Hudson Yards, being built from scratch, had to include all of them from the start.

Working with the city government, 3CDC invested $47 million in renovating Washington Park, which reopened in 2012. This involved moving the Cincinnati Public School for the Creative and Performing Arts to a new building in the southwestern corner of OTR in order to enlarge the park from 6 to 8 acres and add a 450-car garage underneath. Revenue from the garage pays for maintenance of the park. Washington Park, on the western side of OTR, has now been matched by a $32-million 3CDC development, creating Ziegler Park on the eastern side of the neighborhood. Ziegler Park was created on property that had been the parking lot for a public school (now converted to condominium apartments). Like Washington Park, it includes an underground parking garage, whose revenues go toward maintaining the park and its popular swimming pool. Although there is a fee for using the pool, children of low-income families receive free pool passes.

The city and 3CDC also spent $145 million renovating the Cincinnati Music Hall (home of the Cincinnati Symphony Orchestra, the Cincinnati Opera, and Chamber Music Cincinnati) across the street from the park. The Cincinnati Shakespeare Company built a new theater on the DIC site. Because of these investments, the area has become a major cultural activity center, attracting people from the entire metropolitan area. At the same time, $11 million was spent renovating the 556-seat Memorial Hall OTR to provide an up-to-date but smaller venue for the performing arts.

In 2015, the DIC Shelter sold its building (which, like all OTC properties, had appreciated in value), using the revenue along with funds contributed by 3CDC to purchase two new homeless shelters a mile away. They moved homeless adults from the DIC to these two new facilities, which together provided three times as much space, expanded daytime services, and an on-site medical clinic.[43]

Washington Park, Over-the-Rhine, Cincinnati, 2018

When the Saturday flea market (under the white tents in the distance) is in operation, Washington Park attracts customers from the around the metropolitan area, who park in the underground garage and encourage their children to play in the spray fountain. In the background is the renovated Cincinnati Music Hall. (Alexander Garvin)

As a result of the entrepreneurial real estate investments made by 3CDC, the 2006 designation of OTR as a national historic district (which made property restoration eligible for federal historic tax credits), most of the area's huge stock of 19th-century buildings has been restored. Thus, by 2018 OTR was being promoted as "Cincinnati's premiere entertainment district, overflowing with fabulous restaurants, hip bars, breweries, fashionable shops, theatres, and a gorgeous park."[44]

By 2018, 3CDC, with an annual operating budget of $9.4 million and a staff of 70 people, in addition to 17 full-time field staff and another 120 temporary and seasonal workers, had managed to invest $655 million in OTR alone. It had rebuilt Washington Park, created Ziegler Park, renovated two performing arts venues, purchased 369 sites, renovated 147 historic buildings, built 49 new structures, was preparing to renovate or develop 16 sites, and had land banked 32 more sites. This activity resulted in the creation or renovation of 321 apartment units (178, or 56 percent of which were reserved for people of low income), 65 stores and restaurants, and 75,859 square feet of office space occupied by 21 businesses.

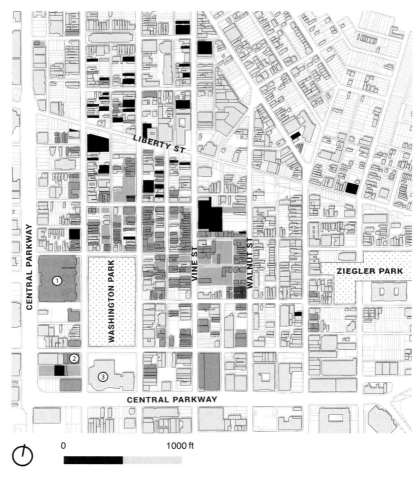

0   1000 ft

New & In Construction

▨ Completed
■ Under construction
■ Land banked

① Cincinnati Music Hall
② Cincinnati Shakespeare Company
③ Cincinnati Public School for the
   Creative + Performing Arts (SCPA)

OVER THE RHINE | Added Between 2004 & Present Day

Development in Over-the-Rhine as of 2018

By 2018, the Cincinnati Community Development Corporation had acquired or renovated more than half the buildings in Over-the-Rhine. (Citiesense and 3CDC)

Despite the amazing transformation of OTR, critics claim the real purpose was not to transform this strategic section of downtown Cincinnati into a cultural center but rather to devise a program to successfully move poor, underprivileged neighborhood residents out.[45] To some degree that is true, but many of the old residents have remained and are enjoying a much improved, safer neighborhood.

By its very nature the Adaptive Reuse Ordinance transformed downtown LA from a business district that, with the exception of the residents of 11,600 apartments, the performance halls on Bunker Hill, and the Staples and LA Convention Centers in its southwest corner, went to sleep at night and reawakened in the morning to, by the end of 2017, a downtown with 71,100 apartments, with another 16,000 in construction.[46] The half a million people who go to work every day in downtown LA share its facilities and programs with the residents and 19 million annual visitors.[47]

Green Market at 5th and Spring streets, Los Angeles, 2013

By 2013 there was activity 24 hours a day, 7 days a week in downtown LA. (Alexander Garvin)

The Boston Seaport, on a smaller scale, is also becoming a high-density, mixed-use downtown. The process began with acceptance of the definitive plan for the Seaport, prepared by Cooper Robertson & Partners for the Boston Redevelopment Authority and issued in 1999.[48] It called for integration with the Silver Line bus rapid transit line (to be opened in two stages, in 2003 and 2016) and advocated creation of three parks (Fan Pier Cove, Pappas Way, and Harbor Walk), establishment of three east–west boulevards and three north–south boulevards, development of an industrial park and a container terminal, and construction of 5,000 to 8,000 housing units. Astonishing as it may seem, most of this had been completed by 2018.

Boston Seaport, 2018

The public promenades, park areas, waterfront recreational facilities, and museums that had been completed by 2018 have transformed what was once a derelict commercial waterfront into a new high-density, mixed-use downtown. (Alexander Garvin)

However, few people expected the major role that two cultural institutions, the Children's Museum and the Institute of Contemporary Art, would play. In 1979, the Children's Museum, established in the Jamaica Plain neighborhood in 1913, moved to the shore of Fort Point Channel, directly across from what eventually became the headquarters of the Federal Reserve Bank of Boston.[49] It was so successful in its new location that in 2006 it began construction of a $47 million,

23,000-square-foot expansion and renovation. More than 600,000 people visit the museum every year.

In 2006, the Institute of Contemporary Art, which had been known under a variety of names and had been in various places in Boston, moved to the Seaport, where it now occupies a sparkling new 65,000-square-foot glass building designed by Diller Scofidio + Renfro. By 2016, annual attendance, which had been only 25,000 at its former home, had risen to 232,000 in the new building.[50]

The private market reaction to these public investments has been awesome. As of 2018, the Seaport included 60 new office buildings with more than 10.1 million square feet of floor area, 11 residential buildings, 7 hotels with more than 1,700 rooms, and 15 mixed office and residential structures.[51] These and other planned developments are expected to provide an estimated $53 billion in tax revenue, more than enough to cover the debt service on the financing of all the public facilities.[52]

The note of cultural institutions in the revival of downtown Dallas is similar to the Boston Seaport. The Dallas Museum of Art, Winspear Opera House, Myerson Symphony Center, Perot Museum of Nature and Science, Booker T. Washington High School for the Performing and Visual Arts, and numerous hotels, apartment towers, and office buildings were already on the blocks surrounding Klyde Warren Park before it opened. The park tied them together into an identifiable district, attracted thousands of daily visitors to the park, and triggered a real estate boom, especially in Uptown. A 20-story and a 25-story office building and a 33-story luxury apartment tower were among the 18 buildings in construction nearby in 2017.[53] In the process, the park has produced a high-density, mixed-use 21st-century downtown never before seen in this part of Texas.

The Hudson Yards also had to tie together all the surrounding properties. But it had to be far more than just a new public park in the midst of what everybody hoped would become a thriving district. Despite two decades of changing plans, before the Related Companies took charge, other than the 2012 Plan for the Olympics there was no vision that combined its millions of square feet of development into an integrated whole.

The Related Companies provided both a development model for large-scale, high-density, mixed-use development and the ability to

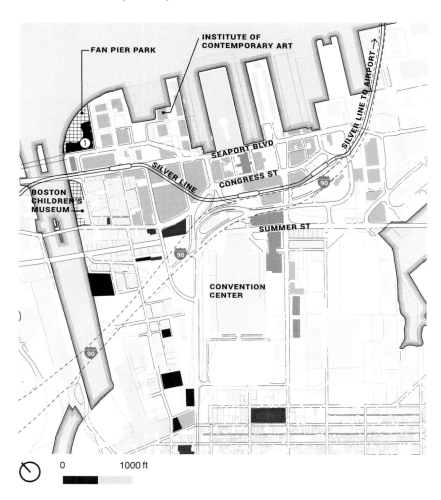

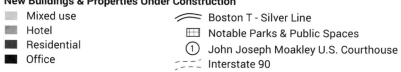

New Buildings & Properties Under Construction

▪ Mixed use		〰	Boston T - Silver Line
▪ Hotel		⊞	Notable Parks & Public Spaces
▪ Residential		①	John Joseph Moakley U.S. Courthouse
▪ Office		⌐ ⌐ ⌐	Interstate 90

BOSTON SEAPORT | Added Between 1998 & Present Day

Map of development in Boston Seaport, 2018

As of 2018, the Seaport included 7 new hotels, 11 apartment buildings, 60 office buildings, and 15 mixed office and residential structures. (Citiesense)

Klyde Warren Park, 2016

Privately financed construction around Klyde Warren Park, Dallas. (Alexander Garvin)

obtain the huge amounts of financing needed to build millions of square feet of expensive towers containing retail, institutional, office, and residential users. Its precedent was the AOL Time Warner Center on New York's Columbus Circle, which had been developed by Stephen M. Ross (chairman and founder of Related Urban) and Kenneth Himmel (president and CEO of Related Urban). Himmel had been involved earlier with the somewhat similar high-density, mixed-use Water Tower Place in Chicago. City Planning chairman Joe Rose was the principal public official responsible for the redevelopment of the Time Warner Center. His advocacy of the inclusion of a performance complex (Jazz at Lincoln Center) and the reconfiguration and redesign of the open space of Columbus Circle transformed the Time Warner Center into the kind of high-density, mixed-use downtown project that inspired the Related Companies' eventual plan for the Hudson Yards.

The Hudson Yards, when it is completed, will be the largest mixed-use, private real estate development in the history of the United States.[54] Kohn Pederson Fox (KPF) prepared the initial master plan for the Related Companies' development of the Hudson Yards and has continually adjusted it to changing market conditions. As of 2018 the plans included 18 million square feet of commercial and residential space, five state-of-the-art office towers, more than 100 shops, approximately 4,000 residences, "The Shed" (a 200,000-square-foot, $455-million center for artistic invention opening in 2019), "The Vessel" (an iconic sculptural monument designed by Thomas Heatherwick with 154 staircases and 80 landings), 14 acres of public open space, a 750-seat public school, and a luxury hotel.

Inclusion of "The Vessel" and "The Shed" is particularly important because they will provide cultural attractions that are increasingly fundamental to high-density, mixed-use downtowns.

Hudson Yards in construction, 2018

Construction under way on the East Hudson Yards and the rezoned surrounding private property. (Alexander Garvin)

The combination of the No. 7 subway, Hudson Yards redevelopment, and rezoning has resulted in billions of dollars of new private investment in the area. As of 2018, excluding the Hudson Yards project itself, the area between 23rd and 43rd streets west of Eighth Avenue included 18.2 million square feet of office space, 17,000 apartments, and 5,900 hotels rooms, either completed or in development.[55] As of 2018, these and other planned developments provided the Hudson Yards Infrastructure Corporation with an estimated $20 billion in revenue, more money than would have been needed to finance the more extensive

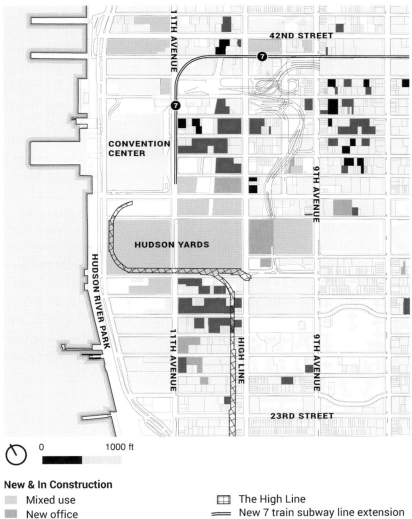

New & In Construction

Mixed use

New office

New residential

New hotel

The High Line

New 7 train subway line extension

DEVELOPMENT AROUND HUDSON YARDS | Over the Past 5 Years

New hotels, apartment buildings, and office towers have been completed, are in construction, or are planned on private property, making the Hudson Yards and the surrounding territory into an extension of Midtown Manhattan. (Citiesense) transportation infrastructure for the area initially proposed as part of the 2012 Olympics Plan.

The development of the Hudson Yards was the product of the persistence and leadership of Daniel Doctoroff, first as the organizer of the bid for a New York Olympics and then as deputy mayor. Nevertheless, his single most important contribution was devising a way to pay for extension of No. 7 subway service, the enabling item that had been missing in every development scheme proposed in the previous seven decades. He demonstrated that when there is enough market demand, if you build it, they will come: thousands of new businesses, employees, and residents using the subway to go to and from home, work, parks, and arts facilities in a genuine 21st-century downtown.

Creating what is now the Hudson Yards has been an unusually complex and difficult task—far more complex that any of the other four downtown expansions discussed in this chapter. It provides the very same components of a vibrant downtown for the new century: a public transportation link connecting it to the rest of downtown, an attractive new public realm, major cultural facilities, new retail outlets, and plenty of new residential apartments—all the ingredients of a mixed-use, high-density downtown. Together they are the heart of the city, and they are creating great American 21st-century downtowns.

Chapter 8

Creating Vibrant Downtowns for a New Generation

In most cities, downtowns are the primary economic engine, repository of knowledge and culture, and generator of new ideas, new technology, and new ventures. They are the very heart of the city. Thus, when its downtown is healthy and vibrant, the entire city benefits; when its downtown is not doing well, the entire city suffers.

Downtowns are altered by their occupants: inspired individuals and well-run organizations, often assisted by carefully crafted government programs. Thus, if we are to keep the heart of our cities vibrant and healthy, we must increase the likelihood that the people and organizations that have the capacity to keep them vibrant keep doing so. They succeed when it is easy to find information needed to respond to changing downtown conditions; it is easy to comply with relevant federal, state, and local government regulations; it is easy to obtain inexpensive financing; and it is difficult for opponents to prevent desirable downtown changes. All the procedural, managerial, and governance changes that are needed to make this possible depend on national institutionalization of the downtown experiment that has worked in hundreds of cities: the business improvement district (BID) (see Chapters 1 and 5). In nearly every downtown a new, "standard" BID would become responsible for maintaining and improving the heart of our cities. This standard

BID would provide all needed information about downtown, make it easy to comply with regulations, improve access to financing, supplement downtown development activities, and restrain undue opposition.

Institutionalizing "Standard" Downtown BIDs Everywhere

The standard downtown BID would be responsible for the entire downtown of every American city. These downtown BIDs will have to be established pursuant to federal statute, state constitutions, and city charters as a legal entity that is responsible for specified activities, financed largely at the local rather than citywide level.

Institutionalizing standard downtown BIDs requires more than cloning the most successful examples. The standard downtown BID would be a permanent, self-sufficient organ of local government (similar to the Philadelphia Center City District), empowered by Congress and state legislatures to perform basic functions. It must include a board of directors elected by the businesses, property owners, and residents of the territory for which it is responsible, plus specified federal, state, and city officials on an ex officio basis. The downtown public realm and infrastructure would be managed and maintained pursuant to a lease from the city government. The standard downtown BID, together with relevant government agencies, would provide specified downtown services (e.g., traffic management, garbage removal, policing) pursuant to an operating agreement with the city government. BID activities would be financed by a dedicated property tax that goes directly to the downtown BID.

This standard downtown BID would be a nonprofit institution similar to the Minneapolis Park and Recreation Board, established nearly a century and a half ago. The rationale for BID creation is similar to the reason the Minneapolis Park and Recreation Board was created. It "will, at comparatively small expense, guarantee that the city will continue to thrive and add many millions of dollars to its real estate value."[1]

During the ensuing 135 years the Minneapolis Park and Recreation Board went from owning and operating nothing to managing 180 properties covering 6,809 acres of park (land and water) organized around 22 major stillwater lakes, 102 miles of designated walking and bicycle paths, 7 public golf courses, 96 supervised playgrounds, 47 recreation centers,

17 supervised beaches, 69 swimming pools, and much more.[2] The $73.7 million that pays for its operations is derived from three sources: a dedicated real estate tax ($52.8 million), additional city aid ($9.3 million), and fees, fines, contributions, and other revenues ($11.6 million). As a result of its guaranteed source of income and board of directors (elected by the people they serve), the Minneapolis Park and Recreation Board operates "the best-located, best-financed, best-designed, and best-maintained public open space in America."[3] Similar legislation would create BIDs that could manage the finest downtowns that any city's leaders could imagine.

Lake Calhoun, Minneapolis, 2009

Lake Calhoun is an important part of the Minneapolis Park System, which includes 6,809 acres of park (land and water) organized around 22 major stillwater lakes, providing exceptional recreational facilities for a population of fewer than 383,000 people. (Alexander Garvin)

The standard downtown BID would automatically be declared a tax increment financing (TIF) district, like the Atlanta BeltLine Inc. (described in Chapter 3); a development corporation, like the Cincinnati Center City Development Corporation (3CDC) (described in Chapter 7), empowered to purchase, sell, and manage property; a state-chartered authority, like many port authorities empowered to perform government functions within the standard downtown district; and an agent of the federal government, empowered by written agreement with federal agencies to certify compliance with their regulations and issue permits.

The development functions of the standard downtown BID would be carried out in its capacity as a state-chartered development authority, which would be empowered to acquire, develop, operate, and maintain private property, exercise eminent domain, issue bonds and notes, grant loans and tax exemptions, create subsidiaries, issue permits, and exempt projects from or override local laws, ordinances, codes, charters, or regulations.

The Standard Downtown BID Enabling Act would be the product of a meeting convened by an impartial organization, such as the U.S. Conference of Mayors, the National League of Cities, or the International Downtown Association, that would bring together all interested parties to discuss what should be included. Based on that meeting the organization would draft a federal and a state BID Enabling Act and then convene the same participants at a second conference at which they would adjust and accept the text. Thereafter, it would go to Congress and every state legislature and relevant city council for approval.

The boundaries of these BIDs would have to include the entire extent of downtown. Standardizing the size and location of a BID would be a mistake, however. Downtowns differ in size and shape. Moreover, size does not with equate with success. America's largest downtown BID, in Memphis, occupies 6 square miles, stretching from northern marshland to southern suburban-style homes.[4] Its generous territory has not given it the edge to dramatically improve downtown Memphis, which has yet to see a significant renaissance. More successful BIDs, such as the 34th Street Partnership in New York, the Center City District in Philadelphia, and the Uptown BID in Houston, are all less than a square mile. Total employment in the 6 square miles of the Memphis BID is only 82,084, whereas more than 240,000 people work in the Alliance for Downtown New York, a BID that encompasses an area one-fourteenth the size.[5]

What is important is that BIDs have boundaries that match downtown's development, including all high-density, mixed-use development related to the central business district. As more development occurs, that territory may well expand beyond previously set borders, thereby requiring redefinition.

In Louisville's downtown BID, a recent expansion was voted in to "serve new and well-established businesses in the eight-block area that is experiencing significant growth and revitalization."[6] BIDs will have to amend their boundaries regularly so that they reflect the changing extent of downtown development. Moreover, because TIF district boundaries match those of the BIDs, expanding boundaries will mean additional revenue.

The existence of a common set of statistics and reports for all downtown BIDs will allow everybody to see what is working well in each downtown BID and learn why those actions have succeeded. Each BID would be able to see what others are achieving, how they went about achieving it, and what benefits it generated. Thus, innovations will quickly spread from one downtown BID to another.

I realize that some cities will not want to create powerful downtown BIDs. Some mayors and city councils may not be ready to give up power over the heart of their city. Others may want to retain control over all city revenues and not cannibalize the city tax base. That is to be expected in any federal democracy. However, I believe that the extraordinary success of the standard downtown BIDs (congruent with a city's entire downtown) will result in increasing those cities' prosperity and provide them with a competitive advantage over those that reject the idea. Consequently, in time, the holdouts will either succumb to competition from other downtown BIDs or adopt the same mechanisms.

The legislation would include a mechanism for deciding the territory covered by the standard downtown BID, the dedicated tax it is entitled to receive on an annual basis, and the specific services it must provide. Each downtown BID would be responsible (at a minimum) for collecting and distributing the same annual statistics and providing the same activities and services. Thus, each BID would be able to learn what had changed during the previous year, as well as where and why those changes had occurred.

Improving Access to Information

The extent, variety, and accessibility of information available on the internet are game changing. Fifty years ago, general information was very difficult to find, collect, or store, much less make easily available. Today, this has improved to an unbelievable extent. Yet while writing this book I discovered that getting information about downtown America was still extremely difficult. Downtown boundaries (unlike incorporated cities) are defined differently, depending on who is reporting on them.

Among the BIDs whose boundaries cover an entire downtown, CCD Philadelphia, the Alliance for Downtown New York, and Downtown LA BID do an exceptionally thorough job collecting and presenting information about their downtown districts. However, even they do not collect consistent data over long periods of time.

The information problem can be easily solved in any downtown that has a BID by redefining its boundaries to include everything within the downtown district and requiring the BID to adjust the boundaries every 5 years. In addition, specific information on an agreed-upon seven sets of set of statistics would have to be issued on an annual basis. There are downtown BID-related facts and maps (boundaries, properties, budgets, expenditures, sources of revenue and staff, and permits, licenses, and approvals issued); residential statistics (population, dwelling units, rents); economic data (employment by category, businesses, office space, hotel rooms, tourist revenue, retail establishments, restaurants); institutional activity (hospitals, educational establishments, cultural and arts organizations); crime; transportation; and historical data comparing records for every decade back to 1950.

Making It Easy to Comply with Regulations

Since the beginning of the republic, every city has enacted regulations and requirements with which its citizens, businesses, property owners, and institutions must comply. Rarely does any city eliminate regulations that have been supplanted by newer statues, have become obsolete, or are no longer needed. This has created various classes of professionals (not just lawyers, architects, and engineers) who specialize in ensuring compliance. The fixers and expediters are the most unfortunate among them, because they often skirt the law and sometimes bribe the public officials who review their clients' compliance.

Most downtown territory is privately owned property. That is where people live and do business. Unfortunately, instead of making it easy for them to do that, government makes it difficult, unnecessarily time-consuming, and expensive. Except in a few cities, such as Houston, property owners have an unnecessarily difficult time adjusting their property to satisfy local regulations.

Having been personally involved in real estate development in New York City, both as a private developer and as a government official, I have strong feelings about what is and is not appropriate government action, how much time should be involved, and how much it costs. The story of one of the properties with which my partners and I were involved is particularly revealing.

In the late 1980s, we purchased a property at a major intersection in lower Manhattan, which I thought correctly could be rezoned to allow for 75 percent more floor area. However, any rezoning in NYC quite appropriately needs environmental analysis, in the form of either a declaration of negative impact or a detailed environmental impact study (EIS) of the zoning change. The Department of City Planning makes the decision about which it should be.

When we purchased the property, a required study demonstrating that our proposed project would have little significant effect on the area might require an expenditure of tens of thousands of dollars. A full EIS might require hundreds of thousands or even millions of dollars (depending on the size of the project). The department assured us that all we needed was a negative declaration. It circulated our application to all city agencies to see whether any of them objected to a negative declaration. After waiting 6 months, the Department of Environmental Protection finally responded with a legitimate concern. The site had once been a gas station. It demanded that we check for any gas or oil leaks that might require detoxification.

I went to discuss the matter with the staff member in charge (who held a PhD in physics). I showed him draft regulations, which the U.S. Environmental Protection Agency had just printed in the Federal Register, and told him that we would comply. He told me that this was not good enough. He wanted a formal test of groundwater on the site to see whether it was contaminated and a commitment to clean up the groundwater if it was polluted. I refused, explaining that the groundwater throughout Manhattan was contaminated, and I would not commit to cleaning all of Manhattan's groundwater, only to eliminate the results of any oil or gas spill from the gas station that had occupied our site. He insisted on assessing groundwater throughout the 17,000-square-foot site. Accordingly, I made an appointment with the city's commissioner of environmental protection, who overruled him.

We did all the federally required tests and found no oil or gas spill. After 8 months we formally entered the city's Uniform Land Use Review Procedure. Then, after 6 months of public hearings and agency review, the City Planning Commission and City Council approved the rezoning. Nevertheless, we were not done with public review.

During the year and a half since we had begun the process, the market in the neighborhood had changed, and there was less demand for apartments at market prices. My partners and I decided to delay starting construction. We wanted some revenue from the site to help in paying real estate taxes, insurance, property maintenance, and interest on our bank mortgage. The solution was to open a parking lot on the site. Based on my reading of the NYC Zoning Resolution, however, that required a City Planning Commission vote after a public hearing. The Planning Department staff disagreed and instructed me to go directly to the Buildings Department for a permit. The Buildings Department refused the permit, saying that my original reading of the text was correct. The two agencies wrangled for 3 months until finally a public hearing was scheduled, and the commission approved temporary parking on the site.

We had spent 2 years on government processing and hundreds of thousands of dollars on government-required studies, construction documents, taxes, fees, insurance, and maintenance costs to get the approvals for a project that had no opposition. By the time we had all the approvals, the market had collapsed, we had run out of capital, and, unfortunately for us, the bank with a mortgage on the property foreclosed.

Our experience involved only three municipal agencies. Doing anything downtown usually involves obtaining approvals from many more entities—not just city agencies but also state and federal agencies, private companies, and other stakeholders (utilities, service delivery companies, a variety of firms that perform functions needed by downtown properties, and neighboring properties), and quasi-public agencies have requirements to which property owners and developers must adhere, all of which are mandated to make sure that nothing is overlooked. These range from distance from utility lines to type and locations for meters measuring activity on the property. Not only do the plethora of rules and procedures waste time and money, they impede all sorts of municipal improvements. They include more than just building codes, zoning regulations, and licensing requirements.

A good example of difficult cross-agency coordination and next-to-impossible regulatory conditions is the recent design and construction of a 20-story combination hotel and condominium in Midtown Manhattan.[7] The site consisted of multiple tax lots, spread across two different zoning, code, and fire districts. The power provider, Con Edison, required that the developers include a very large electrical transformer in their building to compensate for the increased draw of power on the surrounding properties. This transformer required the addition of several large concrete electrical vaults with ventilation grates beneath the public sidewalks on two streets. To fit them in, the basement and lobby had to be redesigned, and the main hotel and condo entrance had to be separated and relocated.

This construction (besides complying with city zoning, building, and fire codes and the New York State Multiple Dwelling Law) required additional approvals from three city agencies, two federal agencies, and one state agency. The NYC Departments of Buildings and Department of Transportation regulated vault placement, and the NYC Department of Health and Mental Hygiene regulated outdoor restaurant seating. The New York State Metropolitan Transit Authority had to approve the sidewalks above the subway platform. The U.S. Postal Service had to approve building entrance doors and street address numbers, and the U.S. Federal Occupational Safety and Health Administration had to verify that management complied with various regulations. Not only were the design and construction approvals exceedingly complicated, costly, and lengthy, but these agency requirements were also complicated and slowed the actual construction process and increased the cost of the developer's various insurance policies.

Although this was a single development project, the NYC Department of Finance and the New York State Attorney General each considered the condominium portion of the building to be a different financial business entity from the hotel portion, so separate paperwork, calculations, and filings were required from start to finish. Surely, time-limited, one-stop service by a single agency would have saved tons of money and time.

Analyzing the environmental impact of a large project is not only wise; it can uncover and prevent harmful results that will affect everybody. But the procedures for doing that analysis can also produce deleterious results. Perhaps the most egregious loss of time and money resulting from required approvals is the EIS. Federal EISs began to be required as part of the National Environmental Policy Act of 1969. The EIS requirement quickly spread to state and local government action. It was soon perverted by opponents to any action under review and has become onerous, in many cases requiring the applicant to spend millions of dollars on studies that take years to complete, and it is used mainly to stall actions that require substantial expenditure and prevent small projects (which cannot afford to spend the needed time or money) from being undertaken on the local level. Moreover, the EIS has been turned into a device that allows one interest group (environmentalists) to prevent other groups with at least as important interests (economic growth, equal opportunity, affordable housing, minimizing public expenditures, the list is endless) from surviving the requirement of preventing any negative environmental impact. Thus, tough trade-offs between competing goals are never made.

As Philip K. Howard explains in *The Rule of Nobody*, "Environmental review has evolved into an academic exercise, like a game of who can find the most complications."[8] As an example he describes the 5 years it took the Port Authority of New York and New Jersey to receive "forty-seven permits from nineteen different governmental entities" to complete an environmental review they needed in order to maintain the existing 80-year-old roadway of the Bayonne Bridge in operation while also replacing it with a higher roadway, one that provided enough clearance for the latest container ships.[9]

The startling and regrettable story of the Bayonne Bridge is duplicated across the country in every place that needs major investment in repairing, replacing, or installing new public facilities. Howard, in *Two Years Not Ten Years: Redesigning Infrastructure Approvals*, estimates the 2018 cost of rebuilding the entire nation's crumbling infrastructure to be $3.7 trillion.[10] Multiagency review, he explains, adds $2 trillion to that cost. It adds trillions more dollars to the millions of individual private sector activities that need government approvals. However, there is no reason that it needs to involve every possible agency that might be affected, particularly those with objectives that have little to do with environmental analysis, or that it should take many years to complete. One-stop service and time limits would result in huge savings of time and money while protecting the environment.

Any of dozens of requirements can stall change. Therefore, I propose national legislation to permit any state-chartered downtown BID (in its capacity as a development authority) to become a one-stop approval entity that has the power to grant approval to any change in procedure or regulation that is impeding development that in the view of the downtown BID will benefit the entire downtown. The cost of analyzing a request for regulatory approval would be paid for with a fee charged to the entity applying for approval.

Few downtown BIDs play the role of a development corporation (like Cincinnati's 3CDC, described in Chapter 7). However, this is the key to allowing downtown activists to make the changes to properties and businesses that are necessary to keep any downtown competitive—and do so as quickly and inexpensively as possible.

There is one set of regulations, zoning, that by its very nature balances competing goals and establishes minimum and maximum requirements. These rules are now an obsolete 20th-century mechanism, created for a world that had neither personal computers nor the internet. New York City's Zoning Resolution (already 3,876 pages long in 2016 and getting longer by the month), for example, has become so complicated that it no longer can be understood by the city residents who live in the buildings it regulates, the property owners who must comply with its instructions, or the public officials who must approve its contents and enforce its provisions.

For those of you who are unfamiliar with the opaque language of the Zoning Resolution, here is a typical quotation:

> However, no existing use shall be deemed non-conforming, nor shall non-conformity be deemed to exist solely because of . . . (c) The existence of conditions in violation of the provisions of either

Sections 32-41 and 32-42, relating to Supplementary Use Regulations, or Sections 32-51 and 32-52 relating to Special Provisions Applying along District Boundaries, or Sections 42-41, 42-42, 42-44, and 42-45 relating to Supplementary Use Regulations and Special Provisions Applying along District Boundaries.[11]

Fortunately, there is a 21st-century remedy to this situation. The city should create a GPS-based application that would automatically provide all the specific requirements that apply to any individual lot in the city and reconfigure them for any assemblage of lots. With this computer system in place, citizens, property owners, government officials, and consultants would have easy access to every regulation that applied to any location in the city. In addition, the users of the computerized system would be able to identify the requirements of any proposed building footprint, building bulk, property use, or occupancy. However, creating this user-friendly application requires a major edit of the text, too much of which is currently indecipherable.

Creating a computerized zoning resolution would save tremendous amounts of time and work. Equally important, it would save millions of dollars currently spent by architects, lawyers, and government employees to determine whether proposals comply with the law. Perhaps most important, it would permit property owners, developers, community leaders, and public officials to evaluate the legality and suitability of any proposed development.

If we were to succeed in creating such a 21st-century computerized zoning system, construction in NYC might well become as cheap as in Houston, where nobody needs to check the zoning because there isn't any. Moreover, creating a standard downtown development BID empowered by the federal, state, and city governments to grant all required approvals for downtown projects would make construction in any downtown even less expensive than in Houston.

Financing the Public Realm

The Atlanta BeltLine (see Chapter 3) and New York's No. 7 subway extension (see Chapter 7) are projects that were financed by their beneficiaries, a technique now called *value recapture*. In each of these downtown projects, infrastructure and public realm improvements cost hundreds of millions of dollars—sums that would have been difficult to charge to any one year of that city's budget. The solution was obvious: Issue bonds that could be repaid on an annual basis over a period of years (say, 25 years), very similar to borrowing from a bank and providing a mortgage payable in regular installments over the life of the mortgage. The problem in issuing bonds for the Atlanta BeltLine or the No. 7 subway extension was that there was no source of revenue that was not explicitly needed for some other expense during that time period.

Value recapture identifies a source for that financing. It establishes the beneficiaries of public projects, estimates the increase in value that will be gained by those beneficiaries, identifies the increase in tax payments that will be generated because of the appreciation in value, and pledges a sufficient portion of those incremental tax payments to cover the annual debt service of the bonds issued to pay for the project. This solution is possible precisely because without the project, there would be no increase in the tax collected. Thus, the city is not losing any revenue that it otherwise would have collected.

Many city capital expenditures are needed to pay for systemwide projects (e.g., water supply, street repaving, fire stations) that must be paid for from citywide tax revenues and cannot be equitably charged to a small number of taxpayers. Other expenditures, such as those for school construction in low-income neighborhoods, require more revenue that can be obtained from taxing the beneficiaries. Consequently, most cities prepare capital budgets that are financed by citywide tax revenue (plus state and federal grants).

Tax increment financing (TIF) is the most straightforward method of recapturing value. TIFs are financing mechanisms that "guarantee" that tax revenue from existing property tax assessments within a specified boundary (at tax rates determined by the city government) will continue to go to the local government. Thus, the local government loses none of the tax revenue it collects to pay for its operations. All future tax revenue from any increase in property tax assessment above the baseline level, however, goes to a specified agency to be used to pay debt service on any outstanding bonds or to pay for new capital or economic investment (not operating expenditures) within the district.

A TIF district's borrowing capacity is established by agreeing to set aside for that purpose the estimated future real estate tax increases from every parcel in the TIF district. Debt service repayment comes from the properties within the TIF district that benefit from the TIF-financed capital improvement. In 1952 California became the first state to use this financing technique, which is now authorized in all 50 states.[12] A good illustration of how this works is the Atlanta BeltLine.

In 2004, in a study published by the Trust for Public, I proposed transforming the rail rights-of-way into a bike and pedestrian system that tied together and expanded existing public parks, reused empty, adjacent land for additional recreational facilities, and opened sites to private development so that they could become prime residential or commercial destinations.[13] The next year, the city council approved the BeltLine Redevelopment Plan and a tax allocation district (a Georgia TAD is similar to a TIF in most other states) to pay for it.

In 2006, Atlanta BeltLine Inc. was established to implement the project.[14] The money generated by the TAD must be spent on property acquisition or development of the BeltLine itself, not on adjacent private development (whether for housing, retail, or business development). The Eastside Trail, which was the first section of the BeltLine to open, served the popular, affluent, and primarily White residential districts south of Piedmont Park and around the Jimmy Carter Presidential Library and Museum, but also the Historic Old Fourth Ward (Martin Luther King Jr.'s birthplace), a historically middle-class African American neighborhood. By the end of 2016, investment the Eastside Trail had already resulted in private development of 33,000 permanent jobs, 28,000 new privately financed residential apartments, and 870,700 new square feet of commercial properties completed within the BeltLine corridor, representing between $10 and $20 billion in privately financed development.[15] By substantially increasing the amount of housing along the Eastside Trail, this level of investment substantially reduced gentrification, but was not enough to prevent it.

Atlanta BeltLine, 2014

New privately financed apartment buildings in construction in 2014 along the Atlanta BeltLine. (Alexander Garvin)

Since the fall of 2017, when the Westside Trail opened, the impact of the BeltLine has also been experienced on the Westside, a largely working-class Black community. Between 2014 and 2017, single-family house and condo apartment prices increased 54 percent in one of the zip codes surrounding the Westside Trail and 110 percent in the other, at a time when the citywide increase in housing costs in Metro Atlanta was 49 percent.[16]

There is an inherent paradox between TIF financing and the objective of retaining or increasing the supply of affordable housing. It assumes that real estate values will increase as a result of TIF expenditures and that the additional taxes will be used exclusively to cover the debt service on the bonds that financed construction of those public works. Increasing property taxes result in increasing property expenses, sometimes increasing those expenses beyond affordability for some residents.

Unless the housing supply in the TIF district and its surroundings exceeds current and future housing demand, the result is area gentrification. If the citywide housing supply is increasing at a rate faster than population growth, the people moving out can still relocate to a more affordable residence somewhere in that city.

Rental tenants in particular will suffer if supply does not increase faster than demand. At least home owners can sell their residences and use the appreciation in value to purchase a home in a retirement area or to move to other suitable accommodations.

The only way to slow gentrification is for government to invest in building additional housing, especially affordable housing within the TIF district, or to mandate that developers of multiple dwellings include a proportion of affordable units in their projects. In NYC, for example, the Lindsay administration (1966–1973) adopted the policy of requiring that 20 percent of the units in redevelopment projects be for "persons of low income." That policy lapsed long ago. There are a few zoning districts in NYC and elsewhere (including Atlanta) that allow construction of additional market-rate housing in exchange for including affordable apartments within a project.

The Atlanta BeltLine Inc. (ABI) TAD has specifically targeted the tax proceeds for property acquisition, park, and trail development. Despite the frequently enunciated objective of creating additional affordable housing, no source of funding for housing was included in the 2005 legislation. Nevertheless, public officials did legislate a commitment to create 5,600 affordable workforce housing units on property within the BeltLine "planning area." Between 2005 and 2017, 2,565 affordable housing units were created by the Atlanta Housing Authority, the State Department of Community Development, and other public and private entities.[17] ABI has promised to invest TAD bond proceeds for additional affordable housing on other sites in the "planning area."

In 2017 the City Council created the Atlanta BeltLine Overlay Zoning District, which requires developers building 10 or more residential units to set aside 10 percent of those units for households earning 60 percent of area median income or less, or 15 percent of the units for households earning 80 percent of area median income or less.[18]

Downtown projects are different. Their beneficiaries are almost entirely businesses, residents, and institutions that generate more than enough revenue to pay for projects from which they benefit. In many cases, these projects are specifically intended to benefit them and would not otherwise be necessary. The same is true of some other capital projects elsewhere in the city. In both cases, the obvious way to finance them is through value recapture. However, downtown value recapture ought to be the primary form of financing downtown capital expenditures because properties in thriving downtowns will generate the incremental increases in taxes to pay for them. Thus, downtown BID boundaries ought to be simultaneously the boundaries of TIF districts that finance downtown capital projects through value recapture.

The Role of TIF- and Community Development Corporation–Enhanced BIDs

New York's Downtown Alliance, CCD Philadelphia, and many other BIDs finance their own improvements to the public realm. They do so out of the annual real estate tax surcharge that they receive to pay for BID operations. That can never be enough to pay for major capital investments such as the Cincinnati Bell Connector streetcar system or the platform over the Hudson Yards.

If a "standard" downtown BID is created by statute that is simultaneously a TIF, every downtown BID will be able to make the capital investments needed to create downtowns for a new generation—and do so without having to compete with or negotiate with other government agencies. Providing this financing capacity guarantees that downtown BIDs will be able to make the necessary investments. Similarly, if the "standard" downtown BID by statute is also a development corporation, it will be able, like the Cincinnati 3CDC, to engage in genuine entrepreneurial activity that includes business activity, real estate development, and property management—in the same manner as do all downtown activists.

The Columbus Downtown Development Corporation, established in Ohio in 2002, is among several U.S. downtown development entities that conceive of and develop their own major capital projects. It does not need to convince a private developer or nonprofit agency to build anything or obtain additional local government action; it does everything itself. In 2011, for example, the corporation used $44 million (half from public sources and half from private sector investments) to transform Scioto Mile (a flood wall topped with a two-lane street and parking) into a popular public park. The project resulted in private financing that replaced cracked asphalt parking lots "with nearly $350 million in new and renovated market-rate buildings that house thousands of downtown residents and helped generate 1,000 jobs."[19]

Scioto Mile, Columbus, Ohio, 2016

The Columbus Downtown Development Corporation conceives, develops, and manages capital projects that have enhanced downtown Columbus. (Alexander Garvin)

Creating powerful BIDs that are simultaneously TIFs and CDCs will provide every downtown with a powerful administering entity created by downtown businesses, residents, and institutions, operated for their benefit and responsible to them. It will ensure that the downtown BID is engaged in activities that will generate widespread and sustained private market activity. That is the best way to create a vibrant downtown for future generations.

Reducing Opposition to Change

In the 19th century, Frederick Law Olmsted, the co-designer New York's Central Park and many other important American public parks and, in my opinion, the nation's greatest city planner, identified the first and most important change in procedure we need to make in order to guarantee vibrant downtowns for a new century: ensuring that citizens (who dislike or will be in some way badly affected by change) are unable to prevent action that will be of great benefit to the city as a whole. One hundred forty years ago he identified the problem, writing,

"Two of the aldermen in succession came to me, and each privately said in effect: 'It is quite plain that the proposition is a good one, and ought to be adopted; the city would undoubtedly gain by it; but the people of the ward I represent have less interest in it than some others: they do not look far ahead, and they are jealous of those who would be more directly benefitted than themselves; consequently I don't think that they would like it if I voted for it, and I shall not, but I hope it will be carried.'"[20]

Olmsted had identified what has become known as NIMBY ("not in my back yard"). The problem goes far beyond that, however, because others insist on NOTE ("not over there either") or even BANANA ("build absolutely nothing anywhere near anybody"). If a property owner, business, or institution wants to do something with its property that is by law as-of-right, opponents cannot legally stop them. If the action is subject to the discretion of a public entity, however, NIMBY, NOTE, and BANANA obstruction is easy and will be particularly effective during formal public hearings.

At most public hearings, the party proposing an action presents the case for that action, as do some of its proponents. The opponents have the same opportunity, but because they believe they are the aggrieved parties, often their feelings are more intense, and their opposition is more vociferous.

The devices that could sufficiently reduce opposition to desirable change include specifying actions that mitigate some of the identified negative impact opponents dislike, giving opponents something that induces them to accept what they perceive as undesirable, identifying a series of alternatives that allows them to select something that is less onerous, and packaging actions together that share burdens across several districts, thereby relieving the local representative from the appearance that his or her district has been (unfairly) singled out. In all these cases, the political process arrives at a compromise solution.

Unfortunately, the process has two flaws: the public dialogue rarely involves an impartial and explicit presentation of the benefits, costs, and beneficiaries of any public action, as well as of the harm, cost, and identity of those who are injured, and it usually takes an overly long period of time to decide to reach a satisfactory result.

The first flaw can be remedied by requiring, *before agency consideration*, a presentation of costs and benefits of any public action, as well as identification of any person, business, or institution that would benefit or be harmed. However, it is neither appropriate nor possible to prevent opponents from ignoring the general interest and promoting their own self-interest or to guarantee that public officials will deal impartially with the identified impacts.

The second flaw, time excessive approval, is easily dealt with by requiring that all agencies be given a maximum of 30 days in which to decide whether to accept a proposed regulatory change.

Afterword

More than half a century ago, Jane Jacobs observed that "cities are an immense laboratory of trial and error, failure and success in city building and city design" and admonished us to study their "success and failure in real life."[1] I have been doing just that since 1961, when I first read those words—but not because I was merely curious "about the reasons for unexpected success." I wanted to learn what could be done to improve our cities.

This book is filled with examples of downtowns that have been changed for the better and, sometimes, for the worse. If people are familiar with these examples, they are more likely to change their downtowns for the better rather than for the worse. Doing that requires being able to diagnose what is going on, being familiar with the prescriptions that have been used to improve downtowns and the prescriptions that have failed, and then providing needed treatment. This book is intended to enable its readers to do all three.

I look forward to seeing the many marvelous changes that this book will enable them to make to their own downtowns.

Notes

Preface

1. Alliance for Downtown New York.
2. Eugenie Birch, "Who Lives Downtown," *Living Cities Census Series*, Washington, DC: The Brookings Institution, November 2005, p. 1.
3. Alliance for Downtown New York, "Residential Market Data," 2018, https://www.downtownny.com/residential-market-data
4. Downtown Center BID, "Downtown LA Market Report," Los Angeles, first quarter 2017.
5. "America's Most Visited Cities," *Forbes*, April 28, 2010, https://www.forbes.com/2010/04/28/tourism-new-york-lifestyle-travel-las-vegas-cities_slide_5.html
6. Jane Jacobs, *The Economy of Cities*, New York, NY: Random House, 1969, p. 6.
7. "Industrial Restructuring and Urban Change in Pittsburgh Region: Developmental, Ecological, and Socioeconomical Trade-offs," https://www.bls.gov/regions/mid-atlantic/data/areaemployment_pittsburgh_table.htm and file:///C:/Users/sandw/Downloads/ES-2005-1261%20(1).pdf
8. F. Scott Fitzgerald, "My Lost City," in Edmund Wilson (ed.), *The Crack Up*, New York, NY: New Directions Paperbook, 1956, pp. 25 and 31.

Chapter 1

1. Eric Homberger, *The Historical Atlas of New York City, Second Edition: A Visual Celebration*, New York, NY: St. Martin's Griffin, 2016, p. 80.
2. *Webster's New Collegiate Dictionary*, Springfield, MA: G&C. Merriam Co., 1953, p. 249.
3. Alexander Garvin, *The American City: What Works, What Doesn't* (3rd ed.), New York, NY: McGraw-Hill Education, 2013, pp. 220–28.
4. U.S. Census website, https://www.census.gov/retail/marts/www/adv45210.txt
5. U.S. Census website, ftp://ftp.census.gov/library/publications/2011/compendia/statab/131ed/tables/12s1061.pdf
6. Josh Sanburn, "Why the Death of Malls Is about More Than Shopping," *Time*, July 20, 2017, http://time.com/4865957/death-and-life-shopping-mall/; Statista Portal website, "Number of Shopping Malls in the United States in 2010, by Size (Gross Leasable Area in Sq. Feet)," https://www.statista.com/statistics/208108/shopping-centers-in-the-us-by-size/
7. Lynn Peisner, "Retail's Next Act," *North East Real Estate Business*, 14, no. 3 (January/February 2018): 1.

8. Michael Corkery, "Hard Lessons (Thanks, Amazon) Breathe New Life into Retail Stores," *New York Times*, September 4, 2018, p. A1.

9. Joseph Berger, "A Purveyor of Fountain Pens and Carbon Paper, Reinvented," *New York Times*, April 8, 2018, Metropolitan Section, p. 1.

10. Alliance for Downtown New York, "Residential Development and Population Growth," updated February 2018, http://www.downtownny.com/sites/default/files/research/2017%20Q4%20Lower%20Manhattan%20Residential%20Pipeline.pdf

11. U.S. Census website, https://www.census.gov/prod/2011pubs/12statab/domtrade.pdf and https://www2.census.gov/library/publications/2001/compendia/statab/120ed/tables/sec27.pdf

12. Terry Pristin, "Venti, Venti, Grande; Starbucks Strikes Deep in a Wary Land of Pushcarts and Delis," *New York Times*, April 29, 2002.

13. Aaron Elstein, "Urban Suburbia: More Local Businesses Are Catering to Suburban Tastes," *Crain's New York Business*, January 15, 2018.

14. Uptown Houston, "Uptown Houston Market Facts & Information," 2015, http://www.uptown-houston.com/images/uploads/2015_Uptown_Houston_Fact_Book.pdf and Harris County Records.

15. U.S. Census website, https://www2.census.gov/library/publications/decennial/1950/population-volume-1/vol-01-14.pdf

16. Bleakly Advisory Group, "Buckhead CID Impact Study," Buckhead Community Improvement District, Atlanta, July 2017.

17. Ellen Creager, "Hotel Prices Reflect Detroit's Trendy Reputation," *Detroit Free Press*, October 22, 2016, https://www.freep.com/story/travel/2016/10/22/hotel-prices-detroit-rates/92367642/

18. Downtown Detroit Partnership, "2016 Annual Report," http://downtowndetroit.org/wp-content/uploads/2014/04/DDP-Annual-Report-WEB.pdf; Hudson-Webber Foundation, "7.2 SQ MI: A Report on Greater Downtown Detroit" (2nd ed.), 2015, http://detroitsevenpointtwo.com/resources/7.2SQ_MI_Book_FINAL_LoRes.pdf

19. Area Vibes website, http://www.areavibes.com/detroit-mi/downtown/demographics/

20. Alliance for Downtown New York website, http://www.downtownny.com/sites/default/files/research/Residential%20Market%20Pipeline%20Q1%202017.pdf

21. Ibid.

22. Alliance for Downtown New York, "Lower Manhattan Indicators Q1 2017," http://www.downtownny.com/sites/default/files/research/Q1%2017%20LM%20Fact%20Sheet.pdf

23. Jon C. Teaford, *The Twentieth Century American City* (2nd ed.), Baltimore, MD: Johns Hopkins University Press, 1993, p. 8.

24. Brian Barth, "Dream Cars," in *Landscape Architecture Magazine, American Society of Landscape Architecture*, November 2017, pp. 79–87.

25. U.S. Bureau of Labor Statistics.

26. Ibid.

27. Alliance for Downtown New York, Uptown Houston District.
28. Denver BID.
29. Garvin, *The American City*, pp. 197–98.
30. New York City Global Partners, "Best Practice: Greenstreets: Greening Roadways," March 24, 2010, http://www.nyc.gov/html/ia/gprb/downloads /pdf/NYC_Environment_GreenStreets.pdf
31. Alexander Garvin, *The Planning Game: Lessons from Great Cities*, New York, NY: W.W. Norton, 2013, p. 33.
32. Garvin, *The American City,* pp. 220–28.
33. Cass Gilbert and Frederick Law Olmsted Jr., *Report of the New Haven Civic Improvement Commission* (facsimile ed.), San Antonio, TX: Trinity University Press, 2012, p. 14.
34. Harland Bartholomew, *Comprehensive City Plan*, St. Louis, MO: City Plan Commission, 1947, p. 1.
35. Katharine L. Bradbury, Anthony Downs, and Kenneth A. Small, *Urban Decline and the Future of American Cities*, Washington, DC: Brookings Institution, 1982.
36. Bernard J. Frieden and Lynne B. Sagalyn, *Downtown Inc.: How America Rebuilds Cities*, Cambridge, MA: MIT Press, 1989, p. 13.
37. It is important to distinguish any downtown from the rest of the city. The U.S. Census stopped tabulating downtown statistics in 1984. Since the 1990s the only sources for tabulated downtown statistics have been BIDs.

Chapter 2

1. Alexander Garvin, *The American City: What Works, What Doesn't* (3rd ed.), New York, NY: McGraw-Hill Education, 2013, pp. 101–3.
2. Ibid., pp. 422–24 and 430–31.
3. Alexander Garvin, *The Planning Game: Lessons from Great Cities*, New York, NY: W.W. Norton, 2013, pp. 54–58.
4. David Stradling and Richard Stradling, *Where the River Burned*, Ithaca, NY: Cornell University Press, 2015, p. x.
5. Patrick Burnson, "Top 20 U.S. Ports: Competition Heats Up for Discretionary Cargo," *Logistics Management*, May 1, 2015, http://www.logisticsmgmt .com/article/top_20_u.s._ports_competition_heats_up_for_discretionary _cargo
6. Downtown Partnership of Baltimore.
7. Cara Mia DiMassa, "Movie Tradition Fading to Black; Seventy Years after Its Neon Heyday, Downtown Los Angeles Is Struggling to Keep Its Last Cinematic Venue Afloat," *Los Angeles Times*, February 17, 2006.
8. Nathan Masters, "Seventh & Broadway: Photos of Downtown's Crossroads through the Decades," KCET website, August 1, 2012, https://www.kcet.org /shows/lost-la/seventh-broadway-photos-of-downtowns-crossroads-through -the-decades
9. Raymond Chandler, *The Little Sister* (1949), quoted in Elizabeth Ward and

Alain Silver (eds.), *Raymond Chandler's Los Angeles*, Woodstock, NY: The Overlook Press, 1987, p. 98.

10. Richard Longstreth, *City Center to Regional Mall: Architecture, the Automobile, and Retailing in Los Angeles, 1920–1950*, Cambridge, MA: MIT Press, p. 204.
11. Jim Heimann, *Los Angeles: Portrait of a City*, Cologne, Germany: Taschen, 2009, p. 305.
12. Ibid., p. 306.
13. NYC Department of City Planning.
14. John Regardie, "State of Darkness: Another Movie Palace Quits Screening Films," *Los Angeles Downtown News*, November 2, 1998.
15. Jane Jacobs, "Downtown Is for People," in Editors of *Fortune*, *The Exploding Metropolis*, New York, NY: Doubleday Anchor Books, 1958, pp. 164–65.
16. Downtown Denver Partnership website, http://www.downtowndenver.com/wp-content/uploads/2017/04/State-of-Downtown-Denver-2017_SPREADS_email.pdf
17. Garvin, *The American City*, pp. 176–78 and 221–22; Alexander Garvin, *What Makes a Great City*, Washington, DC: Island Press, 2016, pp. 36–40.
18. Michael D. Beyard, W. Paul 'O'Mara, et al. *Shopping Center Development Handbook* (3rd ed.), Washington, DC: Urban Land Institute, 1999, p. 8.
19. Ibid.
20. City of Minneapolis website, http://www.ci.minneapolis.mn.us/neighborhoods/northloop/neighborhoods_northloop_population; *Minneapolis Journal* website, http://www.journalmpls.com/focus/neighborhood-spotlight/2016/08/the-north-loop-minneapolis-hippest-neighborhood/
21. North Loop Minneapolis Neighborhood website, http://northloop.org/about/
22. Sophie-Claire Hoeller, "The 12 Coolest Neighborhoods in America," *Thrillist*, February 20, 2015, https://www.thrillist.com/travel/nation/coolest-neighborhoods-in-america-the-mission-wicker-park-and-highland-park-top-our-list
23. Downtown Denver Partnership website, http://www.downtowndenver.com/wp-content/uploads/StateofDowntownDenver_Final_Web_Pages.pdf
24. Joe Rubino, "When Whole Foods at Union Station Opens Next Week, Groceries Will Only Be Half the Story," *The Denver Post*, November 7, 2017.
25. Downtown Denver Partnership, "Center City Housing," Denver, 2017.
26. Downtown Denver Partnership, "2017 State of Downtown Denver," Denver, 2017.
27. J. Mark Souther, *Believing in Cleveland: Managing Decline in "The Best Location in the Nation,"* Philadelphia, PA: Temple University Press, 2017, p. 172.
28. Ibid., p. 201.
29. Cleveland SMSA population as reported by the U.S. Bureau of the Census.
30. Janet H. Cho, "Constantino's Market Opening Its 4th Neighborhood Grocery Store on April 9, at the University of Rochester," *Cleveland Plain Dealer*

website, April 3, 2015, http://www.cleveland.com/business/index.ssf
/2015/04/constantinos_market_opening_its_fourth_store_on_april_9_at
_the_university_of_rochester.html
31. Center City Philadelphia.
32. Minneapolis/St. Paul Business Journal website, https://www.bizjournals.com
/twincities/blog/real_estate/2016/02/downtown-minneapolis-population
-growth-rate.html
33. David J. Wallace, "Real Estate; New Hotel in Downtown Minneapolis,"
New York Times website, November 11, 1992, http://www.nytimes.com
/1992/11/11/business/real-estate-new-hotel-in-downtown-minneapolis
.html
34. Demographia United States Central Business Districts (Downtowns)
website, 2006, http://americandreamcoalition.org/landuse/db-cbd2000.pdf;
Downtown Detroit Partnership website, 2016, http://downtowndetroit.org
/wp-content/uploads/2014/04/DDP-Annual-Report-WEB.pdf
35. John F. McDonald, "What Happened to and in Detroit," draft website,
October 2013, https://www.ccimef.org/pdf/ARES-2014-281-What-Hap
pened-To-and-In-Detroit.pdf
36. Hudson-Webber Foundation, "7.2 SQ MI: A Report on Greater Downtown
Detroit" (2nd ed.), 2015, http://detroitsevenpointtwo.com/resources/7.2SQ_
MI_Book_FINAL_Lo
Res.pdf
37. Julia Beckusen, "Occupations in Information Technology," *American Community Survey Reports* https://www.census.gov/content/dam/Census/library
/publications/2016/acs/acs-35.pdf
38. IEDP website, https://www.iedp.com/articles/the-changing-workplace/
39. Anne Kadet, "Entrepreneurs Are Getting Creative in the Co-Working
Space," *Wall Street Journal*, February 7, 2018.
40. Roger Vincent, "Office Walls Are Closing In on Corporate Workers," *Los
Angeles Times* website, December 15, 2010, http://articles.latimes.com/2010
/dec/15/business/la-fi-office-space-20101215
41. The Mehigan Company Inc. website, http://mehiganco.com/wordpress/?
p=684 and CoreNet Global.
42. Greg David, "Who's More Important in NYC, Tech or Wall Street?" Crain's
New York Business website, February 28, 2018, http://www.crainsnewyork
.com/article/20180301/BLOGS01/180229874/greg-david-on-ny-whos
-bigger-in-nyc-tech-or-wall-street#utm_medium=email&utm_source=cnyb
-morning10&utm_campaign=cnyb-morning10-20180301
43. The first co-working space probably emerged in San Francisco. Curbed
website, https://www.curbed.com/2016/10/25/13400170/real-estate-office
-space-coworking-wework
44. JLL website, "Shared Workspaces," http://www.us.jll.com/united-states/en
-us/Research/US-Shared-workspace-2016-JLL.pdf?fa225063-d93d-49eb
-a389-a6bc00505cca
45. Alliance for Downtown New York, www.downtownny.com

46. U.S. Department of Labor, "Business Employment Dynamics," Bureau of Labor Statistics website, https://www.bls.gov/bdm/entrepreneurship/bdm_chart5.htm
47. Alliance for Downtown New York.

Chapter 3

1. Becky Nicolaides and Andrew Wise, "Suburbanization in the United States after 1945," Oxford Research Encyclopedia website, April 2017, http://americanhistory.oxfordre.com/view/10.1093/acrefore/9780199329175.001.0001/acrefore-9780199329175-e-64
2. PK, "Historical Homeownership Rate in the United States, 1890–Present," DQYDJ website, September 2018, https://dqydj.com/historical-homeownership-rate-in-the-united-states-1890-present
3. "Deaths by Homicide per 100,000 Resident Population in the US from 1950 to 2015," The Statista Portal website, 2018, https://www.statista.com/statistics/187592/death-rate-from-homicide-in-the-us-since-1950/
4. William Schneider, "The Suburban Century Begins," *The Atlantic Monthly*, July 1992, https://www.theatlantic.com/past/docs/politics/ecbig/schnsub.htm
5. That date would have been 10 years later if one includes Higbee's in Tower City Center as the ninth store.
6. U.S. Department of Labor, "Labor Trends in the United States."
7. "FRED Economic Data," Federal Reserve Bank of St. Louis website, updated September 6, 2018, https://fred.stlouisfed.org/series/OUTMS
8. "County and City Data Book: 2007," U.S. Census website, https://www2.census.gov/library/publications/2010/compendia/ccdb07/tabc.pdf
9. "City and County Data Book," University of Virginia website, discontinued 2018, http://ccdb.lib.virginia.edu/
10. U.S. Bureau of Labor Statistics.
11. Alexander Garvin, *The American City: What Works, What Doesn't* (3rd ed.), New York, NY: McGraw-Hill Education, 2013, pp. 283–84.
12. New York State Multiple Dwelling Law Chapter 713 of the Laws of 1929, as amended, Article 7B.
13. Garvin, *The American City*, pp. 347–59.
14. Other reasons for contraction or expansion of freight handling areas and warehousing districts include shifts in the nation's population and economic enterprises and changes in the relative costs of moving freight to and from that location.
15. "Facts & Figures," Port of Oakland Seaport website, 2018, http://www.oaklandseaport.com/performance/facts-figures/
16. Garvin, *The American City*, pp. 107–8.
17. Eric Lipton, "New York Port Hums Again, with Asian Trade," *New York Times*, November 22, 2004.
18. "Facts & Figures," Port of New York and New Jersey website, 2018, https://www.panynj.gov/port/trade-stats.html and http://www.njbiz.com/article/20160520/NJBIZ01

19. Alexander Garvin, *What Makes a Great City*, Washington, DC: Island Press, 2016, pp. 266–71.

20. Garvin, *The American City*, pp. 412–14.

21. Jynnah Radford and Abby Budiman, "Facts on U.S. Immigrants, 2016," Pew Research Center website, http://www.pewhispanic.org/2017/05/03/facts-on -u-s-immigrants/

22. Richard Florida, *The Rise of the Creative Class Revisited*, New York, NY: Basic Books, 2012.

23. Doug Saunders, *Arrival City*, New York, NY: Vintage Books, 2012, p. 1.

24. 2000 US Census Profile of selected social characteristics for Miami-Dade County.

25. Miami-Dade County website, 2018, https://www.miamidade.gov/planning /library/reports/data-flash/2011-hispanics-by-origin.pdf

26. Ibid.

27. "New Americans in San Jose and Santa Clara County," City of San Jose website, 2018, http://www.newamericaneconomy.org/wp-content/uploads /2016/08/SAN-JOSE-Factsheet_FinalDigital.pdf

28. Ibid.

29. Cicero A. Estrella, "S.F.'s Little Saigon: Stretch of Larkin Street Named for Vietnamese Americans," *San Francisco Chronicle*, February 16, 2004.

30. Saunders, *Arrival City*, pp. 76–85.

31. Ibid., p. 80.

32. Phillip Connor and Jens Manuel Krogstad, "For the First Time, U.S. Resettles Fewer Refugees Than the Rest of the World," Pew Research Center website, July 5, 2018, http://www.pewresearch.org/fact-tank/2018/07/05/for -the-first-time-u-s-resettles-fewer-refugees-than-the-rest-of-the-world/

33. Phillip Connor and Jens Manuel Krogstad, "The Number of Refugees Admitted to the U.S. Has Fallen, Especially among Muslims," Pew Research Center website, May 3, 2018, http://www.pewresearch.org/fact-tank/2018 /05/03/the-number-of-refugees-admitted-to-the-u-s-has-fallen-especially -among-muslims/

34. FedEx website, 2018, http://about.van.fedex.com/our-story/history-timeline /history/

35. FedEx website, 2018, http://about.van.fedex.com/our-story/company-struc ture/corporate-fact-sheet/

36. Memphis Freight Infrastructure Plan, October 19, 2009, Greater Memphis Chamber website, http://memphismpo.org/sites/default/files/public/docu ments/freight/memphis-freight-infrastructure-plan.pdf

37. Ibid.

38. Ibid.

39. "Memphis International Airport Maintains Status as World's Second Busiest Cargo Airport; MEM Is Busiest Cargo Airport in North America," Memphis International Airport website, 2018, http://www.flymemphis.com /NewsDetails?newsid=3236

40. Alan Blinder, "The Trouble with the Memphis Airport: No Crowds," *New York Times*, May 23, 2018.

41. Ibid.

42. Memphis Travel website, 2018, http://www.memphistravel.com/mcvb-history

43. Suemedha Sood, "Why Is Atlanta the World's Busiest Airport?" BBC website, February 8, 2013, http://www.bbc.com/travel/story/20130207-why-is -atlanta-the-worlds-busiest-airport

44. Huileng Tan, "If You're Surprised That Atlanta Has the Busiest Airport on Earth, You're Not Alone," CNBC website, December 19, 2017, https://www .cnbc.com/2017/12/19/why-the-atlanta-airport-the-busiest-in-the-world .html

45. Janet R. Bednarek, *Airports, Cities, and the Jet Age*, New York, NY: Palgrave Macmillan, 2016, p. 25.

46. National Travel and Tourism Office.

47. Maria Sheahan, "U.S. Fails to Keep Pace with Global Tourist Boom," Reuters website, March 9, 2018, https://www.reuters.com/article/us-usa-trump-trav el/u-s-fails-to-keep-pace-with-global-tourism-boom-idUSKCN1GL21E

48. Valaer Murray, "List: America's Most-Visited Cities," *Forbes*, April 28, 2010, https://www.forbes.com/2010/04/28/tourism-new-york-lifestyle-travel-las -vegas-cities_slide_5.html

49. Bleakly Advisory Group, "The Economic and Fiscal Impacts of the Buck-head Community Improvement District," Atlanta, July 24, 2017; Uptown Houston District.

50. Patrick McGeehan, "New York City Expects More Tourists but Fewer International Visitors," *New York Times*, November 19, 2017, https://www .nytimes.com/2017/11/19/nyregion/new-york-city-tourism.html

51. Uptown Houston District.

52. "The Economic and Fiscal Impacts of the Buckhead Community Improve-ment District," http://www.buckheadcid.com/wp-content/uploads/2018/01 /buckhead-cid-economic-impact-study-october2017_bag.pdf

53. Ibid.

54. Downtown Denver Partnership website, http://www.downtowndenver.com /wp-content/uploads/2017/04/State-of-Downtown-Denver-2017_SPRE ADS_email.pdf and http://extras.denverpost.com/business/bizreport1218 .htm

55. "Life Expectancy in USA," Google website, 2018, https://www.google.com /search?rlz=1C1CHZL_enUS748US748&ei=ZjKLWuquEsGKggf9_IL4D w&q=life+expectancy+in+usa

56. "Demographic Trends in the 20th Century," U.S. Census website, November 2002, https://www.census.gov/prod/2002pubs/censr-4.pdf

57. Center City District & Central Philadelphia Development Corporation, "2017 Housing Report: Building Optimism," Philadelphia Center City web-site, http://www.centercityphila.org/uploads/attachments/ciziry4x7191nw 1qde5cq0gcw-ccr17-housing.pdf

58. "Share of Cyclists/Bike Riders in the United States in 2018, by Age,"

Statista Portal website, https://www.statista.com/statistics/227415/number-of-cyclists-and-bike-riders-usa/

59. Scott Calver, "Bike Lanes Hit Wall in Many Cities," *Wall Street Journal*, April 19, 2018.

60. Winnie He, "More New Yorkers Opting for Life in the Bike Lane," *New York Times*, July 30, 2017, https://www.nytimes.com/2017/07/30/nyregion/new-yorkers-bike-lanes-commuting.html; Douglas Johnson, "Bike-Share Companies Are Transforming US Cities—And They Are Just Getting Started," *The News & Observer*, April 20, 2018, https://www.newsobserver.com/opinion/op-ed/article209420104.html

61. National Association of City Transportation Officials (NACTO).

62. "Green Lane Project," People for Bikes website, 2017, http://peopleforbikes.org/green-lane-project/inventory-protected-bike-lanes/

63. Janette Sadik-Kahn and Seth Solomonow, *Streetfight: Handbook for an Urban Revolution*, New York, NY: Viking, 2016, p. 152.

64. Ameena Walker, "NYC Added 25 Miles of New Protected Bike Lanes in 2017," *Curbed New York*, December 20, 2017, https://ny.curbed.com/2017/12/20/16798982/nyc-protected-bike-lane-expansion-vision-zero; Andrew Elstein, "Urban Suburbia: More Local Businesses Are Catering to Suburban Tastes," *Crain's New York Business*, January 15, 2018.

65. Garvin, *The American City*, pp. 75–78.

66. Patrick Sisson, "Cycling Success: 10 U.S. Cities Pushing Biking Forward," *Curbed*, April 18, 2017, https://www.curbed.com/2017/4/18/15333796/best-cities-bike-commute-us-cycling; Eric Roper, "Bicycle Commuting Rising in Minneapolis and St. Paul," *Minneapolis Star-Tribune*, September 16, 2016, http://www.startribune.com/bicycle-commuting-at-highest-rate-ever-in-minneapolis-and-st-paul/393618991/

67. Alexander Garvin, "Atlanta's BeltLine, the Emerald Necklace Shaping the City's Future," in Harley R. Etienne and Barbara Faga, *Planning Atlanta*, Chicago, IL: American Planning Association Planners Press, 2014, pp. 204–18.

68. "Deaths by Homicide per 100,000 Resident Population in the US from 1950 to 2015," 2018, Statista Portal website, https://www.statista.com/statistics/187592/death-rate-from-homicide-in-the-us-since-1950/

69. "Fewest Annual Murders and Shooting Incidents Ever Recorded in the Modern Era," New York City Police Department, January 5, 2018, NYC Police Department website, https://www1.nyc.gov/site/nypd/news/pr0105/fewest-annual-murders-shooting-incidents-ever-recorded-the-modern-era#/0; "Total Homicides in Philadelphia: 1960 to 2013," Infogram website, https://infogram.com/total-homicides-in-philadelphia-1960-to-2013-1g90n2oddekjm4y

70. Elstein, "Urban Suburbia."

71. Patrick Sharkey, *Uneasy Peace: The Great Crime Decline, the Renewal of City Life, and the Next War on Violence*, New York, NY: W.W. Norton 2018, pp. xxvii–xviii.

72. "Crime Prevention," Center City District website, https://centercityphila
    .org/ccd-services/public-safety/crime-prevention
73. Ibid.

Chapter 4

1. James M. Lindgren, "Association for the Preservation of Virginia Antiquities," Encyclopedia Virginia website, 2018, https://www.encyclopediavirginia
   .org/Association_for_the_Preservation_of_Virginia_Antiquities
2. Mike McPhee, *Dana Crawford: 50 Years Saving the Soul of a City*, Denver,
   CO: Upper Gulch Publishing Co., 2015.
3. Alexander Garvin, *The American City: What Works, What Doesn't* (3rd ed.),
   New York, NY: McGraw-Hill Education, 2013, pp. 147–48.
4. McPhee, *Dana Crawford*, p. 3.
5. Ibid., p. 4.
6. Ibid.
7. Rachel Sugar, "More Tourists Visited NYC in 2016 Than Ever Before,"
   Curbed New York, December 16, 2016.
8. "Lower Manhattan Tourism 2016," Alliance for Downtown New York
   website, http://www.downtownny.com/sites/default/files/research/LM%20
   Tourism%202016_Fact%20Sheet_0.pdf
9. Alliance for Downtown New York website, www.downtownny.com
10. Two Trees Management Company.
11. Ibid.
12. Ibid.
13. Ibid.
14. Interview with Jed Walentas, December 21, 2017.
15. Letter from Jed Walentas, January 22, 2018.
16. Interview with Jed Walentas, March 6, 2018.
17. Two Trees Management Co. LLC, *Welcome to Dumbo: This Is What Opportu-
    nity Looks Like*, Brooklyn, 2017, https://assets.ctfassets.net/hy1449x19ffb
    /wiWUulIZ5A4suay4uCkEG/9522d866f32554fb7b3b4be097bfec61/retail
    _brochure.pdf
18. Hudson-Webber Foundation, "7.2 SQ MI: A Report on Greater Downtown
    Detroit" (2nd ed.), 2015, http://detroitsevenpointtwo.com/resources
    /7.2SQ_MI_Book_FINAL_LoRes.pdf; Center City District and Central
    Philadelphia Development Corporation, *Center City Reports: 2017 Housing
    Report: Building on Optimism*, Philadelphia, CCD, 2017; Bleakly Advisory
    Group, *Buckhead CID Impact Study*, Buckhead Community Improvement
    District, Atlanta, July 2017.
19. "Dan Gilbert," *Forbes* website, September 20, 2018, https://www.forbes.com
    /profile/daniel-gilbert/
20. Ibid.
21. John Gallagher, "Readers to Dan Gilbert: Name New Skyscraper Hudson's
    as Link to City's Past," *Detroit Free Press*, December 1, 2017.
22. Downtown Detroit Partnership.

23. Margot Gayle, *Cast-Iron Architecture in New York*, New York, NY: Dover Publications, 1974.
24. Garvin, *The American City*, pp. 551–53.
25. "SCAD Economic Impact in the State of Georgia," Savannah College of Art & Design website, 2018, http://www.scad.edu/about/scad-glance/community-impact
26. Mary Thomas, "A Force for Art, Community," *Pittsburgh Post-Gazette*, June 1, 2018, p. 1.
27. Alliance for Downtown New York, www.downtownny.com
28. Uptown Houston BID.
29. "2015 Downtown LA Survey Snapshot," Downtown LA website, https://www.downtownla.com/images/BID.SurveyResults16.infograph.pdf
30. Ibid.
31. Sugar, "More Tourists Visited NYC."
32. "Lower Manhattan Tourism 2016," Alliance for Downtown New York website, http://www.downtownny.com/sites/default/files/research/LM%20Tourism%202016_Fact%20Sheet_0.pdf
33. Alliance for Downtown New York, www.downtownny.com
34. "Los Angeles' Tourism Industry Generates Record $34.9 Billion in Economic Impact," Discover Los Angeles website, updated May 10, 2018, https://www.discoverlosangeles.com/press-releases/los-angeles-announces-tourism-and-visitor-spend-milestones-during-national-travel-and
35. "Tourism," Downtown LA website, 2018, https://www.downtownla.com/do-biz/dtla-by-the-numbers/tourism

Chapter 5

1. "Texas Medical Center Institutions," Greater Houston Partnership website, 2018, https://www.houston.org/newgen/13_Health_Care/13E%20W002%20TMC%20Institutions.pdf; "TMC: Texas Medical Center," Texas Medical Center website, http://www.tmc.edu/about-tmc/facts-and-figures/; Alex Orlando, "Building a City of Medicine: The History of the Texas Medical Center," Texas Medical Center website, August 19, 2014, http://www.tmc.edu/news/2014/08/building-a-city-of-medicine-the-history-of-the-texas-medical-center/
2. Interview with Daniel Biederman, August 14, 2018.
3. Alexander Garvin, *What Makes a Great City*, Washington, DC: Island Press, 2016, pp. 255–66.
4. DTLA consists of the Fashion District, Arts District, Downtown Industrial District, Little Tokyo, Historic Downtown LA, Downtown Center, South Park, and South Park II.
5. "DTLA by the Numbers," DTLA website, 2018, https://www.downtownla.com/do-biz/dtla-by-the-numbers
6. DTLA.
7. Center City District and Central Philadelphia Development Corporation, "Philadelphia Employment," Philadelphia, 2017, p. 1.

8. Center City District and Central Philadelphia Development Corporation, "Plan and Budget for the Center City District 2018–2022," Philadelphia, 2018, p. 5.

9. Center City District and Central Philadelphia Development Corporation and U.S. Census.

10. "2017 Housing Report: Building Optimism," Center City District website, February 2017, http://www.centercityphila.org/uploads/attachments /ciziry4x7191nw1qde5cq0gcw-ccr17-housing.pdf

11. Center City District and Central Philadelphia Development Corporation.

12. Garvin, *The American City*, pp. 311–13.

13. New York City Rent Guidelines Board, "2017 Housing Supply Report," New York City Rent Guidelines Board website, May 25, 2017, https://www 1.nyc.gov/assets/rentguidelinesboard/pdf/17HSR.pdf

14. Statistics derived from Center City District and Central Philadelphia Development Corporation, "Center City Reports: 2017 Housing Report: Building on Optimism," Philadelphia, February 2017.

15. Center City District and Central Philadelphia Development Corporation.

16. Roy Lubove, *Twentieth Century Pittsburgh* (vol. II), pp. 208–14, and Roy Lubove, *Twentieth Century Pittsburgh* (vol. I), New York, NY: John Wiley & Sons, 1969, pp. 106–41.

17. Garvin, *The American City*, pp. 197–99.

18. "Pittsburgh Cultural Trust Background and History," Pittsburgh Cultural Trust website, 2018, https://trustarts.org/pct_home/about/history/

19. Garvin, *The American City*, pp. 342–43.

20. Ibid., pp. 206–9.

21. Alexander Garvin, *The Planning Game: Lessons from Great Cities*, New York, NY: W.W Norton, 2013, pp. 54–58.

22. Tom Jones, *Shelby Farms Park: Elevating a City*, Memphis, TN: Susan Schadt Press, 2017.

23. Judith Rodin, *The University & Urban Revival: Out of the Ivory Tower and Into the Streets*, Philadelphia, PA: University of Pennsylvania Press, 2007, p. 14.

24. "State of Center City 2018," Center City District website, https://www .centercityphila.org/research-reports

25. It includes 54 medicine-related institutions, with 21 hospitals and 8 specialty institutions, 8 academic and research institutions, 4 medical schools, 7 nursing schools, 3 public health organizations, 2 pharmacy schools, and a dental school.

26. "TMC Facts & Figures," Texas Medical Center website, 2018, http://www .tmc.edu/wp-content/uploads/2016/08/TMC_FactsFiguresOnePager_030 7162.pdf

27. "Facts and Figures," Texas Medical Center Corporation, 2016.

28. Kate King, "Hospitals Inject New Life into Communities," *Wall Street Journal*, March 21, 2018, p. A10A.

29. "West Philadelphia Corporation (Philadelphia, Pa.) Records," Temple Uni-

versity website, 2018, https://library.temple.edu/scrc/west-philadelphia-cor
poration
30. Rodin, *The University & Urban Revival*, p. x.
31. Ibid., p. 22.
32. Ibid., pp. 48–49.
33. Tyler Tran, data scientist, University City District.
34. University City District, "2017 Annual Review," Philadelphia, 2018.
35. Yale University Office of New Haven and State Affairs.
36. "Yale Homebuyer Program Renewed through 2019," *Yale News*, December 21, 2017, https://news.yale.edu/2017/12/21/yale-homebuyer-program-re newed-through-2019
37. Interview with Bruce Alexander, April 3, 2018.
38. Arielle Levin Becker, "Schiavone, from the Banjo to the Stump," *Yale News*, October 15, 2001, https://yaledailynews.com/blog/2001/10/15/schiavone -from-the-banjo-to-the-stump/
39. Interview with Bruce Alexander, April 3, 2018.
40. NYC Planning Commission, "Capital Needs and Priorities for the City of New York," New York City, 1981, p. 2.
41. NYC Planning Commission, Robert F. Wagner Jr., Chairman, "Capital Needs and Priorities for the City of New York," New York City, March 1, 1978, p. 4.
42. NYC Planning Commission, "Capital Needs and Priorities for the City of New York," New York City, 1985, p. 1.
43. Robert F. Wagner Jr., Chairman, NYC Planning Commission, "A New Direction in Transit," New York City, December, 1978, p. 4.
44. Alliance for Downtown New York, "Q3 2015 Residential Market Report."
45. Metropolitan Transportation Authority, "Advisory: MTA Celebrates Open-ing of New York Fulton Center," November 4, 2014.
46. David W. Dunlap, "A Sign of Renewal and a Reminder at Ground Zero," *New York Times*, May 23, 2006.
47. "East River Waterfront Esplanade," New York City Economic Development Corporation website, last updated September 12, 2016, https://www.nycedc .com/project/east-river-waterfront-esplanade

Chapter 6

1. Alexander Garvin, *The American City: What Works, What Doesn't* (3rd ed.), New York, NY: McGraw-Hill Education, 2013, pp. 196–99.
2. Ibid., pp. 194–217.
3. Major Anthony Celebrezze, quoted in I. M. Pei and Associates, *Erieview, Cleveland, Ohio: An Urban Renewal Plan for Downtown Cleveland*, New York, NY, 1961, p. 2.
4. Garvin, *The American City*, pp. 149–56 and 193–238.
5. Ibid., pp. 136–39.
6. Raymond Vernon, *Metropolitan 1985*, Cambridge, MA: Harvard University Press, 1960, p. 140.

7. Raymond Chandler, *The Simple Art of Murder*, New York, NY: Vintage Books, 1988, pp. 96–97.

8. John Rechy, "Big Table 3," 1959, quoted in Jim Heimann, *Los Angeles: Portrait of a City*, Cologne, Germany: Taschen, 2009, p. 386.

9. Carla C. Sobala (compiler), *Los Angeles . . . Today*, Washington, DC: Urban Land Institute, 1975, pp. 70–71; Helfeld + Maguire, "Stormy, Controversial Bunker Hill," *Journal of Housing*, March 1978, p. 127; Herbert Ray, "Bunker Hill Urban Renewal," *Los Angeles Times*, April 15, 1979; Cheryl G. Cummins (ed.), *Los Angeles Metropolitan Area . . . Today*, Washington, DC: Urban Land Institute, 1987, pp. 28–35.

10. Chandler, *The Simple Art of Murder*.

11. Garvin, *The American City*, pp. 283–84 and 556.

12. "DRA Retail Up-Fit Grant," Downtown Raleigh Alliance website, 2018, http://www.godowntownraleigh.com/dtretail/dra-retail-up-fit-grant

13. "Raleigh, North Carolina Population, 2018," retrieved September 20, 2018, from http://worldpopulationreview.com/us-cities/raleigh/

14. "Leasing and Financial Incentives," Alliance for Downtown New York website, https://www.downtownny.com/leasing-and-financial-incentives

15. Alliance for Downtown New York.

16. Columbus, 2020, "Downtown Business Incentives," City of Columbus website, https://www.columbus.gov/development/economic-development/Downtown-Business-Incentives/

17. NYC Department of City Planning, "Manhattan Office Space Market 1960–78," New York City, 1979, unpublished.

18. "Uptown Houston Market Facts & Information," Uptown Houston website, 2018, http://www.uptown-houston.com/images/uploads/FactBook.pdf, 08.22.2014.

19. John H. Thompson, "Surveying U.S. Census Bureau Commuting Data in Atlanta," U.S. Census website, April 27, 2016, https://www.census.gov/newsroom/blogs/director/2016/04/surveying-u-s-census-bureau-commuting-data-in-atlanta.html

20. Downtown Denver Partnership, "Employment in International Central Business Districts, 2000," Demographia website, http://www.demographia.com/db-intlcbd.htm

21. Wendell Cox Consultancy, "Analysis of the Proposed Las Vegas LLC Monorail," Belleville, IL, June 6, 2000, p. 12.

22. Hudson-Webber Foundation "7.2 SQ MI: A Report on Greater Downtown Detroit" (2nd ed.), February 2015, http://detroitsevenpointtwo.com/resources/7.2SQ_MI_Book_FINAL_LoRes.pdf

23. Janette Sadik-Kahn and Seth Solomonow, *Streetfight: Handbook for an Urban Revolution*, New York, NY: Viking, 2016, p. xiv.

24. Andrew Tangel and Josh Dawsey, "At Times Square, Fewer Traffic Injuries," *Wall Street Journal*, August 25, 2015.

25. Times Square Alliance.

26. Ibid.

27. Alissa Walker, "The Case against Sidewalks," Curbed Philly website, February 7, 2018, https://www.curbed.com/2018/2/7/16980682/city-sidewalk -repair-future-walking-neighborhood

28. "*Willits V. City of LA* Sidewalk Settlement Announced," City of Los Angeles website, April 1, 2015, https://www.lamayor.org/willits-v-city-la-sidewalk -settlement-announced

29. Umair Irfan, "Cars and Trucks Are America's Biggest Climate Problem for the 2nd Year in a Row," Vox Media website, updated Jan 14, 2018, https: //www.vox.com/energy-and-environment/2018/1/11/16874696/greenhouse -gas-co2-target-2017-paris-trump

30. "Urban Tree Canopy Assessment," St. Paul website, https://www.stpaul .gov/departments/parks-recreation/natural-resources/forestry/urban-tree -canopy

31. Keith Schneider, "To Revitalize a City, Try Spreading Some Mulch," *New York Times*, May 17, 2006.

32. Million Trees NYC, https://www.nycgovparks.org/trees/milliontreesnyc and http://www.milliontreesnyc.org/

33. Alexander Garvin, *What Makes a Great City*, Washington, DC: Island Press, 2016, pp. 175–76.

34. Alexander Garvin, *The Planning Game: Lessons from Great Cities*, New York, NY: W.W Norton, 2013, pp. 81–92 and 132–46.

35. Peggy Noonan, "Over Trump, We're as Divided as Ever," *Wall Street Journal*, March 10, 2018.

36. Ibid.

37. Philip K. Howard, *The Death of Common Sense: How Law Is Suffocating America*, New York, NY: Random House, 1994, p. 174.

Chapter 7

1. Regional Plan Association, *Regional Plan of New York and Its Environs* (seven volumes), New York, 1929.

2. New York City Planning Commission, *Large-Scale Development in New York City*, New York, 1973, pp. 108–9.

3. The title "Hudson Yards" was coined by Daniel Doctoroff. See Daniel L. Doctoroff, *Greater Than Ever: New York's Big Comeback*, New York, NY: Public Affairs, 2017, pp. 164–65.

4. "Hudson Yards Development Information," http://www.hydc.org/downloads /pdf/hy_development_information.pdf

5. Interchange with Daniel Doctoroff, March 18, 2018.

6. The HYIC Tax Increment District included essentially everything west of Eighth Avenue between 42nd and 30th streets, plus the block containing Madison Square Garden and Penn Station but not the Javits Convention Center and the two blocks to its north (see the map on page 197).

7. Jonathan Lerner, "A Freeway Sliced through Central Dallas in 1964. A Park Built over It Is Becoming the City's New Heart," *Landscape Architecture Magazine*, February 2017, pp. 144–57.

8. David Crossley, "Dallas Has Longest Light Rail System in US," *Houston Tomorrow*, December 6, 2010, http://www.houstontomorrow.org/livability /story/dallas-green-line-begins-service/

9. "Facts about Dallas Area Rapid Transit (DART)," http://www.dart.org /about/dartfacts.asp and http://www.dart.org/about/dartreferencebook mar18.pdf

10. Dallas, Texas, M-Line (McKinney Avenue Streetcar), http://www.jtbell.net /transit/Dallas/MLine/

11. "Interactive Estimated Ridership Stats," http://isotp.metro.net/MetroRider ship/Index.aspx

12. Colin Woodard, "How Cincinnati Salvaged the Nation's Most Dangerous Neighborhood," *Politico Magazine,* June 16, 2016.

13. Cincinnati Center City Development Corporation 2016 Annual Report, https://www.3cdc.org/wp-content/blogs.dir/3/files/2017/08/2016-annual -report-FINAL-reduced.pdf

14. City of Boston, "History of Boston's Economy Growth and Transition, 1970–1998," 1999, http://www.bostonplans.org/getattachment/15ca7a2f-56 d1-4770-ba7f-8c1ce73d25b8

15. The Boston Planning & Development Agency, "Boston's Economy Report 2017," http://www.bostonplans.org/getattachment/d835ad4c-e8a9-4f17-b 342-468f02301c58

16. James A. Aloisi Jr., *The Big Dig*, Beverly, MA: Commonwealth Editions, 2004, pp. 26–28.

17. Massachusetts Bay Transportation Authority, "Silver Line SL1," https://mb ta.com/schedules/741/line

18. Interview with Con Howe, September 12, 2017.

19. Ken Bernstein, "A Planning Ordinance Injects New Life into Historic Downtown," in David C. Sloane (ed.), *Planning Los Angeles*, Chicago, IL: American Planning Association, 2012, pp. 253–63.

20. Downtown Center Business Improvement District (DTLA), Los Angeles, June 15, 2018.

21. Zane L. Miller and Bruce Tucker, *Changing Plans for America's Inner Cities: Cincinnati's Over-the-Rhine and Twentieth-Century Urbanism*, Columbus: Ohio State University Press, 1998, p. 166.

22. Over-the-Rhine Foundation, "Guide to OTR Architecture," http://www .otrfoundation.org/OTR_Architecture.htm

23. Alice Skirtz, *Econocide: Elimination of the Urban Poor*, Washington, DC: NASW Press, 2012, p. 127.

24. Ibid., p. 65.

25. Downtown Cincinnati website, https://www.downtowncincinnati.com

26. Skirtz, *Econocide*, pp. 34–41.

27. Ibid., pp. 49–53.

28. Woodard, "How Cincinnati Salvaged the Nation's Most Dangerous Neighborhood."

29. Anne Michaud, "Fast Companies," *Cincinnati Magazine*, March 2000.

30. Walter C. Rucker and James N. Upton, *Encyclopedia of American Race Riots* (Vol. 1), Westport, CT: Greenwood Press, 2006.
31. Cincinnati Center City Development Corporation, "About 3CDC," https://www.3cdc.org/about-3cdc/
32. Shibani Mahtami, "From Ailing to Artisanal: The Transformation of a Cincinnati Neighborhood," *Wall Street Journal*, August 23, 2017.
33. Alexander Garvin, *The American City: What Works, What Doesn't* (3rd ed.), New York, NY: McGraw-Hill Education, 2013, pp. 558–59.
34. Ibid., pp. 141–42.
35. Lerner, "A Freeway Sliced through Central Dallas in 1964."
36. Boston Redevelopment Authority, "A Master Plan for the Fort Point and South Boston Waterfront," Boston, BRA, 1997.
37. "Seaport World Trade Center," Celebrate Boston website, http://www.celebrateboston.com/seaport-world-trade-center.htm
38. "John Joseph Moakley U.S. Courthouse," Clark Construction website, https://www.clarkconstruction.com/our-work/projects/john-joseph-moakley-us-courthouse
39. "Hudson Yards," City of New York website, http://www1.nyc.gov/assets/planning/download/pdf/plans/hudson-yards/hyards.pdf
40. I am indebted to Meredith Kane, partner and co-chair of the Real Estate Department of Paul, Weiss, Rifkind, Wharton & Garrison LLP, for her insights into the role of the MTA in the development of the Hudson Yards.
41. "Mayor Bloomberg and Speaker Quinn Announce Final Rezoning for Redevelopment of Hudson Yards Area," Hudson Yards New York website, http://www.hudsonyardsnewyork.com/press-releases/mayor-bloomberg-and-speaker-quinn-announce-final-rezoning-for-redevelopment-of-hudson-yards-area/
42. The teams consisted of developers Durst Organization and Vornado Realty Trust and designers FXFOWLE Architects; Pelli Clarke Pelli Architects; WRT developer Brookfield Properties and designers Skidmore Owings & Merrill; Thomas Phifer & Partners; ShoP Architects; Diller Scofidio + Renfro; Kazuyo Sejima + Ryue Nishizawa; Handel Architects developers Tishman Speyer Properties and Morgan Stanley and designers Helmut Jahn; landscape architect Peter Walker and developers Related Companies and Goldman Sachs and designers Kohn Pederson Fox; Robert A.M. Stern; Arquitectonica.
43. Mahtami, "From Ailing to Artisanal."
44. "A Local's Guide to Over-the-Rhine, Cincinnati's Cool Cultural Hub," Urban Adventures website, August 23, 2017, https://www.urbanadventures.com/blog/neighbourhood-locals-guide-rhine-cincinnati.html
45. Skirtz, *Econocide*, 2012, pp. 29–41.
46. Downtown Center BID, "Downtown LA Market Report," 2nd quarter 2018, https://www.downtownla.com/images/reports/BID.MarketReport2018.Q2.v5OPT.pdf

47. Downtown Center BID, "Downtown LA Survey, 2018," https://www.down townla.com/images/reports/BID.Survey17.Results.v25.pdf
48. Cooper Robertson & Partners, "South Boston Waterfront Public Realm Plan," Boston, BRA, 1999.
49. Boston Children's Museum website, http://www.bostonchildrensmuseum .org/
50. Institute of Contemporary Art website, http://annualreport.icaboston.org /2016-2017/1_ica_ar_letter_1117/
51. Cushman & Wakefield, "Marketbeat," Q2 2018, Boston_Americas_Market Beat_Office_Q22018.pdf
52. "Office Space in Boston's Seaport District," http://www.bostonofficespaces .com/boston-seaport; Boston Tax Parcel Viewer, http://app01.cityofboston .gov/ParcelViewer/?pid=0602671010
53. Candace Carlisle, "Dallas' Park District Development to Bring 'Top of Market' Luxury to Uptown," *Dallas Business Journal*, 2017 https://www.biz journals.com/dallas/news/2017/04/20/dallas-park-district-development-to -bring-top-of.html
54. "The Story," Hudson Yards New York website, http://www.hudsonyards newyork.com/about/the-story/
55. Citiesense, the neighborhood knowledge platform.

Chapter 8

1. Alexander Garvin, *The American City: What Works, What Doesn't* (3rd ed.), New York, NY: McGraw-Hill Education, 2014, p. 76.
2. Minneapolis Parks and Rec Board website, https://www.minneapolisparks .org/
3. Garvin, *The American City*, p. 75.
4. Downtown Memphis Commission website, http://www.downtownmemphis commission.com
5. Downtown Memphis Commission website.
6. LouisvilleKY.Gov, "Louisville's Business Improvement District to Expand West of 9th Street," July 15, 2015, https://louisvilleky.gov/news/louisvilles -business-improvement-district-expand-west-9th-street
7. I am indebted to Anne Goulet, the person hired by the developer to obtain all the public and private agency clearances described herein. If she had not described exactly what happened, even I would not have believed the story.
8. Philip K. Howard, *The Rule of Nobody*, New York, NY: W.W. Norton, 2014.
9. Ibid.
10. Philip K. Howard, "Two Years, Not Ten Years: Redesigning Infrastructure Approvals," Common Good, 2015, https://www.infrastructureusa.org/two -years-not-ten-years-redesigning-infrastructure-approvals/
11. New York City Planning Commission, "Zoning Resolution," Article V, Chapter 2, Section 52-01.
12. Sherri Farris and John Horbas, "Creation vs. Capture: Evaluating the True Costs of Tax Increment Financing," *Journal of Property Tax Assessment &*

Administration 6 (2008); Kevin Ward, "Tax Increment Financing: Imagining Urban Futures: Research on the Circulation of the Tax Increment Financing Model across North America and the UK," Imagining Urban Futures, https://research.northumbria.ac.uk/urbanfutures/research-projects/urban-development/tif

13. Alex Garvin & Associates, Inc., "The BeltLine Emerald Necklace: Atlanta's New Public Realm," The Trust for Public Land, New York, 2004.

14. Mark Pendergrast, *City in the Verge: Atlanta and the Fight for America's Urban Future*, New York, NY: Basic Books, 2017.

15. Atlanta BeltLine Inc., "Annual Report 2016," Atlanta, 2017; "The Atlanta BeltLine 2030 Strategic Implementation Plan Draft Final Report," Atlanta, August 7, 2013.

16. Cameron McWirther, "Resetting the Atlanta BeltLine's Focus on Equitable Development," *Wall Street Journal*, September 1–2, 2018, p. A3.

17. Atlanta BeltLine website, "Atlanta BeltLine Living Made Easier," https://beltline.org/progress/affordable-housing/

18. Atlanta BeltLine website, "Creating Housing Opportunities for All," https://beltline.org/progress/affordable-housing/#policies-programs

19. Keith Schneider, "Open Spaces Bring Light to Downtown Columbus," *New York Times*, May 31, 2016.

20. Frederick Law Olmsted, "Public Parks and the Enlargement of Towns," originally given as a speech at the American Social Science Association in Boston in 1879, republished in Robert Twombly (ed.), *Frederick Law Olmsted: Essential Texts*, New York, NY: W.W. Norton, 2010, p. 218.

Afterword

1. Jane Jacobs, *The Death and Life of Great American Cities*, New York, NY: Random House, 1961, p. 6.

Index

Rodin, Judith, 112, 114, 115–116
rollerblading, 68
Rose, Joseph B., 123, 166, 167, 195
Ross, Stephen M., 195
Rouse, James, 109
The Rule of Nobody (Howard), 208

Sadik-Khan, Janette, 69, 151–152
Sagalyn, Lynne, 16
San Francisco, California, 50–53
San Jose, California, 59–61, 59t
Saunders, Doug, 58, 61
Savannah, Georgia, 86–87
Schatz, Carol, 99
Schiavone, Joe, 120
schools, critical mass needed for, 34–35
Science Park (New Haven), 120
Scioto Mile (Columbus), 216f
Seaport (Boston), 173–174, 174f, 184–185, 185f, 192, 192f, 194f
Seattle, Washington, 16f, 44, 71, 72f
security measures, 68
"The Shed" (NYC), 196
Shelby Farms Park Conservancy (Memphis), 111–112, 112f
shipping, 50–54, 62–64
shopping malls, 2–4, 22. *See also* Retail space
Silverstein Family Park (Manhattan), 126–127, 126f
16th Street Mall (Denver), 32, 32f, 33f
size of downtowns, 23t
slum clearance, 133–136
Smith, Ken, 128
SoHo district (New York), 48–49, 49f, 86
Southern California Institute of Architecture, 86
Special Lower Manhattan Zoning District, 123
St. Louis, Missouri, 46, 136
St. Paul, Minnesota, 50, 50f, 53
stables, 10
Standard Downtown BID Enabling Act, 202
Staples, 3
Starbucks, 4
stores. *See* Retail space

streetcars, 8
subsidies, 131–132, 140–142
suburbs, flight to, 30, 43–44
subways: Atlanta and, 20f, 147–148, 147f; capacity of, 10; financing of, 210–211; Los Angeles and, 100f, 171–172; New York City and, 122, 125, 125f, 164–165, 165f, 167–169, 185, 196, 198, 207
Sustainable Streets program (NYC), 152

Target, 4
tax increment financing (TIF) districts, 70–71, 201, 211–216
technology, 38–42, 45–46. *See also* Internet
telegraph, 10–11
telephones, 10–11
terrorism, 68
Texas Medical Center (Houston), 95, 113–114, 113f
Third Ward (Milwaukee), 66f, 68f
3CDC. *See* Cincinnati Center City Development Corporation
TIF districts. *See* Tax increment financing districts
Time Warner Center (NYC), 195
Times Square (NYC), 152, 153f
Tompkins, Tim, 152
tourism, 12–13, 64–67, 65t, 91–92
trajectories, 4–8, 24, 43
transportation: Boston and, 167, 173–174; changing forms of, 8–10; Denver and, 13–14, 14f; Hudson Yards and, 166–170; improving, 146–150; Interstate Highway Program and, 137–140; locating downtowns and, 30–33. *See also Specific forms*
trees, 154
Trump, Donald, 61–62, 81, 91, 162
tunnels, 137
Turtle Creek (Dallas), 170–171, 170f
Two Trees Management, 79–82, 182
Tysons Corner, Virginia, 22

University City (Philadelphia), 115–117
University of Pennsylvania, 96, 114, 115–117
unzoning, 176–177